COLLINS
TRAVEL
GEM

KU-043-265

ITALIAN

D I C T I O N A R Y

ITALIAN

D I C T I O N A R Y

COLLINS
London and Glasgow

First published 1986

Consultant
Michela Clari

ISBN 0 00 459436-3

Other Travel Gem
Dictionaries:

French

German

Spanish

Your TRAVEL GEM DICTIONARY will prove an invaluable companion on your holiday or trip abroad. In a genuinely handy pocket or handbag format, this practical two-way dictionary has a double aim. First, it is your key to understanding the foreign words and phrases you are likely to encounter when travelling in Italy. Second, it contains an essential English wordpack with translations and pronunciations.

Understanding foreign signs and notices

With over 6000 Italian words and phrases selected for their relevance to the needs of the traveller, your Travel Gem Dictionary provides essential help towards understanding the basic vocabulary of Italian, and all those important foreign notices, traffic signs, menus and other mystifying items surrounding you on your trip abroad.

Beyond survival communication

In addition, a practical English wordlist of over 3000 items with Italian translations and clear pronunciations allows you to venture beyond basic communication and provides the ideal complement to your Travel Gem Phrase Book, also in this series.

Enjoy your trip!

Notes to help you

In the Italian-English half of the dictionary, you will find that some words *(adjectives and nouns)* are listed with an ending in brackets. This ending is used when the word is *feminine* — i.e. is used with **la** instead of **il** or **lo**, or is marked *(f)* in the dictionary. Thus the entry **caldo(a)** means that both **caldo** and **calda** mean "hot". Most adjectives are made feminine by simply changing the **o** of the basic *(masculine)* form to **a**.

On the English-Italian side we've given only the basic form, whose ending changes to **a** in the feminine.

To make a word plural in Italian, you usually change the **o** ending to **i** for masculine words, and the **a** to **e** for feminine words.

Pronunciation Guide

In the pronunciation system used in this book, Italian sounds are represented by spellings of the nearest possible sounds in English. Hence, when you read out the pronunciation - the line in *italics* after each phrase or word - sound the letters as if you were reading an English word. Whenever we think it is not sufficiently clear where to stress a word or phrase, we have used **heavy italics** to highlight the syllable to be stressed. The following notes should help you:

	REMARKS	EXAMPLE	PRONUNCIATION
ay	As in *day*	**dei**	*day-ee*
ah	As *a* in *father*	**prendiamo**	*prend-**yah**mo*
e	As in *bed*	**letto**	*let-to*
oh	As in *go, low*	**sono**	*sohnoh*
y	As in *yet*	**aiuto**	*a-**yoo**to*

Spelling in Italian is very regular and, with a little practice, you will soon be able to pronounce Italian words from their spelling alone. The only letters which may cause problems are:

i	As *ee* in *meet*	**vino**	*veeno*
	Or as *y* in *yet*	**aiuto**	*a-**yoo**to*
u	As *oo* in *boot*	**luna**	*loona*
	Or as *w* in *will*	**buon**	*bwon*
c	Before *e, i* as *ch* in *chat*	**centro**	*chentro*
	Before *a, o, u* as in *cat*	**cosa**	*koza*
ch	As *c* in *cat*	**chi**	*kee*
g	Before *e, i* as in *gin*	**giorno**	*jorno*
	Before *a, h, o, u* as in *get*	**regalo**	*ray-**gah**lo*
gl	As *lli* in *million*	**figlio**	***feel**-yo*
gn	As *ni* in *onion*	**bisogno**	*beez**ohn**-yo*
h	Silent	**ho**	*o*
sc	Before *e, i*, as *sh* in *shop*	**uscita**	*oo-**shee**ta*
	Before *a, o, u* as in *scar*	**capisco**	*ka-**pee**sko*
z	As *ts* in *cats*	**senza**	*sentsa*
	or *ds* in *rods*	**mezzo**	*medz-zo*

ITALIAN-ENGLISH

A

a at; in; to; **a 30 chilometri** 30 kilometres away; **due volte al giorno** twice a day; **uno a uno** one by one

abbacchio m baby lamb

abbaglianti mpl: **accendere gli abbaglianti** to put one's headlights on full beam

abbagliare to dazzle

abbassare to lower; to turn down; to dip (*headlights*)

abbastanza enough; quite

abbattere to knock down

abbazia f abbey

abbigliamento m clothes; **abbigliamento intimo** underwear; **abbigliamento sportivo** casual wear; **abbigliamento uomo/donna/ bambino** men's/ladies'/ children's wear

abboccato(a) semi-sweet (*wine*)

abbonamento m subscription; season ticket; **spedizione in abbonamento postal** subscription

abbonato(a) m/f subscriber; season ticket holder

abbozzo m sketch; draft

abbracciare to embrace; to hug

abbronzante m suntan oil/ cream

abbronzarsi to tan

abbronzatura f suntan

abete m fir (tree)

abitante m/f inhabitant

abitare to live (*reside*); to live in

abito m dress; suit (*man's*); **abito da sera** evening dress (*woman's*)

abituale usual

abituarsi a to get used to

abitudine f habit

abside f apse

abuso m: **ogni abuso sarà punito** penalty for improper use

accadere to happen

accamparsi to camp

accanto nearby; **accanto a** beside

accappatoio m bathrobe

accelerare to accelerate; to speed up

acceleratore *m* accelerator

accendere to turn on; to light; **vietato accendere fuochi** do not light a fire

accendino *m* cigarette lighter

accensione *f* ignition; **l'accensione della luce rossa segnala il fuori servizio** machine not in use when red light shows

accento *m* accent; stress

acceso(a) on

accesso *m* access; fit; **divieto di accesso** no entry; **divieto di accesso ai non addetti ai lavori** authorized personnel only

accessori *mpl* accessories

accettare to accept; **non si accettano assegni** we do not accept cheques

accettazione *f* acceptance; reception; check-in; **accettazione bagagli** check-in

acchiappare to catch

acciaio *m* steel

acciuga *f* anchovy

accoglienza *f* welcome

accogliere to receive (*guest*); to welcome

accomodarsi to make oneself comfortable

accompagnare to escort; to accompany

accompagnatore *m* escort; **accompagnatore turistico** courier

acconciatura *f* hairstyle; **acconciature** hairdresser's (shop)

acconto *m* down payment

accorciare to shorten

accordare to tune; to grant

accordo *m* agreement; **essere d'accordo** to agree

accostare: accostare (a) to bring near (to); to draw up (at); **accostare la banconota a destra** place the banknote at the right

accreditare to credit

accusa *f* charge; accusation

acerbo(a) unripe; sour

aceto *m* vinegar; **aceto di vino** wine vinegar

ACI *m* ≈ A.A.

acido(a) acid; sour

acqua *f* water; **acqua corrente** running water; **acqua distillata** distilled water; **acqua minerale** mineral water; **acqua potabile** drinking water; **acqua tonica** tonic water; **fare acqua** to leak (*boat*)

acquaio *m* sink

acquazzone *m* shower (*rain*)

acquedotto *m* aqueduct

acquirente *m/f* purchaser

acquistare to acquire

acquisti *mpl* shopping

acquisto *m* purchase

acuto(a) sharp; acute

adattare to adapt

adatto(a) suitable

addebitare to debit

addetto(a): personale addetto relevant staff

addobbi *mpl* decorations

addome *m* abdomen

addormentato(a) asleep

adesione *f* adhesion; agreement

adolescente *m/f* teenager

Adriatico *m* Adriatic (Sea)

adulto(a) *m/f* adult

aereo *m* plane; aircraft; **in aereo** by plane; on the plane

aereo(a) air; **per via aerea** by air

aeromobile *m* aircraft

aeroplano *m* aeroplane

aeroporto *m* airport

aeroportuale: formalità aeroportuali *fpl* airport formalities

afa *f* sultriness

affamato(a) starving

affare *m* affair (*matter*); deal; **affari** business; **per affari** on business

affascinante fascinating; glamorous

affatto at all

afferrare to seize; to grab

affettato *m* (sliced) cold meat

affetto *m* affection

affettuoso(a) affectionate

affidabilità *f* reliability

affilato(a) sharp

affissione *f*: **divieto di affissione** post no bills

affittanze *fpl*: **vendite affittanze** property for sale or rent

affittare to rent; to let

affittasi to let

affitto *m* lease; rent; hire; **affitto ombrelloni** beach umbrellas for hire

affogato(a) drowned; poached (*egg*)

affollato(a) crowded

affondare to sink

affrancare to stamp (*letter*)

affresco *m* fresco

affrettarsi to hurry

affrontare to tackle

affumicato(a) smoked

afoso(a) close (*stuffy*)

agenda *f* diary

agente *m* agent; broker; **agente immobiliare** estate agent; **agente marittimo** shipping agent; **agente di polizia** police officer; **agente verificatore** ticket inspector; **agente di viaggi** travel agent; **agenti portuali** port inspectors

agenzia *f* agency; **agenzia immobiliare** estate agent's (office); **agenzia di navigazione** shipping agency; **agenzia di viaggi** travel agency; **agenzia viaggiatori Ferrovie dello Stato** rail travel agency

aggiornato(a) up-to-date; adjourned

aggiungere to add

aggiustare to repair; to adjust

agire to act

agitare to shake

agitato(a) rough; restless; upset

agli = **a** + **gli**

aglio m garlic

agnello m lamb; **agnello arrosto** roast lamb

agnolotti mpl squares or circles of pasta with meat filling

ago m needle

agosto m August

agricolo(a) agricultural

agricoltore m farmer

agrodolce: in agrodolce in a sweet and sour sauce

ai = a + i

aia f farmyard

aiuola f flowerbed; **è vietato calpestare le aiuole** keep off the grass

aiutare to help

aiuto m help

ala f wing

alba f dawn

albergatore m hotelier

alberghiero(a): catena alberghiera hotel chain

albergo m hotel

albero m tree; mast; **albero di Natale** Christmas tree; **alberi in banchina** overhanging trees

albicocca f apricot

alcolici mpl liquor

alcolico(a) alcoholic (*drink*)

alcolizzato(a) m/f alcoholic

alcool m alcohol; **alcool denaturato** methylated spirits

alcuni(e) some

alcuno(a) any

alghe fpl seaweed

aliante m glider

alici: filetti di alici mpl anchovy fillets

alimentari mpl: **negozio di alimentari** grocer's (shop)

aliscafo m hydrofoil

allacciare to fasten; **allacciare la cintura di sicurezza** to fasten one's seat belt

allappante slightly tart (*wine*)

allarme m alarm; **allarme antincendio** fire alarm

alleanza f alliance

allegare to enclose

allegro(a) cheerful

allenamento m training

allenatore m coach (*instructor*)

allergia f allergy

allestimento m: **mostra/vetrina in allestimento** exhibition/window display in preparation

allevamento m rearing; stock farm

alleviare to ease

alloggiare to put up (*accommodate*); to live (*reside*)

alloggio m lodgings; accommodation

allora then; **d'allora in poi** from then on

allungare to lengthen

almeno at least

Alpi fpl Alps

alpinismo m mountaineering

alt: alt dogana/polizia stop: customs/police

altalena f swing; seesaw

altare m altar

altezza f height

altitudine f altitude

alto high; aloud; **in alto** high; up, upward(s)

alto(a) high; tall; **alta stagione** high season

altoparlante m loudspeaker

altopiano m plateau

altrimenti otherwise

altro(a) other

altrove somewhere else

alunno(a) m/f pupil

alzare to raise; to turn up

alzarsi to get up; to stand up; to rise

amabile sweet (wine)

amaca f hammock

amante m/f lover; mistress

amare to love

amaro(a) bitter

amarognolo(a) slightly bitter

ambasciata f embassy

ambasciatore m ambassador

ambedue both

ambiente m environment

ambulanza f ambulance

ambulatorio m consulting room; **ambulatorio comunale** health centre

America f America; **America del Sud** South America; **America del Nord** North America; **America Latina** Latin America

amianto m asbestos

amichevole friendly

amico(a) m/f friend

amido m starch

ammaccatura f dent; bruise

ammaestrare to train (animal)

ammandorlato(a): vino **ammandorlato** wine with a flavour of almonds

ammettere to admit

amministrazione f administration; **amministrazione statale** civil service

ammiraglia f: (nave) **ammiraglia** flagship

ammirare to admire

ammobiliare to furnish

ammontare a to amount to

ammorbidente m softener

ammortizzatore m shock absorber

amo m (fish) hook

amore m love

ampère m amp

ampio(a) loose; wide; full-bodied (wine)

amplificatore m amplifier

analcolico(a) nonalcoholic; soft (drink)

analisi f analysis; test; **analisi cliniche** medical tests

analizzare to analyse

ananas m pineapple

anatra f duck; **anatra arrosto** roast duck; **anatra in agrodolce** duck in sweet and sour sauce

anca f hip

anche too; also; even

ancora[1] still; yet; again; **ancora del formaggio** more cheese

ancora[2] f anchor

andare to go; **andiamo** let's go;

andare in macchina to drive;
andare in bicicletta to cycle;
andarsene to go away
anello m ring; anello di
fidanzamento engagement ring;
anello di fondo cross-country
skiing circuit
anfiteatro m amphitheatre
angolo m corner; angle
angoscia f distress
anguilla f eel; anguilla in
umido eel stew
anguria f watermelon
anima f soul
animale m animal; animale
domestico pet
animato(a) adj busy (place)
animatore m organizer;
compère
animazione f: programma di
animazione organized
entertainment; animazione
sportiva e ricreativa organized
sports and recreational activities
animelle fpl sweetbreads
annaffiare to water; to wash
down (meal)
annata f vintage; year; vino
d'annata vintage wine
annegare to drown
anno m year; quanti anni ha?
how old are you?
annodare to tie; to knot
annoiare to bore; to annoy
annotare to write down
annotazioni fpl notes
annullamento m cancellation;
spese per l'annullamento del

servizio cancellation fee
annullare to cancel
annuncio m announcement;
advertisement
ansia f anxiety
antenato(a) m/f ancestor
antenna f aerial; antenna;
antenna trasmittente radio
mast
anteprima f preview
anteriore front
antiappannante m demister
antibiotico m antibiotic
antichità f antique; antiquity
anticipare to advance (money)
anticipo m advance (loan); in
anticipo in advance; early
antico(a) antique; ancient
anticoncezionale m
contraceptive
anticongelante m antifreeze
antigelo m antifreeze; de-icer
antincendio: bombola
antincendio f fire extinguisher
antipasto m hors d'œuvre;
antipasto misto mixed hors
d'œuvre, usually containing
cured hams and pickles;
antipasto di pesce fish hors
d'œuvre; antipasto di frutti di
mare seafood starter
antiquario m antique dealer
antiquato(a) out of date;
old-fashioned
antisettico m antiseptic
antistaminico m antihistamine
ape f bee
aperitivo m aperitif

aperto(a) open; on; **all'aperto** in the open (air); open-air

apertura: apertura a spinta push to open

apparecchiare to lay (*table*)

apparecchiatura *f* equipment; device; **apparecchiatura fotografica** photographic equipment

apparecchio *m* appliance; **apparecchio acustico** hearing aid; **apparecchi pubblici** public telephones

apparentemente apparently

apparire to appear

appartamento *m* flat, apartment

appartenere a to belong to

appassionato(a) keen

appena scarcely; just

appendere to hang

appendicite *f* appendicitis

appetito *m* appetite; **buon appetito!** enjoy your meal!

appezzamento *m* plot (of land)

appiccicoso(a) sticky

applaudire to clap; to cheer

appoggiarsi: è pericoloso appoggiarsi do not lean against the door(s); **appoggiarsi a** to lean against

apposta on purpose; specially

apprendista *m/f* apprentice; trainee

apprezzare to appreciate

appropriato(a) suitable

approssimativamente roughly

approvare to approve of

approvazione *f* approval

appuntamento *m* appointment; date

apribottiglie *m* bottle opener

aprile *m* April

aprire to open; to turn on; **non aprire prima che il treno sia fermo** do not open while the train is in motion

apriscatole *m* can-opener

aquila *f* eagle

aquilone *m* kite

arachide *f* peanut

aragosta *f* lobster

arancia *f* orange

aranciata *f* orangeade

arancino *m* rice croquette stuffed with meat

arancione orange

arbitro *m* umpire; referee

arbusto *m* shrub

archeologico(a): museo archeologico archaeological museum

architettura *f* architecture

archivio *m* file; filing cabinet

arco *m* arch; bow (*for arrow, violin*)

ardere to burn

area *f* area; **area di parcheggio** parking area; **area di servizio** service area

argenteria *f* silverware

argento *m* silver

argilla *f* clay

argomento *m* topic

aria *f* air; tune; **con aria condizionata** air-conditioned;

all'aria aperta in the open (air); outdoor

arieggiare to air

aringa f herring

arista f chine of pork

arma f weapon; **arma da fuoco** firearm

armadietto m locker

armadio m cupboard; wardrobe

armeria f armoury; collection of arms

armi fpl arms (weapons)

arnese m tool

aromi mpl seasoning; herbs

arpa f harp

arrabbiato(a) angry

arrampicarsi su to climb (tree, wall)

arrangiarsi to manage

arredare to furnish

arredato(a): appartamento arredato furnished flat

arredo m: **arredo bagno** bathroom furnishings

arretrati mpl arrears

arrivare to arrive; **arrivare a** to reach

arrivederci goodbye

arrivo m arrival; **arrivi/partenze nazionali** domestic arrivals/departures; **arrivi/partenze internazionali** international arrivals/departures

arrostire to roast

arrosto m roast meat; **arrosto di manzo/tacchino/vitello** roast beef/turkey/veal

arrugginirsi to rust

arte f art; craft

articolo m article; **articoli da pesce** fishing equipment; **articoli da spiaggia** beachwear and accessories; **articoli sportivi** sports goods; **articoli di toeletta** toiletries; **articoli di vetro** glassware

artificiale artificial; man-made

artigiano m craftsman

artista m/f artist

artrite f arthritis

ascensore m lift

asciugacapelli m hair-drier

asciugamano m towel

asciugare to dry; to wipe

asciugatoio m hair-drier (at swimming pool)

asciutto(a) dry

ascoltare to listen

asilo d'infanzia m nursery school

asino m donkey

asma f asthma

asparagi mpl asparagus

aspettare to wait; to wait for; to expect

aspetto m appearance

aspirapolvere m vacuum cleaner

aspirina f aspirin

aspro(a) sharp; sour

assaggiare to taste

assalire to attack

assassino m killer

asse[1] m axle

asse[2] f board; **asse da stiro** ironing board

assegnare to allocate

assegno m allowance (*state payment*); cheque

assente absent

assetato(a) thirsty

assicurare to assure; to insure

assicurarsi to make sure; to insure oneself

assicurazione f insurance; **assicurazione contro terzi** third party insurance; **assicurazione casco** comprehensive insurance

assistente m/f assistant; **assistente sanitario** doctor; **assistente sociale** social worker

assistenza f assistance; **assistenza qualificata** expert service; **assistenza sanitaria** health service

assistere to assist; **assistere a** to attend (*meeting etc*)

asso m ace

associazione f society; association; **associazione turistica giovanile** tourist association for young people

assoluto(a) absolute

assomigliare a to resemble

assorbente absorbent; **assorbente igienico** m sanitary towel

assorbire to absorb

assortito(a) assorted

assumere to recruit (*personnel*)

assurdo(a) absurd

asta f auction; **asta dell'olio** dipstick

astenersi to abstain

astice m lobster

astuccio m case

ATG abbreviation of **associazione turistica giovanile**

atlante m atlas

Atlantico m Atlantic Ocean

ATM public transport service

attaccapanni m coat peg; hat stand; coat hanger

attaccare to attach; to attack; to fasten

attacco m attack; **attacco cardiaco** heart attack

atteggiamento m attitude

attendere to wait for

attenti al cane beware of the dog

attenzione f attention; **attenzione allo scalino** mind the step; **attenzione alla corrente elettrica** danger: electricity

atterraggio m landing (*of plane*); **atterraggio di emergenza** emergency landing; **atterraggio di fortuna** crash-landing

atterrare to land (*plane*)

attestare: si attesta che ... it is hereby declared that ...

attestazione f: **attestazione di versamento** proof of payment

attico m attic; penthouse

attività f activity; **attività di bordo** fpl activities on board; **attività sportive** fpl sporting activities

attivo(a) active

atto *m* act; action; deed

attore *m* actor

attracco *m* berthing; berth; **divieto di attracco a imbarcazioni non autorizzate** berths for authorized craft only

attraversamento pedonale *m* pedestrian crossing

attraversare to cross; **vietato attraversare i binari** do not cross the track

attraverso through

attrazione *f* attraction

attrezzatura *f* equipment

attrice *f* actress

attuale present

audace bold

audiovisivo(a) audio-visual

auguri *mpl*: **tanti auguri** all the best; **auguri di buon compleanno** best wishes on your birthday

aula *f* classroom; lecture room; **aula del tribunale** courtroom; **aula magna** main hall

aumentare to increase; to turn up

aumento *m* increase; rise; raise; growth

austriaco(a) Austrian

autentico(a) genuine

autista *m* driver; chauffeur

autobus *m* bus

autocorriera *f* country bus

autocorsa *f* bus

autoforniture *fpl* car parts and accessories

autogrù *f* breakdown van

automatico(a) automatic

automobile *f* car; **automobile decappottabile** convertible

automobilista *m/f* motorist

automotrice *f* railcar

autonoleggio *m* car hire; **autonoleggio con autista** chauffeur-drive service

autopompa *f* fire engine

autopullman *m* bus; coach

autore *m* author

autorimessa *f* garage (*for parking*)

autoritratto *m* self-portrait

autorizzare to authorize

autorizzazione *f* authorization; **autorizzazione scritta** written authorization

autoscuola *f* driving school

autostop *m* hitchhiking

autostoppista *m/f* hitchhiker

autostrada *f* motorway; **autostrada a pedaggio** toll road

autovettura *f* motor car

autunno *m* autumn

avanti in front; forward(s)

avanzare to remain (*be left over*); to advance

avaria *f* breakdown (*of car*); failure

avena *f* oats

avere to have

aviazione *f* air force; aviation

aviogetto *m* jet

avorio *m* ivory

avvenimento *m* event

avvenuto(a): **l'avvenuta accettazione è indicata da un**

segnale acustico an acoustic signal indicates that your money has been accepted

avverso(a): avverse condizioni atmosferiche fpl adverse weather conditions

avvertire to warn

avviarsi to set off

avvicinarsi to approach

avvisare to inform; to warn

avviso m warning; announcement; advertisement; notice; **avviso alla clientela** notice to customers

avvocato m barrister; lawyer

avvolgere to wind; to wrap

azienda f business, firm; **azienda turismo** or **di soggiorno** local tourist board

azione f action

azzurro(a) blue

B

baccalà m dried salted cod; **baccalà alla vicentina** salt cod cooked in milk with white wine, spices, anchovies, onion and garlic

bacheca f display case; notice board

baciare to kiss

bacino m dock; pond

bacio m kiss

badare a to look after; to pay attention to

baffi mpl moustache

bagagliaio m boot (of car);

luggage van

bagaglio m luggage; **bagaglio a mano** hand luggage; **bagaglio personale** personal luggage

bagliore m flash; glare (of light)

bagnare to wet

bagnarsi to get wet; to bathe

bagnino m lifeguard

bagno m bathroom; bath; **bagni** mpl bathing establishment

bagnomaria: cuocere a bagnomaria to cook in a double saucepan

baia f bay

balcone m balcony

balena f whale

ballare to dance

balletto m ballet

ballo m ball; dance

balneazione f: **è proibita la balneazione** bathing strictly prohibited

balsamo m hair conditioner

bambinaia f nurse(maid)

bambino(a) m/f child; baby

bambola f doll

banca f bank

bancarella f stall; stand

bancarotta f bankruptcy

banchetto m banquet

banchina f platform; quay; quayside

banco m counter; bench; **banco di registrazione** check-in (desk); **banco di sabbia** sandbank

bancogiro m bank giro (system)

banconota f bank note

banda f gang; band

bandiera f banner; flag
bandito m gunman
bar m bar; pub
barattolo m tin; jar
barba f beard
barbabietola f beetroot
Barbera m dry, full-bodied, deep-red wine from Piedmont
barbiere m barber
barbo m barbel
barca f boat
barcone m: **barconi per escursioni** boat excursions
Bardolino m light, dry red wine from the area around Verona
barella f stretcher
barile m barrel
barista m/f barman; barmaid
Barolo m dry, full-bodied red wine with a taste of violets, from Piedmont
basare to base
base f base; basis; **pranzo a base di pesce/carne** lunch with fish/meat as the main course
basso(a) low; short
bastare to be enough
bastoncini mpl chopsticks; **bastoncini di merluzzo** cod fish fingers; **bastoncini di pesce** fish fingers
bastone m stick; walking stick
battaglia f battle
battello m boat; **battello da diporto** pleasure boat; **battello di salvataggio** lifeboat
battere to hit; to beat; **battere bandiera inglese** etc to fly the

British etc flag
batteria f battery (in car); heat (sports)
battersi to fight
battesimo m baptism
battistero m baptistry
baule m trunk
beccaccia f woodcock
beccaccino m snipe
bellezza f beauty
bello(a) beautiful; handsome; lovely; fine; **fa bello** the weather's fine
Bel Paese m soft, mild creamy cheese
benché although
benda f blindfold; bandage
bene well; all right; **stare bene** to be well; **va bene** okay; it's okay
beneficiario m payee
beni mpl goods; property
benvenuto(a) welcome
benzina f petrol
bere to drink
berlina f saloon (car)
bernoccolo m bump
berretto m cap
bersaglio m target
bestemmiare to swear
bestiame m cattle
betulla f birch
bevanda f drink
biancheria f linen (for beds, table); **biancheria casa** household linens; **biancheria da letto** bedding; **biancheria intima** underwear

bianco(a) white; blank; **assegno in bianco** blank cheque; **lasciate in bianco per favore** please leave blank; **pesce/carne in bianco** boiled fish/meat

Bibbia f Bible

biberon m baby's bottle

bibita f soft drink

biblioteca f library; bookcase

bicchiere m glass; **bicchiere da vino** wineglass

bicicletta f bicycle

bidone m dustbin

bigiotteria f costume jewellery

bigliettaio m bus conductor

biglietteria f ticket office; **biglietteria aerea** air travel ticket office

biglietto m note; ticket; card; **biglietto di andata e ritorno** return ticket; **biglietto di solo andata** single ticket; **biglietto orario** ticket valid for one hour from time of issue; **il biglietto deve essere convalidato all'inizio del viaggio e conservato per il controllo** tickets must be punched at start of journey and kept ready for inspection

bignè m cream puff

bigodino m curler

bilancia f scales

bilanciare to balance

bilancio m balance sheet; **bilancio preventivo** budget

bilia f marble

biliardo m billiards

bin. abbreviation of **binario**

binario m track; line; platform

binocolo m binoculars

biondo(a) blond(e); fair

birra f beer; **birra alla spina** draught beer; **birra chiara** lager; **birra piccola/grande** half-pint/ pint of beer; **birre estere** foreign beers; **birre nazionali** Italian beers

birreria f brewery; bierkeller

bis m encore

biscotto m biscuit

bisognare to have to

bisogno m need; **avere bisogno di** to need

bistecca f steak; **bistecca ai ferri** grilled steak; **bistecca di filetto** fillet steak; **bistecca alla fiorentina** T-bone steak

bivio m fork

bloccare to block; **bloccare un assegno** to stop a cheque

bloccarsi to jam

blocchetto m notebook; **biglietti in blocchetti** books of tickets

blocco m block; notepad; **per evitare il blocco dell'ascensore ...** to prevent the lift from jamming ...

blu blue

blusa f smock

boa f buoy

bocca f mouth

bocce fpl bowls (game)

boccone m bite (of food)

bolla f bubble; blister

bollettino m bulletin

bollire to boil

bollito m boiled meat; **bollito misto** assorted boiled meats

bollitore m kettle

bombetta f bowler hat

bombola f cylinder (for gas); **bombola spray** spray

bombolone m doughnut

bordo m border; edge; **a bordo** on board; **salire a bordo** to go aboard; **a bordo della nave** aboard ship

borghese middle-class

borgo m district

borsa f handbag; holdall; bag; briefcase; **la Borsa** the stock market; the stock exchange; **borsa dell'acqua calda** hot water bottle; **borsa nera** black market; **borsa per la spesa** shopping bag; **borsa di studio** grant; **borsa da toletta** sponge-bag

borsellino m purse

borsetta f handbag

bosco m wood (forest)

botte f barrel, cask

bottega f shop; **bottega artigiana** crafts shop

botteghino m box office

bottiglia f bottle

bottone m button

bovino(a): carni bovine fpl beef

box m playpen

braccialetto m bracelet

braccio m arm

braciola f chop; **braciola di maiale** pork chop

brandina f camp-bed

brano m passage (from book)

branzino m bass

brasato m braised beef

breve brief

brezza f breeze

briciola f crumb

bricolage m do-it-yourself

briglia f rein; bridle

brillare to shine

brindare a to toast (drink to)

brindisi m toast (drink, speech)

britannico(a) British

brocca f jug

broccoletti mpl broccoli

brodetto m: **brodetto di pesce** spicy fish soup

brodo m stock; **riso/pasta in brodo** rice/noodle soup

bruciare to burn

bruciore di stomaco m heartburn

bruno(a) brown; dark

brusco(a) abrupt; sharp

brutto(a) ugly

buca f hole; **buca per le lettere** letter box

bucato m washing; laundry; **per bucato in lavatrice** for machine washing; **per bucato a mano** for hand washing

buccia f peel, skin

buco m hole; **buco della serratura** keyhole

budino m pudding

bufera f storm; **bufera di neve** blizzard

buffè m buffet
bugia f lie
buio(a) dark
buongustaio m gourmet
buono m voucher; coupon; token
buono(a) good; **buon giorno!**
good morning/afternoon!; **buona
sera!** good evening!; **buona
notte!** good night!; **a buon
mercato** cheap
burrasca f storm
burrascoso(a) gusty; rough
burro m butter
bussare to knock
bussola f compass
busta f envelope
bustina f sachet; **bustina di tè**
tea bag
busto m bust
buttare via to throw away

C

cabina f cabin; beach hut;
cubicle; **cabina interna/esterna**
cabin below/above deck; **cabina
telefonica** telephone booth;
**cabina doppia/tripla/
quadrupla** two-/three-/four-
berth cabin
cabinato m cabin cruiser
cabinovia f two-seater cablecar
cacao m cocoa; **cacao amaro**
cocoa with no added sugar
caccia f hunting; shooting
cacciagione f game (hunting)
cacciare vt to hunt; to chase
away

cacciatora: alla cacciatora with
tomatoes, mushrooms, shallots,
ham and wine
cacciavite m screwdriver
cacciucco m: **cacciucco alla
livornese** spiced fish soup with
garlic and sage
caciocavallo m firm cheese
made from cow's or sheep's milk
cadavere m body (corpse)
cadere to fall; to fall over; to fall
down; to drop
caduta f fall; **caduta massi/
sassi** danger, falling rocks/stones
caffè m café; coffee; **caffè
corretto** coffee containing a
liqueur; **caffè decaffeinato**
decaffeinated coffee; **caffè in
grani** coffee beans; **caffè lungo**
weak black coffee; **caffè
macchiato** coffee with a dash of
milk; **caffè macinato** ground
coffee; **caffè nero** black coffee;
caffè ristretto strong black
coffee; **caffè tostato** roasted
coffee
caffellatte m white coffee
caffettiera f coffeepot
calamaretti ripieni mpl stuffed
baby squid
calamari mpl: **calamari fritti**
fried squid
calamita f magnet
calare to fall
calcestruzzo m concrete
calcio m kick; football (game);
calcium
calcolare to calculate; to allow

calcolo m calculation

caldarroste fpl roast chestnuts

caldo(a) warm; hot; **ho caldo** I'm warm/hot

calendario m calendar; **calendario partenze** departure dates

callo m corn

calma f calm

calmante m painkiller

calmarsi to calm down

calmo(a) calm

calore m warmth; heat

calpestare to tread on

calza f stocking; sock

calzatura f footwear

calzino m sock

calzoleria f shoeshop

calzoncini mpl shorts

calzone m savoury turnover made with pizza dough, usually filled with cheese and ham

calzoni mpl trousers

cambiale f draft (financial)

cambiamento m change;

cambiare to change; to exchange; **cambiare casa** to move house

cambiarsi to change one's clothes

cambio m change; exchange; rate of exchange; gears; **cambio di asciugamani/delle lenzuola** change of towels/sheets; **cambio filtri** oil filter change; **cambio olio rapido** quick oil change; **cambio medio applicato** average rate of exchange

applied; **cambio valute** exchange office

camera f room; **camera (da letto)** bedroom; **camera dei bambini** nursery; **camera blindata** strongroom; **camera di commercio** Chamber of Commerce; **camera libera** vacancy; **camera matrimoniale** double room; **camera degli ospiti** guest-room; **camera singola** single room

cameriera f waitress; chambermaid; **cameriera al banco** barmaid

cameriere m waiter

camerini prova mpl fitting rooms

camiceria f shirt shop

camicetta f blouse

camicia f shirt; **camicia da notte** nightdress; nightshirt

caminetto m mantelpiece

camino m chimney; fireplace

camion m lorry

camionabile for heavy vehicles

camionista m lorry driver

camminare to walk

campagna f country; countryside; campaign

campana f bell

campanello m bell; doorbell

campeggio m camping; camp(ing) site; **campeggio libero** free camp site

campionato m championship

campione m sample; specimen; champion

campo m field; **campo da gioco** playing field; **campo di golf** golf course; **campo sportivo** sports ground; **campo da tennis** tennis court

camposanto m cemetery

canale m canal; channel

cancellare to rub out; to cancel

cancellata f railings

cancellazione f cancellation

cancelleria f stationery

cancello m gate; **cancello motorizzato controllato a distanza** gate operated by remote control

cancro m cancer

candeggina f bleach

candela f spark(ing) plug; candle

cane m dog

canna da pesca f fishing rod

cannella f cinnamon

cannelloni mpl tubes of pasta stuffed with sauce and baked

cannolo m cream horn

cannone m gun; cannon

canoa f canoe

canocchia f squill

canottaggio m rowing

canottiera f vest

canovaccio m teacloth

cantare to sing

cantiere m building site; **cantiere navale** shipyard

cantina f cellar; wine cellar

cantiniere m cellarman

canto m song; singing

canzone f song

capace capable

capacità f ability

capanna f hut

capelli mpl hair; **capelli grassi/ secchi** greasy/dry hair

capello m hair (*single strand*)

capienza f capacity

capire to understand

capitale[1] f capital (*city*)

capitale[2] m capital (*finance*)

capitaneria f: **capitaneria (di porto)** port authorities

capitano m captain; **capitano del porto** harbour master

capitello m capital

capitolo m chapter

capo m head; leader; boss; **capo di vestiario** item of clothing; **detersivo per capi delicati** soap powder for delicates

capocuoco m chef

Capodanno m New Year's Day

capogruppo m group leader

capolavoro m masterpiece

capolinea m terminus

capoluogo m ≈ county town

capotreno m guard (*on train*)

cappella f chapel

cappello m hat

cappotto m overcoat

cappuccino m frothy white coffee

cappuccio m hood

capra f goat

capretto m kid

capriolo m roe deer

carabiniere m (military) policeman

caraffa f decanter; carafe

caramella f sweet
caramello m caramel
caratteristica f characteristic; feature
caratteristico(a) characteristic; typical
carbone m coal
carburante m fuel; **pompa del carburante** fuel pump
carburatore m carburettor
carcere m prison
carciofo m artichoke
cardiologia f cardiology
carenza f shortage
caricare to load; to wind up; to charge (battery)
carico m shipment; cargo; load; **accesso consentito per operazioni di carico e scarico** access for loading and unloading only
carino(a) lovely; pretty; nice
carnagione f complexion
carne f meat; flesh; **carne di cervo** venison; **carne di maiale** pork; **carne di manzo** beef; **carne di montone** mutton; **carne tritata** mince; **carni bianche** white meats; **carni nere** game meats; **carni rosse** red meats
caro(a) dear
carota f carrot
carpa f carp
carpaccio m thin slices of rare beef with oil, salt and pepper and sometimes grated cheese

carpione: pesce in carpione soused fish
carreggiata doppia f dual carriageway
carrello m trolley; **carrello per bagagli** luggage trolley
carriera f career
carro m cart; **carro attrezzi** breakdown van
carrozza f: **carrozza ferroviaria** railway carriage; **carrozza a salone** open-plan carriage; **carrozze cuccette** carriages with couchettes; **carrozze letto** sleepers
carrozzeria f bodywork; body repairer's
carrozzina f pram
carta f paper; card; **alla carta** à la carte; **Carta d'Argento** Senior Citizen's rail card; **carta carbone** carbon paper; **carta di credito** credit card; **Carta Famiglia** Family rail card; **carta geografica** map (of country); **carta da gioco** playing card; **carta d'identità** identity card; **carta igienica** toilet paper; **carta d'imbarco** boarding pass; **carta da lettere** notepaper; **carta nautica** chart (map); **carta da pacchi** wrapping paper; **carta da parati** wallpaper; **carta da regalo** (gift) wrapping paper; **carta da scrivere** writing paper; **carta stradale** road map; **carta verde** green card
cartella f folder; briefcase;

schoolbag

cartello m sign; signpost; cartel

cartoccio m paper bag; **pesce/pollo al cartoccio** fish/chicken baked in tinfoil

cartoleria f stationer's (shop)

cartolina f postcard; greetings card; **cartolina di Natale** Christmas card

cartoncino m card

cartone m cardboard; cardboard box; **cartone animato** cartoon (animated)

cartuccia f cartridge

casa f house; home; **offerto(a) dalla casa** on the house; **casa di cura** nursing home; **casa colonica** farmhouse; **casa dello studente** student hostel

casalinga f housewife

casalinghi mpl household articles

casamento m block of flats

cascata f waterfall

casco m helmet; crash helmet

casella postale f post-office box

casello m: **casello autostradale** motorway tollgate

caserma f barracks; **caserma dei pompieri** fire station

caso m case (instance); **nel caso che** in case; **a caso** at random; **per caso** by accident; by chance; **in caso di necessità rompere il vetro** in an emergency break the glass

cassa f cash desk; cash register;

crate; **cassa chiusa** checkout closed; position closed; **cassa continua** night safe; **cassa da imballaggio** packing case; **cassa di risparmio** savings bank

cassaforte f strongbox; safe

cassata f tutti-frutti ice cream

casseruola f saucepan; casserole (dish)

cassetta f box; cartridge (of tape); cassette; **cassetta di pronto soccorso** first-aid kit; **cassetta per le lettere** letterbox; **cassetta di sicurezza** safe-deposit box

cassetto m drawer

cassiere(a) m/f cashier; teller

castagna f chestnut

castagnaccio m chestnut cake with pine nuts and sultanas

castano(a) brown (hair)

castello m castle

casuale chance

catarifrangente m reflector (on cycle, car)

catena f chain; range (of mountains); **catene (da neve)** snow chains; **obbligo di catene** snow chains compulsory

catrame m tar

cattedrale f cathedral

cattivo(a) bad; nasty; evil; naughty

cattolico(a) Roman Catholic

catturare to capture

causa f cause; case (lawsuit); **a causa di** because of

causare to cause

cauzionale: deposito cauzionale deposit
cauzione f security (for loan); bail (for prisoner); deposit (for key etc); **su cauzione** on bail
cavalcare to ride
cavalcavia m flyover (road)
cavaliere m partner (dancing)
cavallo m horse; **cavallo da corsa** racehorse
cavare to take out; **cavarsela** to manage
cavatappi m corkscrew
caviale m caviar(e)
caviglia f ankle
cavo m cable
cavolfiore m cauliflower
cavolini di Bruxelles mpl Brussels sprouts
cavolo m cabbage; **cavolo cappuccio** spring cabbage; **cavolo rapa** kohlrabi
c'è there is
ce before lo, la, li, le, ne = **ci**
cedere to give in (yield)
cedro m cedar; lime (fruit)
C.E.E. f E.E.C.
cefalo m grey mullet
celibe single (not married: man)
cena f dinner; supper; dinner party
cenere f ash (cinders)
cenno m sign; nod; wave
cenone m: **cenone di Capodanno** New Year's Eve dinner
centesimo(a) hundredth; cent (US)

centinaio m a hundred; about a hundred
cento hundred
centrale central; **centrale telefonica** f telephone exchange
centralinista m/f switchboard operator
centralino m switchboard
centro m centre; **centro arredamenti** furniture centre; **centro assistenza tecnica** after-sales department; **centro città** city centre; town centre; **centro commerciale** shopping centre
ceppo m log (of wood)
cera f wax; polish (for floor)
ceramica f pottery
cerasella f cherry liqueur
cercare to look for; to look up (word); **cercare di fare** to try to do
cerchio m ring; hoop; circle
cernia f: **cernia (gigante)** grouper; **cernia (di fondo)** stone bass
cerniera lampo f zip(-fastener)
cerotto m sticking-plaster
certamente definitely; certainly
certificato m certificate
certo(a) certain; sure; definite
cervella fpl brains (food)
cervello m brain; brains (as food)
cervo m deer; **carne di cervo** venison
cespuglio m bush
cesta f hamper
cestino m waste paper basket

cetriolino m gherkin

cetriolo m cucumber

che that; than; who; whom; which; what; **che c'è?** what's wrong?; **non era che un errore** it was just a mistake

chi who; whom; **di chi è questo libro?** whose book is this?

chiacchierare to chat; to gossip

chiamare to call; **fare chiamare** to page

chiamarsi to be called

chiamata f call; **chiamata d'emergenza** emergency call; **chiamata urbana/interurbana** local/long-distance call

Chianti m dry red/white wine from Tuscany

chiaretto m claret

chiaro(a) clear; light (bright, pale)

chiatta f barge

chiave f key; spanner; **chiave dell'accensione** ignition key

chiavistello m bolt

chiedere to ask; to ask for

chiesa f church

chile m chili

chilo m kilo

chilogrammo m kilogram(me)

chilometraggio m ≈ mileage; **chilometraggio illimitato** unlimited mileage

chilometrico(a): biglietto chilometrico special ticket which can be used to travel a certain number of kilometres

chilometro m kilometre

chimico(a) chemical

chinarsi to bend (person)

chinotto m bitter orange drink

chiocciola f snail

chiodo m nail (metal); stud; **chiodo di garofano** clove

chiosco m kiosk

chirurgia f surgery (operation)

chirurgo m surgeon

chitarra f guitar

chiudere to shut; to close; to turn off; **chiudere a chiave** to lock

chiudersi to shut; to close; **si chiude da sé** door closes automatically

chiunque whoever; anybody

chiusa f lock (in canal)

chiuso(a) shut; off (tap, light etc)

chiusura f end; closure; closing down; lock; **(orario di) chiusura** closing time

ci us; to us; ourselves; one another; there; **ci sono** there are

cialda f waffle

ciao hello; goodbye

ciascuno(a) each

cibo m food

cicatrice f scar

ciclismo m cycling

ciclista m/f cyclist

ciclomotore m moped

cicoria f endive; chicory

cieco(a) blind

cielo m sky

cifra f figure (number); **cifra tonda** round figure/number

ciglio m eyelash

cigno m swan

ciliegia f cherry

cilindro m cylinder

cima f peak; top; **cima alla genovese** cold veal stuffed with sausage, eggs and mushrooms

cimice f (bed)bug

cimitero m cemetery

cincin cheers!

cinepresa f cine-camera

cinese Chinese

cinghia f strap; **cinghia della ventola** fanbelt

cinghiale m wild boar

cinquanta fifty

cinque five

cintura f belt (for waist); **cintura di sicurezza** seat belt; **cintura di salvataggio** lifebelt

cinturato(a) radial(-ply)

ciò this; that; **ciò che** what

cioccolata f chocolate; **cioccolata calda** hot chocolate

cioccolatino m chocolate; **cioccolatini assortiti** assorted chocolates

cioccolato m chocolate; **cioccolato scuro** plain chocolate

cioè that is (to say) . . .

ciottolo m pebble

cipolla f onion

cipollina f spring onion

cipria f face powder

circa about

circo m circus

circolare to move (traffic)

circolazione f circulation; movement; **circolazione stradale** (road) traffic; **valido per la circolazione all'estero** valid for driving abroad; **tassa di circolazione** road tax

circolo m circle

circondare to surround

circonvallazione f ring road; bypass

circostanze fpl circumstances

CIT f Italian Tourist Agency

citazione f quotation (passage); summons

citofono m intercom

città f town; city

clacson m horn (of car)

classe f class; **classe economica** economy class; **classe turistica** tourist class

cliente m/f customer; guest (at hotel); client; **cliente successivo** next customer

clientela f customers; clients

clima m climate

climatizzato(a) air-conditioned

cocco m coconut

coccodrillo m crocodile

cocktail m: **cocktail di scampi** prawn cocktail

cocomero m watermelon

coda f tail; queue; train (of dress); **fare la coda** to queue; **coda di rospo** angler fish

codice m code; **codice fiscale** tax code; **codice postale** postcode; **codice stradale** Highway Code

cofano m bonnet (of car)

cognata f sister-in-law

cognato m brother-in-law

cognome m surname; **cognome da nubile** maiden name

coincidenza f connection (train etc); coincidence; **questo treno fa coincidenza con quello delle 16.45** this train connects with the 16.45; **coincidenze nazionali/internazionali** domestic/international connections

coincidere to coincide

colapasta m colander

colare to strain (tea etc)

colazione f breakfast; **colazione all'inglese** English breakfast; **colazione in stanza** breakfast in one's room

colino m strainer; **colino da tè** tea strainer

colla f glue; paste

collana f necklace

collant m tights

collaudare to test

collega m/f colleague

collegamento m: **collegamenti internazionali** international connections

collera f anger

colletto m collar

collezione f collection

collina f hill

collinoso(a) hilly

collo[1] m neck; **collo alto** polo neck; **collo a V** V-neck

collo[2] m parcel; piece of luggage; **colli a mano** hand luggage

collocare to place

colloquio m interview

colomba f dove

colonia f colony; holiday camp

Colonia f: **(acqua di) Colonia** (eau de) cologne

colonna f column; **colonna sonora** sound track; **colonna dello sterzo** steering column

colonnato m colonnade

colorante m: **senza coloranti** no artificial colouring

colore m colour; **di colore** coloured (person)

colpa f fault (blame)

colpevole guilty

colpire to hit; to beat; to strike; to knock

colpo m knock; blow; hit; shot (from gun); stroke; bang (of gun etc); thump (noise)

coltello m knife

coltivare to grow (plants); to cultivate

comandante m captain (of ship, plane)

comandi mpl controls

combattimento m fight

combustibile m fuel

come like; as; how; **come?** pardon?; **com'è?** what's it like?; **come va?** how are you?

comico m comedian

comignolo m chimney

cominciare to start, begin

comitiva f group; **sconti per comitive** discounts for group bookings

commedia f comedy; play

commensali *mpl* table companions

commerciante *m/f* dealer; trader

commercio *m* commerce; trade

commesso(a) *m/f* assistant; clerk

commettere to commit (*crime*)

commissariato *m* police station

comodità *fpl* amenities

comodo(a) comfortable

compagnia *f* company; **compagnia aerea** airline; **compagnia di navigazione** shipping company

compensato *m* plywood

compito *m* job; duty; task

compleanno *m* birthday; **buon compleanno!** happy birthday!

complesso(a) complex; **complesso pop** *m* pop group

completamente completely

completare to complete

completo(a) complete; full up (*bus etc*); **un completo** a suit; an outfit; a two-piece; **al completo** full; no vacancies

complicato(a) complex; elaborate; complicated

complimento *m* compliment; **complimenti!** congratulations!

comporre to dial (*number*)

comportamento *m* behaviour

comportarsi to behave; to act

compositore *m* composer

comprare to buy

comprensione *f* understanding

compreso(a) including; **servizio compreso** inclusive of service; **... non compreso(a)** exclusive of ...

comune[1] common

comune[2] *m* town council; town hall; municipality

comunicazione *f* communication; **comunicazione telefonica** telephone call; **ottenere la comunicazione** to get through (*on phone*)

comunque in any case; nevertheless; however

con with

concessionario *m* agent; dealer

conchiglia *f* shell

conciliare: conciliare una contravvenzione to settle a fine on the spot

concorrenza *f* competition

concorso *m* contest

condimento *m* dressing; seasoning

condizionamento dell'aria *m* air-conditioning

condizione *f* condition; proviso; **a condizione che ...** on condition that ...

condizioni *fpl* terms (*of contract*); **condizioni del tempo permettendo** weather permitting

condominio *m* block of flats; condominium

condomino *m*: **riservato ai condomini** residents only

conducente *m* driver (*of taxi, bus*)

conduttori elettrici *mpl* jump leads

conferenza *f* lecture; conference

confermare to confirm

confezionato(a) ready-made (*clothes*)

confezione *f* packaging; **confezione gigante** giant economy size; **confezione regalo** gift pack; **confezioni per signora** ladies' wear; **confezioni da uomo** menswear

confine *m* boundary; border

confondere to mix up; to confuse

confrontare to compare

congedo *m* leave (*holiday*); **in congedo** on leave

congelato(a) frozen (*food*)

congelatore *m* deep-freeze

congratularsi con to congratulate

coniglio *m* rabbit; **coniglio stufato** rabbit stew

connazionale *m/f* fellow countryman/woman

cono *m* cone; **cono gelato** ice-cream cone

conoscenza *f* acquaintance; knowledge

conoscere to know

conoscersi to meet

conoscitore *m* connoisseur

consegna *f* delivery; consignment

consegnare to deliver (*goods*)

conseguenza *f* consequence

conservante *m*: **senza**

conservanti no preservatives

conservare to keep; to preserve; **conservare in luogo fresco e asciutto** store in a cool, dry place

conservarsi to keep; **da conservarsi in frigo** keep refrigerated

conservatorio *m* academy of music

consigliare to advise

consiglio *m* advice; **consigli per l'uso** instructions for use

consistere in to consist of

consolato *m* consulate

console *m* consul

consultare to consult; to refer to

consumare to consume

consumarsi: **da consumarsi entro il ...** best before ...

consumatore *m* consumer

consumazione *f* drink; **buono per una consumazione** voucher for one drink; **la consumazione è obbligatoria** customers only, please

contachilometri *m* ≈ milometer

contante *m* cash; **pagare in contanti** to pay cash

contare to count; **contare su** to rely on

contatore *m* meter

contattare to reach (*contact*)

contatto *m* contact; **mettersi in contatto con** to contact

contenere to hold; to contain

contento(a) happy; pleased;

content(ed)

contenuto m contents

contestare to dispute

continuare to continue

continuo(a) continuous; continual

conto m bill; account; **conto corrente** current account; **conto in banca** bank account; **per conto di** on behalf of

contorno m vegetables

contrario m opposite; **al contrario** on the contrary

contratto m contract; **contratto di viaggio** travel agreement terms

contravvenzione f fine

contribuire to contribute

contro against; versus

controllare to check; to control; to inspect (*ticket*)

controllo m check; control; **controllo acque** radiator check; **controllo gomme** tyre check; **controllo passaporti** passport control

controllore m ticket inspector; **controllore di volo** air traffic controller

contusione f bruise

convalidare to punch; to stamp; **convalida** punch (*or* stamp) this side; **il biglietto va convalidato nella obliteratrice all'inizio del viaggio** insert your ticket in the machine at the start of your journey

convegno m conference

convento m monastery; convent

conversazione f talk; conversation

convocazione f: area **convocazione gruppi** group rendezvous point

coperchio m cover; lid

coperta f cover; blanket

coperte fpl bedclothes

coperto m place setting; cover charge; **al coperto** indoor (*games*)

copertura f cover (*insurance*)

copia f copy; print (*photographic*)

copiare to copy

copisteria copy bureau

coppa[1] f cup (*trophy*); dish; **coppa dell'olio** sump (*in car*); **coppa gelato** dish of ice cream; tub of ice cream

coppa[2] f large pork sausage

coppia f pair (*of people*); couple

coprire to cover

coraggio m courage

coraggioso(a) brave

corda f cord (*twine*); rope; string

cordialmente yours sincerely

cornamusa f (bag)pipes

cornice f frame (*of picture*)

corno m horn

coro m choir

corona f crown

corpo m body

corposo(a) full-bodied

corredo m kit; trousseau; **corredi neonato** baby clothes

correggere to correct

corrente f power (*electricity*); current; **corrente d'aria** draught
correntemente fluently
correre to run
correttamente properly
corretto(a) right; correct; proper
corridoio m corridor
corrimano m handrail
corrispondere to correspond
corrompere to corrupt; to bribe
corrotto(a) corrupt
corsa f race; journey; **corsa semplice** single fare; **ultima corsa** last bus; **corse ippiche** horse-racing
corsetteria f corsetry
corsetto m corset
corsia f lane; ward (*in hospital*); **corsia di emergenza** hard shoulder; **corsia di sorpasso** outside lane
corso m course; **corso dei cambi** exchange rates; **corso per corrispondenza** correspondence course; **corso intensivo** crash course; **corso di lingua** language course
corteo m parade
cortile m courtyard; yard; playground
corto(a) short; **essere a corto di qualcosa** to be short of something
cosa f thing; **cosa vuole?** what do you want?
coscia f thigh; **coscia di pollo** chicken leg
cosciotto m leg; **cosciotto**

d'agnello leg of lamb
così so; thus (*in this way*)
cosmetici mpl cosmetics
cospargere di to sprinkle with
costa f coast
Costa Azzurra f French Riviera
costare to cost; **quanto costa?** how much is it?
costata f: **costata di manzo** beef entrecôte
costo m cost
costola f rib
costoletta f cutlet; **costoletta di vitello alla milanese** veal cutlet coated in breadcrumbs and fried
costoso(a) expensive
costringere to force
costruire to build; to construct
costruzione f construction
costume m custom; fancy dress; costume; **costume da bagno** swimsuit; swimming trunks; **costume nazionale** national dress
cotechino m spiced pork sausage
cotoletta f cutlet; **cotoletta alla milanese** chop/cutlet coated in breadcrumbs and fried
cotone m cotton; **cotone idrofilo** cotton wool
cotto(a) done (*cooked*); **poco cotto(a)** underdone
cottura f cooking; baking
cozza f mussel; **cozze alla marinara** breaded mussels cooked in wine with herbs, carrot and onion

crauti mpl sauerkraut
cravatta f tie; **cravatta a farfalla** bow tie
creare to create
credenza f sideboard; belief
credere to believe
credito m credit; **non si fa credito** no credit given; **credito residuo** credit remaining
crema f cream; custard; **crema per barba** shaving cream; **crema per calzature** shoe cream; **crema fredda ai cetrioli** cucumber with yoghurt, milk, cream and parsley; **crema per le mani** hand cream; **crema con pomodori** cream of tomato soup; **crema solare** sun cream; **crema per il viso** face cream
crepuscolo m dusk
crescere to grow; to grow up
crescione m cress
crescita f growth
crespella f fried pastry twist
cric m jack (for car)
crimine m crime
cristallo m crystal
criticare to criticize
croccante crisp
crocchetta f croquette; **crocchette di patate** potato croquettes
croce f cross
crocevia m crossroads
crociera f cruise; **crociera d'altura** sea cruise
croco m crocus
crollare to collapse; to slump

crollo m collapse; slump; **pericolo di crollo** danger: building unsafe
cromo m chrome
cronaca f news
cronista m/f reporter
cronometro m stopwatch
crosta f crust; scab
crostacei mpl shellfish
crostino m crouton
crudele cruel
crudo(a) raw (uncooked)
cruscotto m dash(board)
cubetto di ghiaccio m ice cube
cuccetta f couchette; berth
cucchiaiata f tablespoon (measure); spoonful
cucchiaino m teaspoon
cucchiaio m spoon; dessertspoon
cucina f kitchen; cooker; cooking; **cucina a gas** gas cooker
cucinare to cook
cucinino m kitchenette; **cucinino accessoriato** fully-equipped kitchenette; **cucinino con frigorifero e blocco cottura** kitchenette with fridge and cooker
cucire to sew
cuffia f headphones; **cuffia da bagno** bathing cap
cugino(a) m/f cousin
cui that, which; whose
culla f cradle
cullare to rock
cultura f culture

cumulo m pile; **cumulo di neve** snowdrop
cunetta f gutter (in street)
cuocere to cook; **cuocere al forno** to bake; **cuocere ai ferri** to grill
cuoco(a) m/f cook
cuoio m leather; **cuoio verniciato** patent leather
cuore m heart
cura f care; treatment (medical)
curare to treat; to cure; to look after
curioso(a) curious; funny; quaint
curva f bend; corner; curve; **curva a gomito** hairpin bend; **curva senza visibilità** blind corner
curvare to bend
cuscinetti mpl bearings (in car)
cuscino m cushion
custode m caretaker
custodia valori f valuables accepted for safekeeping
custodire to keep; to guard
C.V. horse power, h.p.

D

da from; by; since; with; **dal giornalaio** at/to the newsagent's
dadi mpl dice
dado m stock cube
dagli = da + gli, **dai** = da + i
dama f draughts; partner (dancing)
danneggiare to spoil; to

damage
danni mpl damages
danno m damage; harm
dappertutto everywhere
dapprima at first
dare to give; **dare su** to overlook to give onto
data f date (day)
dati mpl data
datore di lavoro m employer
dattero m date (fruit)
dattilografo(a) m/f typist
davanti in front; opposite
dazio m customs duty
debito m debt; debit
debole weak; faint
decaffeinato(a) decaffeinated
decennio m decade
decente decent
decidere to decide
decidersi to decide
decimo(a) tenth
decollare to take off (plane)
decollo m takeoff
decorare to decorate
deficienza f shortage
degli = di + gli
degustare to sample (wine)
degustazione f: **degustazione caffè** specialist coffee shop and coffee bar; **degustazione vini** specialist wine bar
dei = di + i, **del** = di + il
delegazione f delegation
delicato(a) delicate; dainty
delitto m crime
delizioso(a) delightful; delicious
deludere to disappoint

deluso(a) disappointed

demi-sec: spumante demi-sec *m* medium-dry sparkling wine

denaro *m* money; **denaro liquido** cash

denominazione f: **denominazione di origine controllata** mark guaranteeing the quality and origin of a wine; **denominazione di origine controllata e garantita** as above, but of a higher standard: awarded to only a few top-quality wines

denso(a) thick; dense

dente *m* tooth

dentiera f dentures

dentifricio *m* toothpaste

dentro in; inside

depositare to settle (*wine*); to deposit

deposito *m* deposit; **deposito bagagli** left luggage office; **deposito valori** place where valuables may be left

deriva: andare alla deriva to drift

derubare to rob

descrivere to describe

descrizione f description

desiderare to wish for; to desire

desiderio *m* wish; desire

destinazione f destination; **con destinazione Messina** bound for Messina

destra f right; **a destra** on/to the right

destro(a) right

detersivo *m* soap powder; detergent

detrarre to deduct

detrazione f deduction

dettagliatamente in detail

dettaglio *m* detail

dettatura f: **dettatura telegrammi** telemessage service

deviare to reroute; to divert; to swerve

deviazione f diversion; detour

di of; some; **di giorno/notte** by day/night; **meglio di lui** better than him

diagnosi f diagnosis

dialetto *m* dialect

diamante *m* diamond

diapositiva f slide (*photo*)

diarrea f diarrhoea

dibattito *m* debate

dicembre *m* December

dichiarare to declare; **niente da dichiarare** nothing to declare

dichiarazione f declaration; statement; **dichiarazione doganale** customs declaration

diciannove nineteen

diciassette seventeen

diciotto eighteen

dieci ten

dieta f diet

dietro behind; after

difendere to defend

difesa f defence

difetto *m* defect; fault

differenza f difference

difficile difficult

difficoltà f difficulty

diffondere to spread (news)

diga f dam; dyke

digestivo m after-dinner liqueur

dilettante m amateur

diluire to dilute

dimagrire to lose weight

dimensioni fpl size; dimensions

dimenticare to forget

diminuire to reduce; to diminish

diminuzione f reduction; fall

dimostrazione f demonstration

dindio m: **dindio ripieno** stuffed turkey

dintorni mpl surroundings

dio m god; **Dio** God

dipendere da to depend on; **dipende** it depends

dipingere to paint

dipinto m painting

diramazione f fork

dire to tell; to say; **si dice che ...** they say that ...

direttamente straight; directly

diretto(a) direct; **treno diretto** through train

direttore m conductor (of orchestra); governor (of institution); manager; president (of company); director (of firm); **direttore di banca** bank manager

direttrice f manageress

direzione f management; direction; **direzione amministrativa** administration; **direzione regionale del turismo** regional tourist board

headquarters

dirigere to manage

dirigersi: dirigersi a or **verso** to make one's way towards

dirimpetto opposite

diritto m right; right side (of cloth etc); **diritto per esazioni in treno** fine payable if not in possession of a train ticket; **diritti portuali/aeroportuali** harbour/airport taxes

diritto(a) straight; **sempre diritto** straight on

dirottare to hijack

disagio m discomfort; difficulty

disapprovare to disapprove of

disarmato(a) unarmed

disastro m disaster

disbrigo m: **disbrigo (di)** dealing (with)

discesa f descent; **in discesa** downhill

disco m disc; record; **disco orario** parking disc

discorso m speech

discoteca f disco(thèque)

discreto(a) discreet; fair

discussione f discussion; **fuori discussione** out of the question

discutere to discuss

disdire to cancel

disegno m plan; design; pattern; drawing

disfare to unpack; to undo; to unwrap

disinfettante m disinfectant

disoccupazione f unemployment

disordinato(a) untidy
disordine m mess
dispari odd (*number*)
dispensa f larder
dispensario m dispensary
disperso(a) missing
dispiacere a to displease; **mi dispiace** (I'm) sorry
disponibile available
disporre to arrange
dispositivo m gadget
disposizione f arrangement; order; measure; **per disposizione di legge** by law; **tempo a disposizione per shopping** you will be allowed time to shop; **siamo a vostra completa disposizione** we are entirely at your disposal
disposto(a) willing
dissenso m disagreement
dissestato(a): strada dissestata road up
distanza f distance; **a poca distanza dal mare** within easy reach of the sea
distinguere to distinguish
distintivo m badge
distorsione f sprain
distrarre to distract
distributore m distributor; **distributore automatico** vending machine; **distributore automatico di benzina** self-service petrol pump; **distributore di benzina** petrol pump
distribuzione f distribution; delivery
distruggere to destroy
disturbare to disturb; **pregasi non disturbare** do not disturb; **non disturbare il conducente** do not distract the driver
disturbarsi to put oneself out
disturbo m trouble; **disturbi di stomaco** stomach trouble
disubbidire to disobey
dito m finger; **dito del piede** toe
ditta f business; firm; company
diurno(a) day(time); **programma diurno** daytime programme; **albergo diurno** public toilets with washing and shaving facilities *etc*
divano m sofa; divan; **divano letto** bed settee
diventare to become
diversi(e) several
diverso(a) different
divertente funny
divertire to amuse
divertirsi to enjoy oneself
dividere to divide; to share
divieto: è fatto severo divieto ... it is strictly forbidden to ...; **divieto di parcheggio** no parking
divisa f uniform; **divisa estera** foreign currency
divo(a) m/f star
divorzio m divorce
dizionario m dictionary
DOC *abbreviation of* **denominazione di origine controllata**

doccia f shower (bath)

DOCG abbreviation of denominazione di origine controllata e garantita

documenti mpl papers (passport etc)

dodicesimo(a) twelfth

dodici twelve

dogana f customs

doganiere m customs officer

dolce[1] sweet; mild

dolce[2] m sweet; dessert; cake; **dolci assortiti** assorted cakes/desserts; **dolci della casa** our own cakes/desserts

dolcelatte m mild, creamy blue cheese

Dolcetto m dry red wine with slightly bitter taste

dolciumi mpl sweets

dolere to hurt

dolore m grief; pain

doloroso(a) painful

domanda f question; demand; application (for job); **fare domanda per** to apply for

domandare to ask; to ask for; to demand

domandarsi to wonder

domani tomorrow

domattina tomorrow morning

domenica f Sunday

domestico(a) m/f servant

donare to donate

donatore m: **donatore di sangue** blood donor

dondolare: non dondolare sit still

donna f woman; **donna delle pulizie** cleaning lady

dono m gift; donation

dopo after; afterward(s); **4 anni dopo** 4 years later; **dopo di che** after which

dopobarba m aftershave (lotion)

dopodomani the day after tomorrow

doppio(a) double

dorato(a) golden

dormire to sleep

dormitorio m dormitory

dosaggio m dosage

dottore m doctor

dove where; **di dove è?** where are you from?

dovere[1] m duty

dovere[2] m to have to; must; to owe (money)

dovunque wherever; everywhere

dozzina f dozen

dragoncello m tarragon

dramma m drama; play

droga f drug

drogheria f grocery shop

droghiere m grocer

dubbio m doubt

dubitare to doubt

duca m duke

due two; **tutti(e) e due** both

dunque so

duomo m cathedral

durante during

durare to last

duro(a) hard; tough; harsh

E

e and

è: Lei è you are; **lui è** he is

E *abbreviation of* **est**; road symbol for international route

ebreo(a) Jewish; Jew

ecc etc

eccedenza f excess; surplus

eccellente excellent

eccesso m excess; **eccesso di velocità** speeding

eccezionale exceptional

eccezione f exception; **fatta eccezione per . . .** except for . . .

eccitazione f excitement

ecco here is/are; **eccolo** here he/it is

economico(a) economic; economical

edicola f newsstand

edificio m building

Edimburgo f Edinburgh

editore m publisher

editrice: casa editrice f publishing house

educato(a) well-mannered

effetto m effect; **effetti personali** belongings

efficace effective

egli he

egoistico(a) selfish

egregio(a) distinguished; **Egregio Signor Smith** Dear Mr Smith

elastico(a) elastic

eleggere to elect

elementare elementary; primary (school)

elemento m unit (of machinery, furniture); element

elencare to list

elenco m list; **elenco telefonico** telephone directory

elettrauto m workshop for car electrical repairs; car electrician

elettricista m electrician

elettricità f electricity

elettrico(a) electric(al)

elettrodomestico m domestic (electrical) appliance

elettronico(a) electronic

elettroricambi mpl electrical spares

elevatore m ramp (in garage)

elezione f election

elicottero m helicopter

ella she

emergenza f emergency

emicrania f migraine

emissione f issue

emorragia nasale f nosebleed

emorroidi fpl haemorrhoids

emozionante exciting

emozione f emotion

energico(a) energetic

enfasi f stress; emphasis

enorme enormous

enoteca f wine bar

ente m body, corporation; **ente nazionale/provinciale turismo** national/provincial tourist board

entrambi(e) both

entrare to come in; to enter; to go in

entrata f entrance; **entrata**

abbonati porta anteriore
season ticket holders' entrance
at front of vehicle

entrate *fpl* takings; income

entusiasta enthusiastic

epidemia *f* epidemic

epilessia *f* epilepsy

epoca *f* age (*era*)

eppure and yet

equilibrio *m* balance; **perdere
l'equilibrio** to lose one's balance

equino(a): carni equine *fpl*
horsemeat

equipaggiamento *m*
equipment; gear

equipaggio *m* crew

equitazione *f* horse-riding

erba *f* grass

erbaccia *f* weed

erbaceo(a): vino erbaceo wine
with a flavour of herbs

erbe *fpl* herbs; **erbe aromatiche**
herbs

erbette *fpl* beet tops

erboristeria *f* herbalist's (shop)

ereditare to inherit

ermetico(a) airtight

ernia *f* hernia

errare to wander

errore *m* error; mistake; **errore
di stampa** misprint

eruzione *f* rash

esagerare to exaggerate

esame *m* examination

esaminare to examine; to test

esatto(a) exact; accurate

esaurimento *m* exhaustion;
esaurimento nervoso nervous

breakdown

esaurito(a) exhausted; out of
print; sold out; **tutto esaurito**
sold out; house full

esausto(a) exhausted

esca *f* bait

esclamare to exclaim

escludere to exclude

esclusivo(a) exclusive

escluso(a): escluso taxi *etc*
except for taxis *etc*; **escluse le
bevande** excluding drinks

escursione *f* excursion;
escursione a piedi hike

eseguire to carry out (*order*)

esempio *m* example

esente exempt; **esente da
dogana/tasse** duty-/tax-free

esercitarsi to practise

esercito *m* army

esercizio *m* exercise; business;
**questo esercizio resta chiuso
nel giorno di ...** this shop (or
restaurant *etc*) is closed on ...

esigenza *f* requirement

esigere to demand

esistere to exist

esitare to hesitate

esito *m* result

espatrio *m*: **valido per
l'espatrio** valid for travel abroad

esperienza *f* experience

esperto(a) expert; experienced

esplorazione *f* exploration

esplosione *f* explosion

esporre to expose; to explain; to
display

esportare to export

esportazione f export
esposto(a) exposed; **esposto(a) a nord** facing north
espresso m express letter; express train; espresso (coffee)
esprimere to express
essere to be
essi(e) they; them
esso(a) it
est m east
estate f summer
esterno(a) outside; external
estero(a) foreign; **all'estero** abroad
estetista m/f beautician
estintore m fire extinguisher
estratto m: **estratto di carne** meat extract
estremi mpl details, particulars
estremo(a) extreme
età f age
etichetta f etiquette; tag; label
eventuale possible
evitare to avoid
extrasec: spumante extrasec m extra-dry sparkling wine

F

fa¹ ago
fa²: Lei lo fa you do it; **lui lo fa** he does it
fabbrica f factory
fabbricante m manufacturer
fabbricare to manufacture; **fabbricato in serie** mass-produced
facchino m porter (for luggage)

faccia f face
facciata f façade
facile easy
facilmente easily
facoltativo(a) optional
faggio m beech
fagiano m pheasant
fagioli mpl beans; **fagioli borlotti** kidney beans; **fagioli con le cotiche** beans in a ham and tomato sauce with onion, garlic, basil and parsley
fagiolini mpl runner beans
falegname m carpenter; joiner
fallimento m failure; bankruptcy
fallo m error; **senza fallo** without fail
falò m bonfire
falsificazione f forgery
falso false; fake
fama f fame; reputation
fame f hunger; **avere fame** to be hungry
famiglia f family
familiare family; familiar; m relative
fanale m light (on car); **fanali di posizione** sidelights; **fanali dei freni** stoplights
fango m mud
fantascienza f science fiction
fantasma m ghost
fantino m jockey
faraona f guinea fowl
farcito(a) stuffed (chicken etc)
fare to do; to make; **ti fa bene** it's good for you; **fa caldo** it is

warm/hot

farfalla f butterfly

farina f flour; **farina di granturco** cornflour

farmacia f chemist's shop; **farmacie di turno** duty chemists

faro m headlight; lighthouse

farsa f farce

fascia f band; bandage; **fascia oraria** time band

fascino m charm

fascio m bundle

fastidio m bother; **dare fastidio a** to annoy

fatelo da voi m do-it-yourself

fatto m fact

fattore m factor

fattoria f farm

fattorino d'albergo m bellboy

fattura f invoice; **la fattura si richiede all'atto del pagamento** an invoice should be requested when making payment

fave fpl broad beans

favore m favour; **per favore** please; **per favore silenzio** quiet please

fazzolettino di carta m tissue (handkerchief)

fazzoletto m handkerchief; (head)scarf

febbraio m February

febbre f fever; **avere la febbre** to have a temperature; **febbre da fieno** hay fever

fede f faith; belief; wedding ring

fedeltà f faithfulness; **ad alta fedeltà** hi-fi

federa f pillowcase, pillowslip

fegatelli mpl: **fegatelli alla fiorentina** pig's liver kebabs with fried croutons, bay leaves, fennel and garlic

fegatini mpl: **fegatini d'anatra** duck livers; **fegatini di pollo** chicken livers

fegato m liver; **fegato di maiale/ vitello** pig's/calf's liver; **fegato alla veneziana** calf's liver fried with onions

felice glad

felicissimo(a) delighted

felicità f happiness

felicitazioni fpl congratulations

feltro m felt (cloth)

femmina f female

femminile feminine

fendinebbia: (proiettori) **fendinebbia** mpl fog lamps

feriale: giorno feriale working day, weekday

ferie fpl holiday(s)

ferita f wound; injury; cut

ferito(a) injured

fermaglio m: **fermaglio per capelli** hair slide

fermare to stop

fermarsi to stop; **si ferma automaticamente** (it) stops automatically

fermata f stop; **fermata dell'autobus** bus stop; **fermata a richiesta** request stop; **divieto di fermata** no waiting

fermo(a) firm; steady; stationary; off (machine); **ferme restando le**

condizioni di cui sopra in accordance with the terms as set out above

feroce fierce; **animali feroci** wild animals

ferramenta *fpl* hardware; **(negozio di) ferramenta** ironmonger's (shop)

ferri: ai ferri grilled

ferro *m* iron; **ferro da calza** knitting needle; **ferro da stiro** iron (*for clothes*)

ferrovia railway; **ferrovia pacchi dogana** border customs office for rail parcels

ferroviario(a) rail(way); **carta ferroviaria** rail map

fesa f: **fesa di vitello** rump of veal

fessura f slot; crack

festa f party; holiday (*day*); **festa danzante** dance

festeggiare to celebrate

fetta f slice; **fette biscottate** rusks

fettuccine *fpl* ribbon-shaped pasta

FF SS Italian State Railways

fiamma f flame

fiammifero *m* match

fiasco *m* straw-covered flask

fiato *m* breath

fibbia f clasp; buckle

fibra f fibre

fico *m* fig

fidanzato(a) engaged; fiancé(e)

fidarsi di to trust

fidato(a) reliable

fiducia f confidence (*trust*)

fieno *m* hay

fiera f fair

fieristico(a): sede fieristica trade fair centre

figlia f daughter

figliastra f stepdaughter

figliastro *m* stepson

figlio *m* son

figura f figure

fila f row; queue; **fare la fila** to queue

filetto *m* fillet; **filetto alla Carpaccio** raw strips of fillet steak with mayonnaise, cream, Worcester sauce, red peppers, capers and brandy; **filetto di manzo alla griglia** grilled fillet steak; **filetto al pepe verde** fillet steak with green peppercorns; **filetti di merluzzo/sogliola** cod/sole fillets

filiale f branch; subsidiary

film *m* film; **film per soli adulti** film for adults only; **film giallo/di fantascienza** detective/science fiction film; **film dell'orrore** horror film

filo *m* thread; flex; wire; edge (*of blade*)

filo di ferro *m* wire; **filo di ferro spinato** barbed wire

filone *m*: **filone di vitello** veal marrow bone

filtro *m* filter; **con filtro** tipped (*cigarettes*); **filtro dell'olio** oil filter; **filtro dell'aria** air filter

finalmente finally

finanza f finance

finanziario(a) financial

finanziera f sauce made with truffles, mushrooms, offal and Marsala

finché as long as; until

fine[1] f end; **alla fine** at last; eventually; **fine settimana** weekend

fine[2] m purpose

fine[3] fine; thin

finestra f window

finestrino m window (in car, train)

fingere to pretend

finire to finish

fino even; **fino a** until; as far as; **fino a 6** up to 6

fino(a) fine

finocchio m fennel; **semi di finocchio** fennel seeds

finora up till now

fiocco m flake; bow (in ribbon)

fioraio(a) m/f florist

fior di latte m cream

fiore m flower; **fiori di zucca fritti** fried courgette flowers

fiorista m/f florist

Firenze f Florence

firma f signature

firmare to sign

fiscale fiscal

fischio m whistle

fisco m Inland Revenue

fissare to stare at; to fix; to arrange

fitta f stitch (pain)

fitto(a) dense

fiume m river

flauto m flute

flipper m pinball

flotta f fleet

flusso m flow

focaccia f kind of pizza; bun

focolare m fireplace

fodera f lining

foglia f leaf

foglio m sheet (of paper)

fogna f drain

folaga f coot

folclore m folklore

folla f crowd

folle mad; **in folle** in neutral (car)

fondale m bottom; **attenzione basso fondale** warning: shallow water

fondamentalmente basically

fondare to establish

fondere to melt

fondersi to melt; to merge

fondi mpl funds

fondo m back (of room); bottom; **fondi di caffè** coffee grounds

fonduta f melted cheese with milk, egg yolk and truffles

fontana f fountain

fonte f source; **fonte battesimale** baptismal font

fontina f soft, creamy cheese from Piedmont

footing m jogging

forare to pierce; to punch (ticket etc)

foratura f puncture

forbici fpl scissors

forchetta f fork

forcina f hairpin

forfora f dandruff

forma f form; **in forma** in good shape

formaggio m cheese; **formaggi piccanti/teneri** strong/mild cheeses

formica f ant

fornaio m baker

fornello m stove; hotplate; ring; **fornello a gas** gas ring; camping stove

fornire to provide; to supply

fornitore m supplier

forno m oven

foro m hole; forum; law court; **foro competente** court of jurisdiction

forse perhaps

forte strong; loud; **forte nel golf** good at golf

fortuna f fortune (*wealth*); luck

forza f strength; force; **per causa di forza maggiore** by reason of an act of God; due to circumstances beyond one's control

foschia f mist

fossa f pit

fossato m ditch

foto f photo; **foto ritratto** portrait photo

fotocopia f photocopy

fotografare to photograph

fotografia f photography; photograph

foto-ottica f photographic and optical instruments dealer

fototessera f passport(-type) photo

fra between; among(st); **fra 2 giorni** in 2 days

fracasso m crash (*noise*)

fragola f strawberry; **fragole al limone** strawberries with lemon juice and sugar; **fragole con la panna** strawberries and cream

fragore m roar; rumble

frana f landslide

francese French

franchigia f: **in franchigia** duty free; **franchigia bagaglio** luggage allowance

Francia f France

francobollo m (postage) stamp

frangia f fringe

frappé m milk shake

Frascati m dry or medium-dry white wine from the Frascati area near Rome

frase f phrase; sentence

fratello m brother

frattaglie fpl offal; giblets

frattura f fracture

frazione f village

freccette fpl darts

freccia f arrow; indicator (*of car*); **mettere la freccia** to use one's indicator

freddo(a) cold; **ho freddo** I'm cold

fregare to rub; to cheat

frenare to brake

freno m brake; **freno a mano** handbrake; **freno a pedale**

footbrake; **freni a disco** disc
brakes

fresco(a) cool; fresh; wet (*paint*)

fretta *f* rush; haste; **avere fretta**
to be in a hurry

fricassea *f*: **coniglio/pollo** *etc* **in
fricassea** rabbit/chicken *etc*
fricassee

friggere to fry

frigo *m* fridge

frigorifero *m* refrigerator

frittata *f* omelette; **frittata con
le erbe/le verdure** omelette
with herbs/vegetables

frittella *f* fritter

frizzante fizzy; sparkling

fritto *m*: **fritto misto** mixed fry

fritto(a) fried

frizione *f* clutch (*of car*)

frontale head-on

fronte *f* forehead; **di fronte**
facing; **la casa di fronte** the
house opposite

frontiera *f* frontier; border

frullato *m* milkshake

frullatore *m* blender

frullino *m* whisk

frumento *m* wheat

frusta *f* whip

frutta *f* fruit; **frutta secca** dried
fruit

fruttato(a) fruity (*wine*)

frutteto *m* orchard

fruttivendolo *m* greengrocer

frutto *m* fruit; **frutti di mare**
seafood; **frutti di bosco** fruits of
the forest (blackberries *etc*)

FS Italian State Railways

fu late (*deceased*)

fucile *m* rifle; gun

fuga *f* escape; leak (*gas*)

fuggire to run away; to escape

fumare to smoke

fumatore *m* smoker

fumo *m* smoke

fungere da to act as

fungo *m* mushroom; **funghi
ovoli** royal agaric mushrooms;
funghi porcini boletus
mushrooms; **funghi secchi** dried
mushrooms

funzionare to work
(*mechanism*); **funziona a nafta** it
runs on diesel; **fare funzionare**
to operate (*machine*)

funzionario(a) statale *m/f*
civil servant

fuoco *m* fire; focus; **fuochi
d'artificio** fireworks; **mettere a
fuoco** to focus

fuori outside; out (*not at home*)

fuoribordo *m* outboard

furgone *m* van

furto *m* robbery

fusibile *m* fuse

fuso orario *m* time zone

futuro *m* future

G

gabbia *f* cage; crate

gabinetto *m* toilet; **gabinetto
medico** doctor's surgery

galleggiante *m* float

galleria *f* tunnel; gallery; circle
(*in theatre*); arcade; **prima**

galleria dress circle; **galleria interi/ridotti** full-price/concessionary circle tickets; **galleria d'arte** art gallery

Galles m Wales

gallese Welsh

gallina f hen

gallo m cock

gamba f leg

gamberetto m shrimp; prawn

gambero m crayfish

gamma f range

gancio m hook; **gancio per rimorchio** tow-bar (on car)

garanzia f guarantee; warranty; **garanzia assicurativa** insurance cover; **garanzie infortuni al conducente** cover in the event of an accident to the driver

garofano m carnation

garza f gauze; lint

gas m gas; **gas di scappamento** exhaust (fumes)

gasolio m diesel oil

gassato(a): bevanda gassata fizzy drink

gassoso(a) fizzy

gatto m cat

gelare to freeze

gelateria f ice-cream shop

gelatina f jelly

gelato m ice-cream

gelo m frost

geloso(a) jealous

gemelli mpl twins; cuff links

genere m kind (type); gender

generi alimentari mpl foodstuffs

genero m son-in-law

gengiva f gum

genitori mpl parents

gennaio m January

Genova f Genoa

gente f people

gentile kind; polite

geometra m surveyor

gergo m slang

Germania f Germany; **Germania Occidentale** West Germany; **Germania Orientale** East Germany

gesso m chalk; plaster (for limb); plaster of Paris

gesto m gesture

gettacarte m wastepaper basket

gettare to throw; **non gettare alcun oggetto dal finestrino** do not throw anything out of the window

gettone m token (for machine); chip (in gambling); counter; **gettone telefonico** telephone token; **gettoni esauriti** telephone tokens sold out

gettoniera f telephone-token dispenser

ghiacciaia f icebox

ghiaccio m ice

ghiacciolo m ice lolly

ghiaia f gravel

ghiandola f gland

ghisa f cast iron

già already

giacca f jacket; **giacca a vento** anorak; **giacca di salvataggio** life jacket; **giacca sportiva**

sports jacket; **in giacca e cravatta** a jacket and tie must be worn

giallo m detective story/thriller

giallo(a) yellow

giardinetta f estate (car)

giardiniere m gardener

giardino m garden; **giardino botanico** botanical gardens

giarrettiere fpl suspenders

giglio m lily

ginepro m juniper; **bacche di ginepro** juniper berries

Ginevra f Geneva

gingerino m drink similar to ginger ale

ginnastica f gymnastics; **ginnastica presciistica** pre-ski exercises

ginocchio m knee; **mettersi in ginocchio** to kneel down

giocare to play; to gamble

giocatore(trice) m/f player

giocattolo m toy

gioco m game; **essere in gioco** to be at stake; **gioco d'azzardo** gambling; **giochi di società** parlour games

gioia f joy

gioielli mpl jewellery

gioielliere m jeweller

gioiello m jewel

giornalaio m newsagent

giornale m newspaper; **giornale a fumetti** comic; **giornale radio** radio news; **giornale della sera** evening paper

giornalista m/f journalist

giornata f day

giorno m day; **di giorno in giorno** day by day; **giorno festivo** holiday; **giorno feriale** weekday; **giorno di mercato** market-day

giostra f merry-go-round

giovane young; young person

giovedì m Thursday

gioventù f youth

giradischi m record-player

girare to turn; to spin

giro m tour; turn; rev (in engine); lap (of track); **fare un giro in macchina** to go for a drive

gita f trip; excursion; **gita di gruppo** group excursion

giù down; downstairs

giudicare to judge

giudice m judge

giugno m June

giuntura f joint

giurare to swear

giustizia f justice

giusto(a) right; fair

glassa f icing

gli the; to him/it; **glielo dia** give it to him/her

gliela = gli + la

gliele = gli + le

glieli = gli + li

glielo = gli + lo

gliene = gli + ne

globale inclusive (costs); global

gnocchi mpl small dumplings made of potato or semolina; **gnocchi di semolino alla romana** semolina dumplings made with butter, egg yolks, milk and nutmeg

goccia f drop (of liquid); drip

gocciolare to drip

gola f throat

golf m golf; cardigan

golfo m gulf

goloso(a) greedy

gomito m elbow

gomitolo m ball (of string, wool)

gomma f rubber; tyre; **gomma per cancellare** rubber (eraser); **gomma da masticare** chewing gum

gommone m dinghy (inflatable)

gonfiare to inflate

gonfiarsi to swell (up)

gonfio(a) swollen

gonfiore m swelling

gonna f skirt

gorgonzola m rich, soft blue-veined cheese with a pungent smell

governante f housekeeper

governare to govern; to rule; to steer (boat)

governo m government

GR abbreviation of **giornale radio**

gradazione f: **a bassa gradazione alcolica** low in alcohol

gradevole pleasant

gradinata f flight of steps; terracing

gradino m step; stair

gradire to accept; to like; **gradisce qualcosa da bere?**

would you like something to drink?

grado m grade; standard; degree; **a 2 gradi sotto zero** at minus 2 degrees; **un whisky di 40 gradi** a 70° proof whisky

graffetta f paper clip; staple

graffiare to scratch

grafico m graph; chart

grammatica f grammar

grammo m gram(me)

grana m hard cheese similar to Parmesan

granaio m barn

Gran Bretagna f Great Britain

grancevola f spiny spider crab

granchio m crab; **polpa di granchio** crab meat

grande great; large; big; **di gran lunga** by far

grandine f hail

granita f water ice

grano m grain

granturco m maize

grasso(a) fat; greasy; grease

grata f grating

gratinato(a) sprinkled with grated cheese and breadcrumbs and browned in the oven

grato(a) grateful

grattacielo m skyscraper

grattugia f grater

gratuito(a) free; **il servizio è gratuito** the service is free of charge

grazie thank you

grazioso(a) charming; graceful

Grecia f Greece

greco(a) Greek

grezzo(a) raw (*unprocessed*); crude (*oil etc*)

gridare to shout

grigio(a) grey

griglia *f* grill (*gridiron*); **alla griglia** grilled

grigliata *f* grill; **grigliata mista** mixed grill

Grignolino *m* dry red wine from Piedmont, with the scent of roses

grissino *m* bread-stick

grondaia *f* gutter

grongo *m* conger eel

grossista *m/f* wholesaler

grosso(a) big; thick

grossolano(a) rude

groviera *f* mild cheese with holes: Italian version of the Swiss cheese, gruyère

gru *f* crane

gruccia *f* crutch; coat hanger

grumo *m* lump (*in sauce*)

gruppo *m* group; **gruppo sanguigno** blood group

gruviera *f* = **groviera**

guadagnare to earn; to win

guado *m* ford

guai *mpl* trouble (*problems*)

guancia *f* cheek

guanciale *m* pillow

guanto *m* glove

guardacoste *m* coastguard

guardare to watch; to look at; to look

guardaroba *m* wardrobe; cloakroom

guardia *f* guard; **guardia del corpo** bodyguard; **Guardia di Finanza** Customs and Excise

guardiano *m* warder; caretaker

guardrail *m* crash barrier

guarire to cure; to heal; to recover

guarnizione *f* gasket

guastarsi to go bad (*food*); to fail (*brakes*); to break down (*car etc*)

guasto *m* failure (*mechanical*); **guasto al motore** engine trouble; **guasto tecnico** technical failure

guasto(a) out of order

guerra *f* war

guida *f* directory; guide; guidebook; **guida a sinistra** left-hand drive; **guida telefonica** telephone directory

guidare to drive; to steer

guidatore *m* driver

guinzaglio *m* lead, leash; **cani al guinzaglio** dogs must be on a lead

guscio *m* shell

gustare to taste; to enjoy

gusto *m* taste; flavour

H

ha: Lei ha you have; **lui ha** he has

ho: io ho I have

I

i the

idraulico m plumber

ieri yesterday; **ieri l'altro** the day before yesterday

igienico(a) hygienic

ignorare to ignore (*person*); to be unaware of

il the

illimitato(a) unlimited

illuminato(a) floodlit

illuminazione f lighting; illumination; **illuminazione elettrica** electric lighting; **illuminazione al neon** strip-lighting

imballaggio m packing

imballare to pack (*goods*); to wrap up (*parcel*); to rev

imbarazzato(a) embarrassed

imbarcarsi to embark

imbarcazione f boat

imbarco m boarding; **carta d'imbarco** boarding card

imbattibile unbeatable

imbottigliato(a) bottled

imbottito(a) stuffed (*cushion etc*)

imbrogliare to mix up; to cheat

imbucare to post

immagazzinare to store

immaginare to imagine

immangiabile inedible

immediato(a) immediate; instant

immergere to dip (*into liquid*)

immersione f: **immersione in apnea** diving without breathing apparatus

immobile still

immondizie fpl rubbish

imparare to learn

impasto m mixture

impaziente impatient

impedire to hinder; to prevent

impegnarsi a to undertake

impegno m undertaking; commitment

imperatore m emperor

impermeabile m waterproof; m raincoat

impero m empire

impiegare to employ; to spend; to take

impiegato(a) m/f employee

impiego m use; employment; job

imporre to impose

importanza f importance

importare to import; to matter; **non importa** it doesn't matter

importazione f import

importo m (total) amount

imposta f tax (*on income*); shutter (*on window*); **imposta sul valore aggiunto** value-added tax

impresa f venture; enterprise; undertaking

impressionare to impress; to upset

improbabile unlikely

improvviso(a) sudden

in in; to; into; **in treno/macchina** by train/car; **in marmo** made of marble; **siamo in quattro** there are four of us

inadatto(a) unsuitable

inadempienza f: **eventuali**

inadempienze dei nostri agenti di viaggio . . . any negligence on the part of our travel agents . . .

incantevole charming

incaricarsi di to take charge of

incendio m fire

incerto(a) uncertain; doubtful

inchino m bow

inchiodare to nail

inchiostro m ink

inciampare to trip

incidente m accident; **incidente stradale/aereo** road accident/ plane crash

incinta pregnant

inclinare to tip

incluso(a) included; enclosed; inclusive

incollare to glue

incolpare to blame

incontrare to meet

incrinarsi to crack

incrocio m crossroads; **incrocio a T** T-junction

incubo m nightmare

indicare to show; to point to

indicatore m gauge; indicator

indicazioni fpl directions

indice m index; contents

indietro backwards; back; behind; **il mio orologio va indietro** my watch is slow; **fare marcia indietro** to reverse

indigesto(a) indigestible

indirizzare to send; to address

indirizzo m address

indivia f endive

indomani m: **l'indomani** the next day

indossare to put on (clothes)

indossatrice f (fashion) model

indovinare to guess

indumento m garment

industria f industry

infatti in fact; actually

infelice miserable; unhappy

inferiore inferior; lower

infermiera f nurse

infettivo(a) infectious

infezione f infection

infiammabile inflammable

infiammazione f inflammation

influenza f influence; flu

influire su to influence

informare to inform; **informarsi (di)** to inquire (about)

informazioni fpl information; **per informazioni e prenotazioni di gruppi . . .** for information and group bookings . . .

infortunio m accident

infrangibile unbreakable

ingannare to trick; to deceive

inganno m trick; deceit

ingegnere m engineer

Inghilterra f England

inghiottire to swallow

inginocchiarsi to kneel

ingiusto(a) unfair

inglese English

ingombrante: bagaglio ingombrante luggage exceeding the dimensions allowed

ingombrare: non ingombrare l'uscita do not obstruct the exit

ingorgo m blockage; **ingorgo stradale** traffic jam
ingrandire to enlarge
ingresso m entry; entrance; **prezzo d'ingresso** admission fee; **ingresso libero** admission free; no obligation to buy; **ingresso a pagamento** admission charge; **ingresso pedonale** pedestrian entrance; **ingresso riservato al personale** staff only; **ingresso vietato ai non addetti ai lavori** no entry to unauthorised personnel; **vietato l'ingresso alle persone sprovviste di biglietto di viaggio** ticketholders only beyond this point
ingrosso: all'ingrosso wholesale
iniezione f injection
inizio m start
innamorarsi to fall in love
innestato(a) in gear
inno m hymn; **inno nazionale** national anthem
innocuo(a) harmless
inoltre besides
inondazione f flood
inossidabile rustproof; stainless (steel)
inquilino(a) m/f tenant; lodger
inquinamento m pollution
insaccati mpl sausages
insalata f salad; **insalata verde** green salad; **insalata mista/di pomodori/di riso/di cetrioli** mixed/tomato/rice/cucumber salad; **insalata di pesce** seafood salad; **insalata russa** mixed boiled vegetables in mayonnaise

insegna f sign
insegnante m/f teacher
insegnare to teach
inseguire to chase
inserire to insert; **inserire le banconote una per volta** insert the banknotes one at a time
inserzione f advertisement
insettifugo m insect repellent
insetto m insect
insieme together; m outfit
insistere to insist
insolazione f sunstroke
insolito(a) unusual
insopportabile unbearable
installarsi to settle in
insuccesso m failure
insulina f insulin
intanto meanwhile
intelligenza f intelligence
intenzionale deliberate
intenzione f intention
interessante interesting
interessarsi a to be interested in
interesse m interest
internazionale international
interno m inside; telephone extension; flat number
interno(a) internal
intero(a) whole
interpretazione f interpretation; performance (of actor)
interprete m/f interpreter
interrompere to interrupt
interruttore m switch

interurbano(a) long-distance

intervallo *m* half-time; interval (*in performance*)

intervento *m* intervention; operation (*medical*)

intervenuto *m*: **gli intervenuti** those present

intervista *f* interview

intestato(a) a registered in the name of; made out in the name of

intimi donna *mpl* ladies' underwear

intingolo *m* sauce; tasty dish

intirizzito(a) numb (*with cold*)

intonaco *m* plaster

intonarsi to match

intorno round

intossicazione alimentare *f* food poisoning

intraprendere to undertake

intrattenere to entertain

introdurre to introduce

inutile unnecessary; useless

invalido(a) disabled; invalid

invano in vain

invecchiamento *m* ageing; maturing

invece instead; but; **invece di** instead of

inventario *m* inventory; stocktaking

inverno *m* winter

inversione *f* U-turn

investigatore *m* detective

investire to run down; to invest

invidiare to envy

invitare to invite

invito *m* invitation

involtino *m* stuffed meat roll

io I

iodio *m* iodine

ipermercato *m* hypermarket

ipoteca *f* mortgage

ippodromo *m* racecourse

Irlanda *f* Ireland

irlandese Irish

irruzione *f* raid (*by police*)

iscritto *m* member; **per iscritto** in writing

iscrizione *f* inscription; enrolment; registration

isola *f* island; **isola pedonale** pedestrian precinct

isolato *m* block

isolato(a) isolated

ispettore di polizia *m* police inspector

ispezione *f* inspection

istituto *m* institute; **istituto di bellezza** beauty salon

istruttore(trice) *m/f* instructor/ instructress

istruzione *f* education

istruzioni *fpl* instructions; directions

Italia *f* Italy

Italia Nostra *f* ≈ National Trust

itinerario *m* route; **itinerario di massima** general itinerary; **itinerari d'arte** routes of artistic interest; **itinerario turistico** scenic route

I.V.A. *f* V.A.T.

J

jolly *m* joker (*cards*)

L

l' the; him; her; it; you
la the; her; it; you
là there; **per di là** that way
labbro *m* lip
laboratorio *m* laboratory;
  workshop; **laboratorio orafo**
  goldsmith's
lacca *f* lacquer; hair spray
laccio *m* lace (*of shoe*)
lacrima *f* tear
ladro *m* thief
laggiù down there; over there
lagnarsi to complain
lago *m* lake
lama *f* blade
Lambrusco *m* sparkling red
  wine from Emilia-Romagna
lamentarsi (di) to complain
  (about)
lametta *f* razor blade
lamiera *f* sheet (*of metal*)
lampada *f* lamp; **lampada a
  raggi ultravioletti** sunlamp;
  lampada a stelo standard lamp
lampadina *f* light bulb;
  lampadina tascabile torch
lampione *m* streetlamp;
  lamppost
lampo *m* flash of lightning
lampone *m* raspberry
lana *f* wool; **di lana** woollen;
  pura lana vergine pure new

wool; **lana di vetro** fibre-glass
lancetta *f* needle (*on dial*); hand
  (*of clock*)
lanciare to throw; to launch
larghezza *f* width; breadth
largo(a) wide; broad; **al largo**
  offshore
lasagne *fpl* thin layers of pasta
  with meat sauce, white sauce
  and grated cheese, baked in the
  oven; **lasagne verdi** thin layers
  of spinach pasta, served as
  above
lasciare to leave; to let go of; to
  let (*allow*); **lasciare libero il
  passaggio** keep clear
lassativo *m* laxative
lassù up there
lastra *f* slab; plate
lastricato *m* paving
**lastricato(a): stradine
  lastricate** *fpl* narrow, paved
  streets
laterale: via laterale *f* side
  street
lato *m* side
latta *f* can
lattaio *m* milkman
latte *m* milk; **latte condensato**
  condensed milk; **latte
  detergente** cleansing milk; **latte
  evaporato** evaporated milk;
  latte intero full-cream milk;
  latte macchiato hot milk with a
  dash of coffee; **latte in polvere**
  dried milk; **latte scremato**
  skimmed milk
latteria *f* dairy

lattuga f lettuce; **lattuga romana** cos lettuce
laurea f degree (university)
laureato(a) m/f graduate
lavabile washable
lavabo m washbasin
lavacristallo m windscreen washer
lavaggio m washing; **qui lavaggio rapido** rapid car wash; **per lavaggi frequenti** for frequent shampooing
lavanderia f laundry (place); **servizio lavanderia e stireria** laundry and ironing service
lavandino m sink
lavare to wash; **lavare a secco** to dry-clean
lavarsi to wash (oneself)
lavasecco m dry-cleaner's (shop)
lavastoviglie m dishwasher
lavatrice f washing machine
lavorare to work
lavoratore(trice) m/f worker
lavoro m work; **lavori domestici** housework; **lavori stradali** road works; **lavori in corso** work in progress; road works ahead
le the; them; to her/it; to you
lecca-lecca m lollipop
leccare to lick
legare to tie
legenda f key
legge f law
leggere to read; **leggere attentamente le avvertenze** read the instructions carefully

leggero(a) light (not heavy); weak; mild; slight; minor
legno m wood (material); **di legno** wooden
legumi mpl: **legumi secchi** dried pulses
lei she; her; you; **Lei** you
lente f lens (of glasses); **lenti a contatto** contact lenses
lenticchie fpl lentils
lento(a) slow; slack
lenzuolo m sheet
leone m lion
lepre f hare; **lepre in salmì** jugged hare
lesso m boiled meat
lettera f letter; **lettera di accompagnamento** covering letter; **lettera raccomandata** registered letter
letteratura f literature
lettino m cot
letto m bed; **letto a una piazza** single bed; **letto matrimoniale** double bed; **letti a castello** bunk beds; **letti gemelli** twin beds
lettura f reading
leva f lever
levare to remove; to take away; to take off
levata f collection (of mail); **orario della levata** collection times
lezione f lesson; lecture
li them
lì there
libbra f pound (weight)
liberare to release

libero(a) free; clear (*not blocked*); vacant (*seat, toilet*)
　giorno libero day off
libreria f bookshop; **libreria antiquaria** shop selling old and rare books
libretto m booklet; **libretto di circolazione** logbook (*of car*); **libretto degli assegni** chequebook; **libretto di banca** bankbook
libro m book; **libro di grammatica** grammar (book); **libro tascabile** paperback; **libro paga** payroll
licenziare to dismiss; to lay off
liceo m secondary school (*for 14- to 19-year-olds*)
lieto(a) glad; **molto lieto** pleased to meet you
lievito m yeast
lima f file (*tool*)
limetta f nailfile
limitare to restrict
limite m limit; boundary; **limite di velocità** speed limit
limonata f lemonade
limone m lemon
linea f line; **linea urbana** urban bus service; **linee marittime** sea routes; shipping lines; **Linee FS** Italian State railway network
lingeria f ladies' underwear
lingua f language; tongue; **lingua salmistrata** pickled ox tongue
linguaggio m language
lino m linen

liofilizzato(a) freeze-dried
liquidazione f liquidation
liquido(a) liquid; **denaro liquido** cash
liquirizia f licorice
liquore m liqueur
liquori mpl spirits
liquoroso(a): **vino liquoroso** dessert wine
liscio(a) smooth; straight
lista f list; **lista dei vini** wine list; **lista d'attesa** waiting list; **lista delle pietanze** menu
listino prezzi m price list
lite f argument; quarrel
litigare to argue; to quarrel
litro m litre
livello m level; **livello del mare** sea level
lo the; him; it
locale m room; place; **locale notturno** nightclub
località f: **località balneare/di villeggiatura** seaside/holiday resort
locanda f inn
locomotiva f engine (*of train*)
loggione m: **il loggione** the gods (*in theatre*)
logorare to wear out
logoro(a) worn; worn-out
Londra f London
lontananza f distance
lontano far
lordo(a) gross; pretax
loro they; them; to them; you; to you; **Loro** you; to you; **il loro padre** their/your father

lotta f struggle; wrestling

lotto m lottery; lot (at auction)

lozione f lotion

lucchetto m padlock

luccio m pike

luce f light

lucidare to polish

lucido m polish (for shoes)

luglio m July

lui he; him

lumache fpl snails

luna f moon; **luna di miele** honeymoon

luna-park m amusement park

lunedì m Monday

lunghezza f length

lungo(a) long; **lungo la strada** along the street; **a lungo** for a long time

lungomare m promenade; seafront

lungometraggio m feature film

luogo m place; **in nessun luogo** nowhere; **sul luogo** on the spot

lupo m wolf

lusso m luxury; **di lusso** de luxe; luxury

M

ma but

maccheroni mpl macaroni; **maccheroni alla siciliana** macaroni in a sauce containing tomato, capers, garlic, green and black olives, chilli pepper; **maccheroni alla chitarra** macaroni in a sauce containing bacon, tomato, cheese, onion, basil

macchia f spot; stain; blot

macchiare to stain; to mark

macchina f car; machine; **macchina da scrivere** typewriter; **macchina per cucire** sewing machine; **macchina fotografica** camera; **macchina della polizia** police car; **macchina sportiva** sports car

macchinetta per il caffè f percolator

macedonia f fruit salad

macellaio m butcher

macelleria f butcher's (shop)

macinare to mill; to grind

macinato(a) ground (coffee)

macinino m mill (for coffee, pepper)

madera m Madeira (wine)

madre f mother

madrelingua f mother tongue

madrina f godmother

maestra f teacher (primary school)

maestro m master; teacher (primary school)

magazzino m store room; warehouse; **grande magazzino** department store

maggio m May

maggioranza f majority

maggiorazione f increase

maggiore larger; greater; largest; greatest; elder; eldest

magia f magic

maglia f jersey (sweater);

lavorare a **maglia** to knit
maglieria f knitwear
maglietta f T-shirt
maglione m sweater
magnetofono m tape recorder
magnifico(a) great (*excellent*);
magnificent; grand
magro(a) thin (*person*); lean
(*meat*)
mai never; ever
maiale m pig; pork; **maiale al
latte** pork cooked in milk with
bacon, garlic, cinnamon and
rosemary; **maiale arrosto** roast
pork
maialino m: **maialini da latte**
suckling pigs
maionese f mayonnaise
mais m maize
maiuscola f capital letter
mal m see **male²**
malato(a) ill; sick; sick person;
patient
malattia f illness; disease
male¹ badly (*not well*)
male² m pain; ache; **fare male** to
hurt; **mal d'auto** car-sickness;
mal di mare seasickness; **mal di
cuore/di fegato** heart/liver
complaint; **mal di denti/di gola/
d'orecchi/di stomaco/di testa**
toothache/sore throat/earache/
stomach ache/headache
malgrado in spite of
maltempo m bad weather
malva mauve
malvagio(a) wicked
Malvasia f sweet, aromatic

dessert wine
mamma f mum(my)
mancanza f lack; shortage
mancare to miss
**mancato(a): mancate
coincidenze** fpl missed (rail/air
etc) connections
mancia f tip (*money given*)
mancino(a) left-handed
mandare to send
mandarino m mandarin
(orange)
mandorla f almond
maneggio m riding school
manette fpl handcuffs
mangia-e-bevi m ice cream
with nuts, fruit and liqueur
mangiare to eat; **vietato dare
da mangiare agli animali** do
not feed the animals
manica f sleeve
Manica f Channel
manico m handle
maniere fpl manners
manifestazione f
demonstration (*political*); rally
manifesto m poster
maniglia f handle; strap (*on
bus*)
mano f hand; trick (*in cards*);
fatto(a) a mano handmade
manopola f knob (*on radio etc*);
mitt(en); **manopola di spugna**
facecloth
manovale m labourer
manovella f handle (*for
winding*)
mantello m cloak; coat

mantenere to support (*financially*); to keep

Mantova f Mantua

manubrio m handlebar(s)

manutenzione f upkeep; maintenance

manzo m beef

marca f brand; brand name

marchio m hallmark; **marchio di fabbrica** trademark; **marchio depositato** registered trademark

marcia f march; gear (*of car*); **quarta/prima marcia** top/bottom gear

marciapiede m pavement

marcio(a) rotten (*wood etc*)

marcire to rot; to go bad

mare m sea; seaside; **avere mal di mare** to be seasick

marea f tide; **c'è alta/bassa marea** the tide is in/out

margine m margin

marina f navy

marinaio m sailor

marito m husband

maritozzo m sort of currant bun

marmellata f jam; **marmellata d'arance** marmalade

marmitta f silencer (*on car*)

marmo m marble (*material*)

marrone brown; m chestnut

Marsala m red dessert wine from Sicily

martedì m Tuesday; **martedì grasso** Shrove Tuesday

martello m hammer

marzo m March

mascarpone m soft, creamy

cheese often served as a dessert

mascella f jaw

maschera f mask; usherette

maschile masculine

maschio male

massaggiare to massage

massiccio(a) massive

massimale m maximum sum insurable

massimo(a) maximum

masticare to chew

mastro m ledger

materassino m air bed

materasso m mattress

materia f subject (*in school*); **materie prime** raw materials

maternità f maternity hospital

matita f pencil

matrice f stub (*counterfoil*)

matrimonio m wedding; marriage

matterello m rolling pin

mattina f morning

mattino m morning

mattone m brick

maturarsi to ripen; to accrue

maturo(a) ripe; mature

mazza f club; bat

mazzo m pack (*of cards*); bunch

me me; to me; myself

meccanismo m mechanism; works

medaglioni mpl: **medaglioni di filetto/di pollo** round fillets of beef/chicken

media f average

medicina f medicine; **medicina d'urgenza** emergency treatment

medicinale m drug (*medicine*)

medico m doctor; **medico generico** general practitioner, G.P.

medusa f jellyfish

meglio better; best

mela f apple; **mela cotogna** quince

melagrana f pomegranate

melanzana f aubergine; **melanzane alla parmigiana** aubergines baked with tomatoes, Parmesan cheese and spices; **melanzane ripiene** stuffed aubergines

melassa f treacle

melo m apple tree

melone m melon; **melone ghiacciato** iced melon

membro m member

memoria f memory; **a memoria** by heart

mendicante m/f beggar

meno less; minus; **a meno che** unless; **il meno caro** the least expensive; **meno errori** fewer errors

mensa f canteen

mensile monthly

menta f mint (*herb*)

mente f mind

mentire to lie (*tell a lie*)

mento m chin

mentre while; whereas

menù m: **menù del giorno** menu of the day; **menù turistico** tourist or low-price menu; **menù vegetariano** vegetarian menu

menzione f mention

meraviglioso(a) wonderful, marvellous

mercante m merchant

mercatino m: **mercatino dell'usato** flea market

mercato m market; **Mercato Comune** Common Market; **mercato ittico** fish market

merce f: **la merce si paga alle casse del piano dove è stata scelta** goods must be paid for on the floor from which they have been selected

merceria f haberdashery

merci fpl freight; goods

mercoledì m Wednesday

merenda f snack

meridionale southern

meritare to deserve

merlango m whiting

merlo m blackbird

Merlot m dry red table wine

merluzzo m cod

meschino(a) mean

mescolanza f mixture

mescolare to blend; to mix

mescolarsi to mix

mese m month

messa f mass (*church*); **messa in piega** set (*of hair*)

messaggio m message

mestiere m job; trade

mestruazioni fpl menstruation

metà f half

metro m metre; **metro a nastro** tape measure

metropolitana f underground

mettere to put; to put on
(*clothes*); **mettere in
comunicazione** to put through
(*on phone*); **mettersi in posa** to
pose

mezzanotte *f* midnight

mezzi *mpl* means

mezzo *m* means; means of
transport; middle; **per mezzo di**
by means of; **mezzo di trasporto**
means of transport

mezzo(a) half; **di mezza età**
middle-aged

mezzogiorno *m* midday, noon;
il Mezzogiorno the south of
Italy

mezz'ora *f* half-hour; half-an-
hour

mi me; to me; myself

mia my; mine

microfono *m* microphone

mie my; mine

miei my; mine

miele *m* honey

mietere to harvest (*grain*)

miglio *m* mile

migliorare to improve

migliore better; best

miliardo *m* thousand million

milione *m* million

militare *m* serviceman

mille thousand

mina *f* lead (*in pencil*)

minacciare to threaten

minatore *m* miner

minestra *f* soup; **minestra in
brodo** clear soup with rice or
noodles; **minestra di verdura**
vegetable soup

miniera *f* mine (*for coal etc*)

minigonna *f* miniskirt

minimo(a) minimum

ministero *m* ministry (*political*)

ministro *m* minister (*political*)

minoranza *f* minority

minore less; smaller; lower;
younger; **vietato ai minori di
anni 18** no admission to anyone
under 18 years of age

minorenne under age

mio my; mine

miope shortsighted

mira *f* aim

mirtillo *m* cranberry

miscela *f* blend

misto *m*: **misto mare** mixed fish
salad

misto(a) mixed

misura *f* measure; measurement;
fatto(a) su misura made-to-
measure

mite mild; gentle

mitili *mpl* mussels

mittente *m/f* sender

MM abbreviation of
metropolitana

mobile *m* piece of furniture

mobili *mpl* furniture

moda *f* fashion; **l'ultima moda**
the latest fashions; **di moda**
fashionable

modalità *f*: **secondo le
modalità previste** according to
what has already been agreed;
modalità di pagamento method
of payment; **seguire le modalità**

d'uso follow the instructions
modificare to modify
modisteria f milliner's shop
modo m way; manner; **ad ogni modo** in any case; **in tutti i modi** at all costs; **in qualche modo** somehow
modulo m form (*document*)
mogano m mahogany
moglie f wife
molla f spring (*coil*)
molletta f clothes-peg; **molletta per capelli** hairgrip
mollica f: **mollica (di pane)** crumb
molluschi mpl molluscs
molo m pier; **molo per attracco** docking pier
molti(e) many
moltiplicare to multiply
molto a lot; much; very
molto(a) much; **molta gente** lots of people
momento m moment; **per il momento** for the time being
monaca f nun
monaco m monk
monastero m monastery
mondo m world
moneta f coin
monorotaia f monorail
montagna f mountain
montare to go up; to put up; to assemble (*parts of machine*); to whip (*cream, eggs*)
montatura f frames (*of glasses*)
montone m: **carne di montone** mutton; **giacca di montone** sheepskin jacket
montuoso(a) mountainous
moquette f wall-to-wall carpet(ing)
mora f blackberry
morbido(a) soft
morbillo m measles
mordere to bite
morire to die
morso m bite (*by animal*)
mortadella f type of salted pork meat
morte f death
morto(a) dead
mosca f fly
moscato m muscatel: red or white dessert wine; **moscato spumatizzato** sparkling muscatel; **Moscato d'Asti** sweet, sparkling white wine
moscerino m gnat
moscone m pedalo (with oars)
mosella m Moselle (*wine*)
mostarda f mustard
mostra f show; exhibition; **mostra permanente** permanent exhibition; **mostra convegno** conference and exhibition
mostrare to show
motocicletta f motorbike
motociclista m/f motorcyclist
motociclo m motorbike
motolancia f launch
motonautica f speedboat racing
motore m engine; motor; **vietato tenere motori e luci non elettriche accese** switch off engine and extinguish any

cigarettes
motorino d'avviamento *m*
starter (*in car*)
motoscafo *m* motorboat
movimento *m* motion;
movement
mozzarella *f* moist Neapolitan
curd cheese; **mozzarella in
carrozza** mozzarella with either
anchovies or ham between
2 slices of bread, fried in
batter
mucchio *m* pile; heap
mulino *m* mill; **mulino a vento**
windmill
multa *f* fine; **multa per sosta
vietata** parking ticket
municipio *m* town hall
muovere to move
muoversi to move
muratura *f*: **villette in
muratura** stonebuilt or
brickbuilt villas
muro *m* wall
muscolo *m* muscle
museo *m* museum; **museo
civico di storia naturale**
municipal museum of natural
history; **museo storico** museum
of history
musica *f* music; **musica
leggera/da camera/di
sottofondo** light/chamber/
background music
musicista *m/f* musician
mutande *fpl* underpants
mutandine *fpl* panties
muto(a) dumb

N

nafta *f* diesel oil
nailon *m* nylon
Napoli *f* Naples
narrativa *f* fiction
nascere to be born
nascita *f* birth
nascondere to hide
nasello *m* hake
naso *m* nose
nastro *m* ribbon; tape; **nastro
adesivo** sellotape
Natale *m* Christmas
nato(a) born
naufragio *m* shipwreck
navata *f* nave
nave *f* ship; **nave cisterna**
tanker (*ship*)
nave-traghetto *f* ferry
navigare to sail
nazione *f* nation
ne of him/her/it/them
né . . . né neither . . . nor; **né
l'uno né l'altro** neither
neanche not even; neither
nebbia *f* fog
Nebbiolo *m* light, dry red wine
from Piedmont
negare to deny
negli = in + gli
negoziante *m* shopkeeper
negozio *m* shop
nei = in + i, **nel** = in + il
nemico *m* enemy
nemmeno, neppure not even;
neither
nero(a) black

nervetti *mpl*: **nervetti in insalata** thin strips of sinewy beef or veal served cold with beans, shallots and pickles

nessuno(a) no; any; nobody; none; anybody

netto(a) net; **al netto di IVA** net of VAT

neve *f* snow

nevicare to snow

nevischio *m* sleet

nido *m* nest; **nido d'infanzia** day nursery, crèche

niente nothing; anything

nipote *m/f* grandson/granddaughter; nephew/niece

Nizza *f* Nice

no no (*as answer*)

nocciolo *m* stone (*in fruit*)

noce *f* walnut

nocivo(a) harmful

nodo *m* knot; bow (*ribbon*); **nodo ferroviario** junction (*railway*)

noi we; us

noioso(a) dull; boring; annoying

noleggiare to hire; to rent; to charter (*plane, bus*); **si noleggiano biciclette** bicycles for hire

noleggio *m*: **noleggio biciclette** bicycles for hire; **noleggio furgoni** vans for hire

nolo *m* = **noleggio**

nome *m* name; first name; **nome di battesimo** Christian name

nominare to appoint; to mention

non not

nondimeno all the same

non-fumatore *m* nonsmoker (*person*)

nonna *f* grandmother

nonno *m* grandfather

nono(a) ninth

nord *m* north

norma *f* norm; par (*golf*)

nostalgia *f* homesickness; nostalgia

nostro(a) our; ours

nota *f* note; memo(randum)

notaio *m* notary (*public*)

notare to notice

notevole remarkable

notiziario *m* news (*on TV etc*)

notizie *fpl* news

notte *f* night

novanta ninety

nove nine

novembre *m* November

novità *f* novelty; news

nubile single (*woman*)

nudo(a) naked; nude; bare

nulla nothing; anything

nullo(a) void (*contract*)

numero *m* number (*figure*); act (*at circus etc*); issue (*of magazine*); size (*of shoes*)

nuora *f* daughter-in-law

nuotare to swim

nuovo(a) new; **di nuovo** again

nutrire to feed

nuvola *f* cloud

nuvoloso(a) cloudy

O

o or; **o...o** either...or
obbligo m obligation
obiettare a to object to
obiettivo m lens (of camera);
target; objective; **obiettivo
grandangolare** wide angle lens
obliterare to stamp (ticket); **lato
da obliterare** side to be stamped
obliteratrice f stamping
machine
oblò m porthole
oca f goose
occasione f opportunity;
occasion; bargain
occhiali mpl glasses; goggles;
occhiali da sole sunglasses
occhio m eye
Occidente m: **l'Occidente** the
West
occorrere to be necessary
occuparsi to occupy oneself; **me
ne occupo io** I'll take care of it
occupato(a) busy; engaged
odiare to hate
odierno(a): in data odierna
today
odio m hatred
odore m smell; scent
offerta f bid; offer; **in offerta
(speciale)** on (special) offer
officina f workshop; **officina
autorizzata** authorized garage;
**officina per autovetture
nazionali ed estere** repairs
carried out on all makes of car
offrire to offer; to bid (amount)

oggettistica f fancy goods;
oggettistica regalo giftware
oggetto m object; **oggetto
d'antiquariato** antique
oggi today
oggigiorno nowadays
ogni every; each
ognuno everyone
Olanda f Holland
oleodotto m pipeline
olio m oil; **olio solare** suntan oil;
olio di ricino castor oil; **olio
d'oliva** olive oil
oltre beyond; besides
oltremare overseas
ombra f shadow; shade
ombrello m umbrella
ombrellone m sunshade (over
table); beach umbrella
ombretto m eyeshadow
omettere to omit
omicidio m murder
omissione di soccorso f
failure to stop and give
assistance
omogeneizzati mpl baby foods
oncia f ounce
onda f wave; **onde medie**
medium wave; **onde corte** short
wave; **onde lunghe** long wave
onesto(a) decent (respectable);
honest
onorario m fee
opera f work (art, literature);
opera
operaio m workman
operaio(a) working-class
opuscolo m brochure

ora¹ now
ora² f hour; **ora di pranzo** lunchtime; **ora di punta** rush hour; **che ora è?** what's the time?
orario m timetable; schedule; **in orario** punctual; on schedule; **orario di apertura/chiusura** opening/closing times; **orario di cassa** banking hours; **orario definitivo/indicativo** final/approximate schedule; **orario delle partenze** timetable for departures; **orario degli uffici per il pubblico** hours of opening to the public; **orario di vendita** opening hours; **orario per visitatori** visiting times
orata f sea bream
ordinare to order (goods, meal)
ordinato(a) neat, tidy
ordinazione f order (for goods)
ordine m command; order; **di prim'ordine** high class
orecchino m earring
orecchio m ear
orecchioni mpl mumps
oreficeria f jeweller's (shop)
organizzare to organize
orgoglio m pride
orientarsi to take one's bearings
Oriente m: **l'Oriente** the East
origano m oregano
orizzontale level; horizontal
orizzonte m horizon
orlo m hem; verge
ormeggiare to moor
ornare to decorate

oro m gold; **oro massiccio** solid gold; **placcato oro** gold-plated
orologeria f watchmaker's (shop)
orologio m watch; clock
orso m bear
ortaggi mpl vegetables
ortofrutticolo(a): mercato ortofrutticolo fruit and vegetable market
Orvieto m light, straw-coloured wine from Umbria: dry, sweet or semi-sweet
orzo m barley; **orzo tostato solubile** instant barley coffee
osare to dare
oscuro(a) dim; obscure
ospedale m hospital; **ospedale infantile/psichiatrico** children's/mental hospital
ospite m/f guest; host; hostess
osservazione f remark; observation
ossigeno m oxygen
osso m bone
ossobuco m marrowbone; stew made with knuckle of veal in tomato and wine sauce
ostacolare to obstruct; to hinder
ostacolo m obstacle
ostaggio m hostage
ostello m hostel; **ostello della gioventù** youth hostel
osteria f inn
ostrica f oyster
ostruzione f blockage
ottanta eighty
ottavo(a) eighth

ottenere to obtain; to get;
  ottenere la linea to get through
  (*on phone*)
ottico m optician
otto eight
ottobre m October
ottone m brass
otturatore m shutter (*in camera*)
otturazione f filling (*in tooth*)
ovatta f cotton wool
ovest m west
ovino(a): carni ovine fpl lamb
  and mutton
ovvio(a) obvious
ozio m leisure

P

pacchetto m pack; packet
pacco m package; parcel
pace f peace
padella f frying pan
Padova f Padua
padre m father
padrino m godfather
padrona f landlady
padrone m landlord
paesaggio m scenery;
  countryside
paese m country; land
paesino m village
paga f pay
pagaia f paddle (*oar*)
pagamento m payment;
  pagamento alla consegna cash
  on delivery; **pagamento
  anticipato** payment in advance

pagare to pay; to pay for
pagina f page
paglia f straw
pagliaccio m clown
pagnotta f round loaf
paio m pair; **un paio di** a pair of;
  a couple of
pala f shovel
palasport m sports stadium
palazzo m building; palace;
  palazzo comunale town hall;
  palazzo dei congressi
  conference centre; **palazzo dello
  sport** sports stadium
palco m platform
palcoscenico m stage
palestra f gym(nasium)
paletta f dustpan
palla f ball
pallacanestro f basketball
pallavolo f volleyball
pallido(a) pale
pallone m balloon; football
pallottola f bullet
palma f palm-tree
palo m pole; post
palpebra f eyelid
palude f swamp; bog
panca f bench
pancetta f bacon
panciotto m waistcoat
pandoro m type of sponge cake
  eaten at Christmas
pane m bread; loaf (of bread);
  pane carrè sandwich bread;
  pane e coperto cover charge;
  pane integrale wholemeal
  bread; **pan di Spagna** sponge;

pane di segale rye bread

panetteria f bakery

panettone m very light cake containing sultanas and crystallized fruit, traditionally eaten at Christmas

panforte m nougat-type delicacy from Siena

pangrattato m breadcrumbs

paniere m basket; hamper

panificio m bakery

panino m roll; **panino imbottito** sandwich; **panini caldi** hot rolls

panna f cream; **panna montata** whipped cream; **panna da cucina** ≈ double cream

panno m cloth

pannocchia f corn-on-the-cob

pannolino m nappy

pantaloni mpl trousers

pantofola f slipper

panzarotto m fried savoury turnover with a filling of mozzarella, bacon, egg and sometimes tomatoes and anchovies

papa m pope

papà m dad(dy)

pappardelle fpl wide strips of pasta; **pappardelle con la lepre** wide strips of pasta with spiced hare

parabrezza m windscreen

paracadute m parachute

parafango m mudguard

paralume m lampshade

paraspruzzi m mudguard

paraurti m bumper

paravento m screen (*partition*)

parcheggiare to park

parcheggio m car-park; **parcheggio custodito/incustodito** attended/unattended car-park

parchimetro m parking meter

parco m park; **parco demaniale** public park; **parco giochi bambini** children's play park; **parco marino** nature reserve for marine life

parecchi(ie) several

parente m/f relation; relative; **parente stretto** next of kin

parentesi f bracket

parere[1] to seem, appear

parere[2] m opinion

parete f wall

pari: numero pari even number

Parigi f Paris

parlare to talk; to speak

parmigiano m Parmesan: hard, tangy cheese often used in cooking

parola f word

parrucca f wig

parrucchiere(a) m/f hairdresser

parte f share; part; side; **d'altra parte** on the other hand

partenza f departure

particolare particular; m detail

partire to go; to leave

partita f match; game

partito m party (*political*)

Pasqua f Easter

passaggio m passage; gangway;

dare un passaggio a to give a lift to; **passaggio a livello** level crossing; **passaggio pedonale** pedestrian crossing

passaporto m passport; **passaporto collettivo** group passport

passare to pass; to spend; to put through (on phone); **passare avanti** move forward

passatempo m interest; hobby

passato m past; **passato freddo di pomodoro** chilled tomato soup; **passato di patate/piselli** creamed potatoes/peas; **passato di verdura** cream of vegetable soup

passato(a) past; off (meat)

passeggero(a) m/f passenger

passeggiare to walk

passeggiata f walk; stroll; **passeggiata a mare** promenade

passeggino m pushchair

passe-partout m master key

passera f plaice

passerella f gangway

passero m sparrow

passito m sweet wine made with raisins

passo m pace; step; pass (in mountains); **passo carrabile** keep clear

pasta f pastry; pasta; dough; **pasta di acciughe** anchovy paste; **pasta e ceci/fagioli** chick pea/bean and pasta soup; **pasta frolla** shortcrust pastry; **pasta di mandorle** almond paste; **pasta**

sfoglia puff pastry; **pasta all'uovo** egg pasta

pastasciutta f pasta served in a sauce, not in soup

pastello m crayon

pasticceria f cake shop

pasticciere m confectioner

pasticcino m petit four

pasticcio m muddle; pie (meat); **pasticcio di lasagne** wide strips of pasta in layers, with meat sauce, white sauce and cheese

pastiglia f tablet; pastille

pasto m meal

pastore m shepherd; minister (of religion)

pastorizzato(a) pasteurized

pastoso(a): vino pastoso mellow wine

patata f potato; **patate arrosto/al forno** roast/baked potatoes; **patate fritte** chips; **patate lesse/novelle/in padella/saltate** boiled/new/fried/sautéed potatoes

patatine fpl crisps

pâté m: **pâté di fegato** liver pâté

patente f licence; driving licence

patrimonio m estate; heritage

patta f flap

pattinare to skate

pattino m skate; **pattini a rotelle** roller skates

pattumiera f dustbin

paura f fear

pausa f pause; break

pavimento m floor

paziente patient

pazienza f patience

pazzo(a) mad

peccato m sin; **che peccato!** what a shame!

pecora f sheep

pecorino m hard, tangy sheep's-milk cheese

pedaggio m toll

pedalò m pedalo

pedicure m chiropodist

pedone m pedestrian; **pedoni sul lato opposto** pedestrians please use the other pavement

peggio worse

peggiore worse; worst

pelati mpl: **(pomodori) pelati** peeled tomatoes

pelle f skin; hide; leather; **pelle scamosciata** suede

pelletterie fpl leather goods

pellicceria f furrier's (shop); furs

pelliccia f fur coat; fur

pellicola f film (for camera)

pelo m hair; fur

pena f sentence; sorrow

penale f penalty clause

pendenza f slope

pendere to hang; to lean

pendio m hill; slope

pendolare m commuter

penna f pen; **penna stilografica** fountain pen

pennarello m felt-tip pen

penne fpl quill-shaped tubes of pasta; **penne all'arrabbiata** penne in a spicy sauce of tomatoes, mushrooms, bacon, chilli pepper, basil and garlic; **penne ai funghi** penne with mushrooms, parsley, cream, whisky and butter

pennello m brush; **pennello da barba** shaving brush

pensare to think

pensiero m thought

pensionato(a) m/f pensioner

pensione f boarding house; pension; **pensione completa** full board; **mezza pensione** half board

Pentecoste f Whitsun; Whitsunday

pentola f pot; saucepan

peoci mpl mussels

pepato(a) peppery

pepe m pepper; **pepe bianco/nero** white/black pepper

peperonata f stew of peppers, aubergines, tomatoes, onion, garlic, oregano and basil

peperoncino m chilli pepper

peperone m pepper (capsicum); **peperone verde/rosso** green/red pepper; **peperoni ripieni** stuffed peppers

per for; per; in order to; **per le 4** by 4 o'clock; **3 metri per 3** 3 metres square

pera f pear

percentuale f percentage

perché why; because; in order that

percorrenza f: **biglietto con percorrenza superiore/inferiore a 100 chilometri** ticket for journeys of more than/less than 100 kilometres

percorrere to travel; to cover

percorribilità f: **percorribilità strade** traffic information service

percorso m journey; route; **percorso panoramico** scenic route

perdere to lose; to miss (train); **perdere tempo** to waste one's time

perdita f leak; loss

perdonare to forgive

pericolante unsafe

pericolo m danger

pericoloso(a) dangerous

periferia f outskirts; suburbs

perizia f survey (of building)

perla f pearl; bead

permanente f perm; **permanente continua** parking restrictions still apply

permanenza f: **buona permanenza!** enjoy your stay!

permesso m permission; permit; **permesso di soggiorno** residence permit

permettere to permit

pernice f partridge

pernottamento m overnight stay

pernottare to stay the night

perquisire to search

perquisizione f: **sono previste perquisizioni personali** searches will be carried out

persiana f shutter

persona f person

personale m staff; personnel; **personale di sicurezza** security personnel

pertinente a relevant to

pertosse f whooping cough

p. es. e.g.

pesante heavy

pesare to weigh

pesca f angling; fishing; peach; **divieto di pesca, pesca vietata** no fishing; **pesche al vino rosso** peaches in red wine with cinnamon and sugar

pescatore m angler; fisherman

pesce m fish; **pesce persico** perch; **pesce spada** swordfish

pescecane m shark

pescheria f fishmonger's shop

pescivendolo m fishmonger

peso m weight; **peso a pieno carico** weight when fully loaded

pessimo(a) awful

pesto m: **pesto alla genovese** sauce made with fresh basil, pine kernels, garlic and cheese

petardo m banger

petroliera f oil tanker

petrolio m oil

pettinare to comb

pettine m comb; scallop

petto m breast; chest

pezza f patch; rag

pezzo m piece; cut (of meat); **pezzo di ricambio** spare (part)

pezzuola f cloth; rag

piacere[1] to please

piacere[2] m enjoyment; pleasure; **piacere di conoscerla** pleased to

meet you
piacevole pleasant
pianerottolo m landing (on stairs)
pianeta m planet
piangere to cry
piano[1] slowly; quietly
piano[2] m floor; storey; plan; **al primo piano** on the first floor; **ai piani inferiori/superiori** on the lower/upper floors
piano(a) level
pianobar m bar offering musical entertainment
pianta f plant; sole (of foot); map (of town); plan
piantare to plant; to pitch
pianterreno m ground floor
pianura f plain
piastra f: **panini alla piastra** toasted sandwiches; **formaggio alla piastra** grilled cheese
piastrella f tile
piattaforma f platform
piatti: **piatti pronti/da farsi** prepared dishes/dishes requiring preparation
piattino m saucer
piatto m dish; course; plate; **primo piatto** entrée
piatto(a) flat
piazza f square
piazzale m open square; service area
piazzola f: **piazzola (di sosta)** lay-by
piccante spicy; hot
picchetto m peg; picket; tent peg

picchiare to hit; to knock (engine)
piccione m pigeon
picco m peak; **a picco sul mare** rising straight from the sea
piccolo(a) little; small
piccone m pick; pickaxe
piede m foot; bottom (of page, list)
piega f crease; fold; pleat
piegare to fold; to bend
pieno(a) full; **il pieno, per favore!** fill it up! (car)
pietra f stone
pietrina f flint (in lighter)
pigiama m pyjamas
pigro(a) lazy
pila f battery (for radio etc)
pilastro m pillar
pillola f pill
pineta f pinewood
pinne fpl flippers
pino m pine
pinoli mpl pine kernels
Pinot m: **Pinot bianco** dry, aromatic white wine from north-east Italy; **Pinot grigio** dry, aromatic and full-bodied white wine from the same area as 'Pinot bianco'; **Pinot nero** dry, red wine with a fruity flavour, from the same area as the white Pinot
pinze fpl pliers
pinzette fpl tweezers
pioggia f rain
piombo m lead
pioppo m poplar

piovere to rain; **piove** it's raining

pioviggine f drizzle

piovoso(a) rainy; wet

pipa f pipe (for smoking)

piroscafo m steamer

piscina f swimming pool; **piscina comunale** public swimming pool

piselli mpl peas

pista f track; race track; **pista d'atterraggio** runway; **pista da ballo** dance floor; **pista di pattinaggio (su ghiaccio)** (ice-) skating rink; **pista per principianti** nursery slope; **pista da sci** ski run

pistola f gun; nozzle

pittore m painter

pittoresco(a) picturesque

più more; most; plus; **i più** most people; **in più** extra

piuma f feather; down

piumino m duvet; eiderdown; quilted jacket

piuttosto quite; fairly; rather

pizza f: **pizza alla diavola** pizza with spicy salami; **pizza margherita** pizza with tomato, mozzarella and oregano; **pizza napoletana** pizza with tomato, garlic and oregano; **pizza ai quattro formaggi** pizza with four kinds of cheese melted on top

pizzaiola: alla pizzaiola with tomato, garlic and oregano sauce

pizzico m pinch; sting

pizzo m lace

placcato(a): placcato oro/ argento gold-/silver-plated

platano m plane (tree)

platea f stalls; **platea interi/ ridotti** full-price/concessionary seats in the stalls

plico m parcel

pneumatico m tyre

po' see **poco(a)**

pochi(e) few

poco(a) little; not much; **un po'** a little; **fra poco** shortly

poesia f poem; poetry

poggiatesta m headrest

poi then

poiché because; since

polenta f sort of thick porridge made with maize flour; **polenta e osei** small birds, spit-roasted and served with polenta; **polenta e salsiccia** polenta with sausages

politica f policy; politics

polizia f police; **polizia ferroviaria** railway police; **polizia stradale** traffic police

poliziotto m policeman

polizza f policy; **polizza di assicurazione** insurance policy

pollame m poultry

pollice m thumb

pollo m chicken; **pollo alla diavola** grilled chicken, highly spiced

polmone m lung

polmonite f pneumonia

polo *m* polo; pole; terminal (*electricity*)

polpette *fpl* meatballs

polpettone *m* meat loaf

polpo *m* octopus

polsino *m* cuff (*of shirt*)

polso *m* wrist

poltrona *f* armchair

polvere *f* dust; powder

pomeriggio *m* afternoon

pomo *m* doorknob

pomodoro *m* tomato

pompa *f* pump; **pompa di benzina** petrol pump

pompelmo *m* grapefruit

pompiere *m* fireman

ponce *m* punch (*drink*)

ponte *m* bridge; deck; **ponte a pedaggio** toll bridge; **fare il ponte** to make a long weekend of it

pontile *m* jetty

popolo *m* people

porcellana *f* china; porcelain

porchetta *f* roast suckling pig

porpora *f* purple

porre to put

porro *m* leek

porta *f* door; gate; goal; **porta antipanico/di sicurezza** emergency exit

portabagagli *m* luggage rack; roof rack

portabottiglie *m* wine rack

portacenere *m* ashtray

portachiavi *m* key ring

portafoglio *m* wallet

portale *m* portal

portaombrelli *m* umbrella stand

portare to carry; to bring; to wear

portasigarette *m* cigarette case

portata *f* course; range; capacity; **fuori portata** out of reach

portatile portable

portatore *m*: **pagabile al portatore** payable to the bearer

portauovo *m* egg cup

portavoce *m* spokesman

portellone posteriore *m* tailgate

porticciolo *m* marina

portico *m* porch

portiera *f* door

portiere *m* porter (*doorkeeper*); janitor

portineria *f* caretaker's lodge

porto *m* port; harbour; **porto franco** carriage free; **porto fluviale** river port; **porto di scalo** port of call

porzione *f* portion; helping

posare to put down

posate *fpl* cutlery

posologia *f* dosage

posporre to postpone

possedere to own

posta *f* mail; stake; odds; **per posta aerea** by air mail; **posta raccomandata** registered mail; **fermo posta** poste restante

postagiro *m* post office giro

Poste *fpl* Post Office

posteggio *m* car park; **posteggio per tassi** taxi rank

posteriore rear; later
postino m postman
posto m place; position; job; seat; **posto di blocco** road block; border post; **posto riservato ad invalidi di guerra e del lavoro** seat reserved for disabled persons; **posto di soccorso** first-aid centre; **posto telefonico pubblico** public telephone; **posti in piedi** standing room; **posti a sedere** seating capacity; **posti prenotati** reserved seats
potabile drinking; drinkable; **acqua non potabile** this is not drinking water
potente powerful
potenza f power (of machine)
potere[1] to be able to; can
potere[2] m power; authority
povero(a) poor
pozzanghera f puddle; pool
pozzo m well
pranzo m lunch
prassi f normal procedure
pratica f practical experience; file
pratico(a) practical; handy
preavviso m advance notice; **soggetto a cambiamenti senza preavviso** subject to change without notice; **comunicazioni con preavviso** person-to-person calls
precedente previous; earlier
precedenza f right of way (on road); **dare la precedenza to give way

precipitarsi to rush
preciso(a) precise; exact; accurate
precotto(a) ready-cooked
predeterminare: **predeterminare l'importo desiderato** select the amount required
preferire to prefer
prefisso m prefix; **prefisso (teleselettivo)** dialling code
pregare to pray; **si prega di chiudere la porta/non fumare** please close the door/do not smoke
preghiera f prayer
prego don't mention it!; after you!
prelievo m withdrawal; collection; blood sample; **prelievo gettoni e monete respinti** returned tokens and coins
preludio m overture
pré-maman m maternity dress
premere to push; to press
premio m bonus; premium; prize
prendere to take; to get; to catch
prenotare to book; to reserve
prenotazione f reservation; **prenotazione obbligatoria** seats must be booked
preoccupato(a) worried
preparare to prepare
prepararsi to get ready
preparativi mpl preparations

presa f socket; outlet; **presa di corrente** power point
presbite long-sighted
presentare to introduce
presentarsi to report; to check in (at airport)
presentazione f introduction; presentation
preservativo m sheath, condom
preside m/f headmaster; headmistress
presidente m president; chairman
pressione f pressure
presso near; care of
prestare to lend
prestazione f performance; **prestazioni** services; **prestazioni ambulatoriali** outpatients' department
prestigiatore m conjuror
prestito m loan; **prendere in prestito** to borrow
presto early; soon; **faccia presto!** hurry up!
prete m priest
prevendita f: **biglietti in prevendita** tickets may be purchased in advance
preventivo m estimate
previo(a): **previa autorizzazione delle autorità competenti** upon authorization from the relevant authorities
previsione f forecast; **previsioni del tempo** weather forecast
previsto(a): **all'ora prevista** at the scheduled time; **come**

previsto as expected
prezioso(a) precious
prezzemolo m parsley
prezzo m price; **prezzo del coperto** cover charge; **a prezzo di costo** at cost; **prezzo della corsa** fare; **prezzo fisso** set price; **prezzo di catalogo** list price; **prezzo al minuto** retail price; **prezzo d'ingresso** entrance fee
prigione f prison
prigioniero(a) m/f prisoner
prima[1] before; first; earlier
prima[2] f première
primato m record
primavera f spring
primo(a) first; top; early; **prima classe** first class; **solo prima classe senza prenotazione** only first-class passengers may travel without a reserved seat
principale major; main
principalmente mainly
principe m prince
principessa f princess
principiante m/f beginner
privato(a) private; personal
privo(a) di lacking in
probabile probable; likely
procedimento m procedure; process
processo m trial (in law); process
prodotti mpl produce; products
prodotto m product; commodity
produrre to produce
produzione f production;

output; **gelati di produzione propria** our own ice cream
professore m professor; teacher (*secondary school*)
professoressa f teacher (*secondary school*)
profondità f depth
profondo(a) deep
profumeria f perfumery; perfume shop
profumo m scent; perfume
progetto m plan; project
programma m programme; syllabus; schedule; **fuori programma** supporting programme (*at cinema*)
proibire to ban; to prohibit
proiettare to show (*film*)
proiettore m headlight; floodlight; projector
proiezione f: **proiezioni cinematografiche** film shows
promessa f promise
promettere to promise
promosso(a) promoted; **essere promosso(a)** to pass (*exam*)
pronostico m forecast
pronto(a) ready; **pronto!** hello! (*on telephone*); **pronto intervento** emergency services; **pronto soccorso** first aid
pronunciare to pronounce
proporre to propose; to suggest
proposito m intention; **a proposito di** with regard to
proposta f proposal; suggestion
proprietà f ownership; property; land

proprietario(a) m/f owner
proprio just; really
proprio(a) own
proroga f extension; deferment
prosciutto m ham; **prosciutto affumicato** smoked ham; **prosciutto crudo/cotto** raw/cooked ham; **prosciutto di Parma (con melone/fichi)** cured ham from Parma (with melon/figs)
Prosecco m dry, sweet white wine with a natural sparkle, from the Trieste area
proseguimento m: **volo con proseguimento per ...** flight with onward connection for ...
proseguire to continue
prospettiva f prospect; outlook
prossimamente coming soon
prossimo(a) next; **prossima apertura** opening soon
proteggere to protect; to guard
prova f proof; evidence; rehearsal; test
provare to prove; to try; to try on
provenienza f origin; **luogo di provenienza** place of origin
provolone m medium-hard white cheese
provvedere a to provide for
provvisorio(a) temporary
provvista f supply
prudente wise; careful
prudere to itch
prugna f plum
prurito m itch

psichiatra m/f psychiatrist
psicologo(a) m/f psychologist
PTP abbreviation of **posto telefonico pubblico**
pubblicare to publish
pubblicità f publicity; advertising
pubblico m public; audience
pubblico(a) public
pugilato m boxing
pugnale m dagger
pugno m fist; punch
pulire to clean
pulito(a) clean
pulitura f: **pulitura a secco** dry cleaning
pulizia f cleaning
pullman m coach
pullmino m minibus
pummarola f: **spaghetti alla pummarola** spaghetti in tomato sauce
pungere to prick; to sting
punire to punish
punizione f punishment
punta f point; tip
puntare to point; to aim; **puntare su** to bet on
punteggio m score
puntina f drawing pin
punto m point; spot; stitch; full stop; **punto d'incontro** meeting place; **punto interrogativo** question mark; **punto di riferimento** landmark; **punto vendita** sales outlet
puntualmente on time
puntura f bite; sting

pupazzo m puppet
purché provided; providing
purè m purée; **purè di patate** mashed potatoes
puro(a) pure

Q

qua here
quaderno m exercise book
quadrato(a) square
quadretti: a quadretti checked
quadro m picture; painting
quaglia f quail
qualche some; **qualche volta** sometimes
qualcosa something; anything
qualcuno somebody; anybody; **qualcun altro** somebody else
quale what; which; which one
qualificato(a) qualified
qualsiasi any
qualunque any
quando when; **di quando in quando** occasionally
quanto(a) how much; **quanti(e)** how many; **quanto a** as for
quaranta forty
quarantena f quarantine
quartiere m district; **quartiere popolare** working-class district
quarto m quarter; **un quarto d'ora** quarter of an hour
quarto(a) fourth; **la quarta (marcia)** top gear
quasi nearly; almost
quattordici fourteen
quattro four

quei those

quel(la) that

quelli(e) those

quello(a) that; **quello(a) che** what; the one who

quercia f oak

questi(e) these

questione f issue; question

questo(a) this; this one

questura f police headquarters; police force

qui here

quindi then; therefore

quindici fifteen

quindicina di giorni f fortnight

quinto(a) fifth

quota f subscription; quota; height; **quota d'iscrizione** enrolment fee; entry fee; membership fee; **quota di partecipazione** cost (of excursion etc); **quota per persona** amount per person; **prendere/perdere quota** to gain/lose height (plane)

quotazione f: **quotazione dei cambi** exchange rates

quotidiano m daily (paper)

quotidiano(a) daily

R

rabarbaro m rhubarb

rabbia f anger; rabies

racchetta f racket; bat; **racchetta da neve** snowshoe; **racchetta da sci** ski stick

raccogliere to gather; to collect; to pick up

raccolta f collection; **raccolta vetro** bottle bank

raccolto m crop; harvest

raccomandare to recommend

raccontare to tell (story)

raccordo m connection; slip road; **raccordo anulare** ring road

raddoppiare to double

radersi to shave

radice f root

radiografia f X-ray

radiotelefono m radiophone

radunarsi to gather

raffermo(a) stale

raffica f squall; gust

raffineria f refinery

raffreddare to cool; to chill (wine, food)

raffreddore m cold (illness); **raffreddore da fieno** hay fever

ragazza f girl; girlfriend; **ragazza squillo** call girl

ragazzo m boy; boyfriend

raggio m beam; ray

raggiungere to reach

ragione f reason

ragioneria f accountancy

ragionevole sensible; reasonable

ragioniere m accountant

ragno m spider

ragù m: **ragù (di carne)** meat sauce; **ragù vegetale** vegetable sauce

RAI f Italian State broadcasting

company

rallentare to slow down or up

rame m copper

rammendare to darn

ramo m branch

rana f frog

rango m rank

rapa f turnip

rapidamente quickly

rapido m express train

rapido(a) high-speed; quick

rapire to kidnap

rapporto m ratio; report; relationship; **i rapporti sessuali** sexual intercourse

rappresentante m/f representative

rappresentazione f performance; production

raro(a) rare; scarce

raso m satin

rasoio m razor

rassomigliare to look like

rastrello m rake

rata f instalment

ratto m rat

ravanello m radish

ravioli mpl square cushions of pasta with meat or other filling; **ravioli panna e prosciutto** ravioli with cream and ham

razza f race; breed

razzia f raid

razziale racial

razzo m rocket

re m king

reagire to react

reale royal; real

realizzare to carry out; to realize (assets)

realmente really

reazione f reaction

recapito m address; delivery

recarsi: recarsi alla cassa pay at the cash desk

recensione f review

recentemente lately; recently

recinto m fence

Recioto m sparkling red wine from the Verona area

recipiente m container

réclame f advertisement

reclamo m complaint

recluta f recruit

recupero m: **recupero monete** returned coins

redditizio(a) profitable

reddito m income; yield

redigere to draw up (document)

referenze fpl reference (testimonial)

regalare to give (as a present); to give away

regalo m present, gift

reggere to support; to carry

reggipetto, reggiseno m bra

regina f queen

regione f region; district; area

regista m/f producer (of play); director (of film)

registrare to tape; to register; to record

Regno Unito m United Kingdom, U.K.

regola f rule

regolamento m regulation
regolare[1] regular; steady
regolare[2] to regulate; to settle; to adjust
relativo(a) relevant; relative
relazione f relationship; report
reliquia f relic
remare to row (boat)
remo m oar
rendere to return; to render; to make; **rendersi conto di** to realize
rendimento m performance (of car); profitability; output
rene m kidney (of person)
reparto m department (in store); unit
repellente m insect repellent
residenza f residence
residenziale residential
resistente hardwearing; durable; tough
resistenza f resistance; strength
resistere to resist
respingere to reject
respirare to breathe
respiratore m breathing apparatus
responsabile responsible
responsabilità f: **responsabilità civile** civil liability
restare to stay; to remain; to be left
restituire to return
restituzione f return; repayment; **dietro restituzione dello scontrino** on presentation

of the receipt
resto m remainder; change
restringersi to shrink
restrizione f restriction
rete f net; goal
retro m back; **Vedi retro** P.T.O.
retromarcia f reverse (gear)
revisione f review; service (for car)
rialzo m upturn; rise
rianimare to revive
riattaccare to reattach; to hang up (telephone)
ribasso m fall (in price)
ribes m blackcurrant
ricambio m: **ricambi auto** car spares; **ricambi originali** car manufacturers' spare parts
ricamo m embroidery
ricchezza f wealth
ricciolo m curl
ricciuto(a) curly
ricco(a) wealthy; rich
ricerca f research
ricetta f prescription; recipe
ricevere to receive; to welcome; **si riceve solo per appuntamento** visits by appointment only
ricevimento m reception; reception desk
ricevitore m receiver (phone)
ricevitoria f Inland Revenue office; **ricevitoria del lotto** lottery office
ricevuta f rreceipt; **ricevuta di itorno** acknowledgement of receipt

ricezione f reception

richiesta f request

ricompensa f reward

riconoscere to recognize

riconoscimento m: **documento di riconoscimento** means of identification

ricordare to remember; to remind; **ricordarsi di** to remember

ricordo m souvenir; memory

ricorrere a to resort to

ricotta f soft white unsalted cheese

ricuperare to recover; to retrieve

ridere to laugh

ridicolo(a) ridiculous

ridurre to reduce

riduzione f reduction

riempire to fill; to fill in/out/up

rientro m return; return home

rifare to do again; to repair; **rifare i letti** to make the beds

riferimento m reference

rifiutare to refuse; to reject

rifiuti mpl rubbish; waste

rifiuto m refusal

riflettere to reflect; to think

riflettore m spotlight; floodlight

rifornimento m: **fare rifornimento (di benzina)** to fill up (car); **posto di rifornimento** filling station

rifugio m refuge; shelter

rigido(a) stiff

riguardare to concern

riguardo m care; respect; **riguardo a . . .** as regards . . .

rilascio m: **data di rilascio** date of issue

rilassarsi to relax

rimandare to send back; to postpone

rimanere to stay; to remain; to be left

rimbalzare to bounce

rimborsare to repay; to refund

rimborso m refund; **rimborso spese mediche a seguito infortunio** refund of medical expenses following an accident

rimedio m remedy

rimescolare to shuffle (cards); to stir

rimessa f remittance; garage

rimettere to put back; to return; to remit; to postpone

rimettersi to recover

rimorchio m trailer; **a rimorchio** on tow

rimozione f: **divieto di parcheggio con zona rimozione** no parking: offenders' cars will be towed away; **rimozione forzata** illegally parked cars will be towed away

rimpatrio m repatriation

rincrescere: mi rincresce che . . . I regret that . . .

rinforzare to strengthen

rinfreschi mpl refreshments

ringhiera f rail; banister

ringraziare to thank

rinnovare to renew

rinunce fpl cancellations

rinunciare to give up

rinviare to send back; to postpone; to adjourn

rinvio m return; postponement; adjournment

riparare to mend; to repair

riparazione f repair; **riparazione gomme** tyre repairs

ripassare to revise

ripetere to repeat

ripido(a) abrupt; steep

ripieno m stuffing

ripieno(a) stuffed; filled

riposarsi to rest

riposo m rest

riprendere to take back; to resume; **riprendere i sensi** to come round

risa fpl laughter

risalita f: **impianto di risalita** ski lift(s)

risarcimento m compensation

riscaldamento m heating

rischio m risk; **il bagaglio viaggia a rischio e pericolo del partecipante** luggage is carried at owner's risk

risciacquare to rinse

riscuotere to collect; to cash

riserva f reserve; reservation; **riserva di caccia** game reserve; **riserva naturale** nature reserve

riservare to reserve

riservato(a): **riservato alle ambulanze** reserved for ambulances

risi e bisi m rice and peas cooked in chicken stock

riso m laugh; rice; **riso in bianco** boiled rice with butter; **riso alla greca** rice salad with olives

risolvere to solve; to work out

risorse fpl resources

risotto m dish of rice cooked in stock with various ingredients; **risotto ai funghi/alla marinara** risotto with mushrooms/fish; **risotto alla milanese** risotto with saffron and Parmesan cheese; **risotto nero alla fiorentina** risotto with cuttlefish, garlic and white wine

risparmiare to save

rispetto m respect

rispondere to answer; to reply; to respond; **la compagnia non risponde di . . .** the company cannot be held responsible for . . .

risposta f reply; answer

ristabilirsi to recover

ristorante m restaurant

ristorazione f: **servizi di ristorazione** refreshments

ristoro m: **servizio ristoro** refreshments

risultato m result

ritardare to delay; to be late; to be slow (clock, watch)

ritardo m delay; **essere in ritardo** to be late

ritenere to hold back; to consider

ritirare to withdraw

ritirata f WC

ritiro m retirement; withdrawal;

ritiro bagagli baggage claim
ritmo m rhythm
ritorno m return
riunione f meeting; conference
riuscire to succeed; to manage
riva f bank
rivale m/f rival
rivedere to see again; to revise
rivendita f resale; retailer's shop
riviera f: **la Riviera ligure** the Italian Riviera
rivista f magazine; revue
roba f stuff; belongings
roccia f rock
rodare to run in
rognone m kidney
rollino m spool
romanzo m novel
rombo m turbot; roar; rumble
rompere to break
rompersi to break
rompicapo m puzzle; worry
rosa pink; rose
rossetto m lipstick
rosso(a) red
rosticceria f shop selling roast meat and other prepared food
rotaie fpl rails
rotolo m roll
rotonda f roundabout
rotondo(a) round
roulotte f caravan
rovesciare to pour; to spill; to turn upside down; to turn over
rovesciarsi to spill; to overturn
rovescio m reverse side; wrong side
rovina f ruin

rovinare to wreck; to ruin
rovine fpl ruins
rubare to steal
rubinetto m tap
rubino m ruby
rudemente roughly
ruga f wrinkle
ruggine f rust
rumore m noise
ruota f wheel; **ruota di scorta** spare wheel
ruscello m stream
ruvido(a) rough; coarse

S

sabato m Saturday
sabbia f sand
sabbioso(a) sandy
sacchetto m (small) bag
sacco m bag; sack; **sacco a pelo** sleeping bag
saggio m essay
sala f hall; auditorium; **sala d'aspetto** or **d'attesa** waiting room; airport lounge; **sala da gioco** gaming room; **sala giochi** games room; **sala di lettura** reading room; **sala TV** TV lounge; **sale di intrattenimento** reception rooms
salame m salami
salario m wage, wages
salato(a) salted; salty; savoury
saldare to settle (bill); to weld; **da saldare** to be paid
saldi mpl sales (cheap prices)
saldo m payment; balance

sale m salt; **sale fino** table salt; **sale grosso** cooking salt; **sali e tabacchi** tobacconist's shop

saliera f salt cellar

salire to rise; to go up; **salire a bordo (di)** to board

saliscendi m latch

salita f climb; slope; **in salita** uphill

salmì m game stewed in a rich brown sauce

salmone m salmon; **salmone affumicato** smoked salmon

salone m lounge; salon; **salone dell'automobile** motor show; **salone di bellezza** beauty salon; **salone di ritrovo** lounge

salotto m living room; sitting room

salsa f gravy; sauce; **salsa di pomodoro** tomato sauce; **salsa rubra** ketchup; **salsa tartara** tartare sauce; **salsa verde** sauce made with parsley, anchovy fillets, gherkins, potato, garlic and onion

salsiccia f sausage

saltare to jump; to explode; to blow (fuse)

saltato(a) sautéed

saltimbocca m: **saltimbocca (alla romana)** veal escalopes with ham, sage and white wine

salumeria f delicatessen

salumi mpl cured pork meats

salutare to greet

salute f health

saluto m greeting; **distinti saluti** yours sincerely

salvagente pedonale m traffic island

salvaguardia f safeguard

salvare to save; to rescue

salvataggio m rescue

salvia f sage

salvo except; unless; **salvo imprevisti** barring accidents

salvo(a) safe

sanato m young calf

sangue m blood; **al sangue** rare (steak)

sanguinaccio m black pudding

sanguinare to bleed

Sangiovese m dry red table wine from Emilia-Romagna

sanitari mpl bathroom fittings

sano(a) healthy

santo(a) holy; m/f saint

sanzioni fpl sanctions

sapere to know; **sa di pesce** it tastes of fish

sapone m soap; **sapone da barba** shaving soap

saponetta f bar of soap

sapore m flavour; taste

saporito(a) tasty

sarago m bream

Sardegna f Sardinia

sardella f pilchard

sarto m tailor

sartoria f tailor's; dressmaker's

sasso m stone

sbagliarsi to make a mistake

sbagliato(a) incorrect; wrong

sbaglio m mistake

sbalordire to amaze

sbandare to swerve

sbarcare to land

sbarco m: **al momento dello sbarco** on landing

sbarra f bar

sbarrare to cross (*cheque*)

sbattere to slam; to whisk

sbiadire to fade

sbornia f drunkenness

sbrigare: sbrigare le formalità to deal with the formalities

sbrinare to defrost

sbucciare to peel

scacchi mpl chess

scadenza f expiry; **a lunga scadenza** long-term

scadere to expire

scaduto(a) out-of-date

scaffale m shelf

scaglia f scale (*of fish*); flake

scala f scale; ladder; staircase; **scala mobile** escalator

scaldabagno m water heater

scaldare to warm

scale fpl stairs

scalinata f flight of steps

scalino m step

scalo m stopover; **scali intermedi** intermediate stops

scaloppa f: **scaloppa milanese** veal escalope fried in egg and breadcrumbs

scaloppina f veal escalope; **scaloppine al limone/al Marsala** veal escalopes in a lemon/ Marsala sauce

scalzo(a) barefoot

scamiciato m pinafore dress

scampi mpl: **scampi ai ferri** grilled scampi; **code di scampi dorati e fritti** scampi tails, breaded and fried

scampoli mpl remnants

scantinato m cellar

scapolo m bachelor

scappare to escape

scarafaggio m beetle

scaricare to unload

scarico(a) flat (*battery*)

scarpa f shoe; **scarpe da pioggia** waterproof shoes

scarpette fpl sneakers

scarpone da sci m ski boot

scassinatore m burglar

scatola f box; carton; **in scatola** tinned (*food*)

scatolame m tinned food; tins

scattare to take (*photograph*)

scatto m (telephone) unit

scavare to dig; to dig up

scegliere to choose

scelta f range; selection; choice

scena f scene

scendere to go down

scheda f slip (*of paper*); **vendita schede telefoniche** phonecards sold here

scheggia f splinter

schermo m screen

scherzo m joke

schiacciare to crush; to squash; to mash

schiaffo m smack

schiantarsi to shatter

schiavo(a) m/f slave

schiena f back

schienale m back (of chair); **mantenere lo schienale in posizione eretta** ensure your seat back is in the upright position

schiuma f foam

schizzare to splash

sci m ski; skiing; **sci accompagnato** skiing with instructors; **sci di fondo** cross-country skiing; **sci nautico** or **d'acqua** water-skiing

scialle m shawl; wrap

scialuppa di salvataggio f lifeboat

sciare to ski

sciarpa f scarf

sciatore(trice) m/f skier

scienza f science

scienziato(a) m/f scientist

scimmia f ape; monkey

sciocchezze fpl nonsense; rubbish

sciogliere to untie; to dissolve

sciogliersi to dissolve; to melt

sciolto(a) loose

sciopero m strike

sciovia f ski lift

sciroppato(a): prugne/ciliegie sciroppate plums/cherries in syrup

sciroppo m syrup; **sciroppo per la tosse** cough mixture

sciupato(a) ruined; spoilt; shop-soiled

scivolare to slip; to slide; to glide

scodella f bowl; basin

scogliera f cliff

scoiattolo m squirrel

scolapiatti m draining-board

scolare to drain

scommessa f bet

scomodo(a) uncomfortable; inconvenient

scompartimento m compartment

sconfitta f defeat

sconosciuto(a) unknown; m/f stranger

scontabile: tariffa non scontabile no discount on this rate

sconto m discount; **non si fanno sconti** no discounts given

scontrino m ticket; receipt; **esigete lo scontrino** ask for a receipt; **scontrino alla cassa** pay at the cash desk first and bring your receipt to the bar; **scontrino fiscale** receipt for tax purposes

scontro m collision; crash

sconveniente improper

scopa f broom; brush

scoperto m overdraft

scopo m aim; goal; purpose

scoppiare to burst; to explode

scoppio m explosion; bang

scoprire to discover; to find out; to uncover

scorciatoia f short cut

scorcio m glimpse; **scorcio panoramico** vista

scorrere to flow; to pour

scortese unkind; rude

scossa f shock
scottarsi to scald oneself
scottatura f burn; sunburn
Scozia f Scotland
scozzese Scottish
scrittore(trice) m/f writer
scrittura f writing
scrivania f desk
scrivere to write; to spell
scultura f sculpture
scuola f school; **scuola elementare** primary school; **scuola media** ≈ junior comprehensive school; **scuola (di) sci** ski school
scuotere to shake
scuro(a) dark
scusa f excuse
scusare to excuse
scusarsi to apologize
sdraiarsi to lie down
drucciolevole slippery
se if; whether
sé himself; herself; itself; oneself; themselves
sebbene though
seccare to dry; to annoy
seccarsi to dry up
secchio m pail; bucket
secco(a) dried; dry
secolo m century
secondo(a) second; according to; **di seconda mano** secondhand
sedano m celery
sede f seat; head office
sedere[1] m bottom
sedere[2] to sit, be seated

sedersi to sit down
sedia f chair; **sedia a rotelle** wheelchair; **sedia a sdraio** deckchair
sedici sixteen
sedile m bench; seat
segale f rye
seggiolone m highchair
seggiovia f chair-lift
segnalazione f: **segnalazioni guasti** reporting of faults
segnale m signal; road sign; **segnale di linea libera** dial(ling) tone; **un segnale acustico preannuncia l'avviamento del nastro** an acoustic signal precedes any movement of the conveyor belt
segnaletica f road signs; **segnaletica orizzontale in rifacimento** road markings being renewed
segnare to mark; to score (goal)
segno m sign; mark
segretario(a) m/f secretary
segreteria f secretary's office; **segreteria telefonica** answering service
segreto(a) secret
seguente following
seguire to follow; to continue
sei six
sella f saddle
selvaggina f game (hunting)
selvaggio(a) wild
selvatico(a) wild
selz m soda water
semaforo m traffic lights

sembrare to look; to seem
seme m seed; suit (cards)
semifreddo m chilled dessert made with ice cream
seminario m seminar; seminary
seminterrato m basement
semola f: semola di grano duro durum wheat
semolino m: semolino al latte semolina pudding
semplice plain; simple
sempre always; ever
senape f mustard
seno m breast
sensibilità f feeling
senso m sense; strada a senso unico one-way street
sentiero m path; footpath
sentinella f sentry
sentire to hear; to feel; to smell; to taste
senza without
separare to separate
sepoltura f burial
seppia f cuttlefish; seppie in umido stewed cuttlefish
seppioline fpl baby cuttlefish
sera f evening
serata f: serata di gala gala evening
serbatoio m tank; cistern
serie f series
serio(a) serious; reliable
serpeggiante winding
serpente m snake
serra f greenhouse
serratura f lock
servire to attend to; to serve;

servire a to be of use to; to be used for
servizio m service; service charge; report (in press); servizi facilities; bathroom; in servizio in use; on duty; fuori servizio out of order; off duty; servizio di buffet buffet service; servizio interurbano/internazionale con prenotazione booking service for long-distance/international calls; servizio pubblico bus public bus service; servizio al tavolo waiter/waitress service; servizi igienici bathroom fittings; camera con servizi privati room with private bathroom; servizi di pubblica utilità public facilities
sessanta sixty
sesso m sex
sesto(a) sixth
seta f silk
setaccio m sieve
sete f thirst; avere sete to be thirsty
settanta seventy
sette seven
settembre m September
settentrionale northern
settimana f week; settimana bianca week's skiing holiday
settimanale weekly
settimo(a) seventh
severo(a) harsh; strict
sfinito(a) worn out
sfoderato(a) unlined
sfondo m background

sfortuna f bad luck
sfortunatamente unfortunately
sforzare to force; **sforzarsi di** to struggle to
sforzo m effort
sfuso(a) in bulk; loose
sgabello m stool
sganciarsi: sganciarsi adesso let go of the bar now
sgelare to thaw
sghiacciare to de-ice
sgombro m mackerel
sgonfio(a) flat
sgradevole unpleasant
sguardo m look; glance
si himself; herself; oneself; each other; themselves
sì yes
siccità f drought
Sicilia f Sicily
sicuramente surely
sicurezza f safety; security
sicuro(a) safe; sure
sidro m cider
siepe f hedge
sigaretta f cigarette
sigaro m cigar
significato m meaning
Signor m Mr
signora f lady; madam; **Signora** Mrs
signore m gentleman; sir
signorina f young woman; miss
silenzio m silence
simile similar; alike
simpatico(a) pleasant; nice
sinagoga f synagogue
sincero(a) sincere

sindacato m syndicate; trade union
sindaco m mayor
sinfonia f symphony
singhiozzo m sob; hiccup
singola f single room
singolarmente individually
singolo(a) single
sinistra f left; **a sinistra** on/to the left
sinistro m accident
sinistro(a) left
sintomo m symptom
SIP f Italian telephone company
sirena f siren
sistema m system
sistemazione f: **sistemazione alberghiera** hotel accommodation
sito m site
skai m® Leatherette®
slacciare to unfasten; to undo
slavina f snowslide
slegare to untie
slip m briefs
slitta f sledge; sleigh
slittare to slip; to skid
slogare to dislocate
smacchiatore m stain remover
smagliatura f ladder
smalto m nail polish, nail varnish; enamel
smarrirsi to lose one's way
smarrito(a) lost
smeraldo m emerald
smettere to stop; to cease
smoking m dinner jacket
snello(a) slim

Soave m dry white wine from the Verona area

sobborgo m suburb

soccorso m assistance; **soccorso pubblico di emergenza** emergency police service

società f society

socio m associate; member

soddisfare to satisfy

sodo hard; hard-boiled

soffiare to blow

soffice soft

sofficini mpl small savoury fritters

soffitta f loft; attic

soffitto m ceiling

soffrire to suffer

soggiorno m visit; stay; sitting room; **soggiorno balneare** stay at the seaside

sogliola f sole; **sogliola ai ferri** grilled sole; **sogliola alla mugnaia** sole lightly fried in butter with lemon juice and parsley

sogno m dream

solamente only

solare solare; **crema/olio solare** suntan cream/oil

solco m track; furrow

soldato m soldier

soldi mpl money

sole m sun; sunshine

soleggiato(a) sunny

solido(a) strong; solid; fast (dye)

solito(a) usual; **di solito** usually

sollevare to raise; to lift; to relieve

sollievo m relief

solo only

solo(a) alone; lonely

solubile soluble; **caffè solubile** instant coffee

somigliare a to be like; to look like

somma f sum

sommario m summary; outline

sommelier m wine waiter

sonnifero m sleeping pill

sonno m sleep

sono: io sono I am; **loro sono** they are

sontuoso(a) luxurious

sopportare to bear; to stand

soppressata f type of sausage

soppresso(a): corsa soppressa nei giorni festivi no service on holidays

sopra on; above; over; on top; **di sopra** upstairs

sopracciglio m eyebrow

soprattassa f surcharge

sopravvivere to survive

sordo(a) deaf

sorella f sister

sorgente f spring

sorgere to rise; to arise

sorpassare to overtake

sorpresa f surprise

sorridere to smile

sorriso m smile

sorvegliante m/f supervisor

sorvegliare to watch; to supervise

sospensione f adjournment; postponement; **sospensione voli**

(per avverse condizioni atmosferiche) flights postponed (due to adverse weather conditions)
sospeso(a): corsa sospesa service cancelled
sospirare to sigh
sosta f stop; **divieto di sosta, sosta vietata** no waiting
sostanza f substance; stuff
sostanzioso(a) filling; nourishing
sostare: vietato sostare nei passaggi di intercomunicazione do not stand in the passageway
sostegno m backing; support
sostenere to support; to maintain
sostituire to substitute; to replace
sostitutivo(a): servizio sostitutivo con autocorsa back-up coach service
sottaceti mpl pickles
sottana f underskirt
sotterraneo(a) underground
sottile thin; fine; subtle
sotto underneath; under; below; **di sotto** downstairs
sottoesposto(a) underexposed
sottolineare to emphasize; to underline
sottopassaggio m underpass
sottoporre to subject; to submit
sottosviluppato(a) underdeveloped
sottotitolo m subtitle

sottoveste f petticoat
sottrarre to subtract
sovraesposto(a) overexposed
sovvenzionare to subsidize
spaccio m shop; **spaccio di carni fresche** butcher's shop
spada f sword
spaghetti mpl: **spaghetti all'amatriciana** spaghetti in tomato sauce with garlic and Parmesan cheese; **spaghetti alla bolognese** spaghetti in a meat and tomato sauce; **spaghetti alla carbonara** spaghetti with bacon, eggs and Parmesan cheese; **spaghetti alla ciociara** spaghetti with black olives, tomatoes, peppers and cheese; **spaghetti al pomodoro** spaghetti in tomato sauce; **spaghetti alle vongole** spaghetti with clams
spago m string
spalla f shoulder
spallina f strap (of dress etc)
spalmare to spread
sparare to fire; to shoot
sparire to disappear
spartitraffico m central reservation
spaventare to frighten
spazio m space; room
spazzaneve m snowplough
spazzola f brush
spazzolino m brush; **spazzolino da denti** toothbrush
specchietto retrovisore m rear-view mirror

specchio m mirror
specializzato(a) skilled
specialmente especially
specie f kind
specificare to specify
spedalità f hospital admissions
  office; hospital expenses
spedire to send; to dispatch; to
  ship
spegnere to turn off; to put out
spellarsi to peel
spendere to spend
spento(a) off; out
speranza f hope
sperare to hope
spesa f expense; **fare la spesa** to
  go shopping
spese fpl expenditure; expenses;
  costs; **spese mediche** or
  sanitarie medical expenses;
  spese di spedizione postage
spesso often
spesso(a) thick
spettacolo m show;
  performance
spezie fpl spices
spezzatino m stew; **carni
  bianche in spezzatino** poultry
  stew
spia f spy; warning light; **con la
  spia spenta non selezionate** do
  not use when light is out
spiacente sorry
spiacere = dispiacere
spiacevole unpleasant
spiaggia f beach; shore;
  spiaggia libera public beach
spicchio d'aglio m clove of

garlic
spiccioli mpl (small) change
spiedino m skewer; **spiedini di
  calamari** squid kebabs
spiedo m spit; **pollo allo spiedo**
  spit-roasted chicken
spiegare to explain; to unfold; to
  spread out
spiegazione f explanation;
  **spiegazione segni
  convenzionali** explanation of
  symbols
spilla f brooch
spillo m pin
spina f bone (of fish); plug
  (electric); **spina dorsale**
  backbone; **togliere la spina**
  remove the plug
spinaci mpl spinach; **spinaci al
  burro** spinach in butter
spingere to push; **spingere i
  carrelli all'uscita** please leave
  trolleys at the exit
splendere to shine
spogliarello m striptease
spogliarsi to undress
spogliatoio m dressing room
spolverare to dust
sporcizia f dirt
sporco(a) dirty
**sporgersi: è pericoloso
  sporgersi** it is dangerous to lean
  out
sport: sport invernali mpl
  winter sports
sportello m counter, window;
  door (of car); **servizio sportelli
  automatici** automatic banking

service
sposa f bride
sposato(a) married
sposo m bridegroom
spostare to move
sprecare to waste
spremere to squeeze
spremuta f fresh juice;
  **spremuta d'arancia/di limone/
  di pompelmo** fresh orange/
  lemon/grapefruit juice
spruzzare to spray
spugna f sponge
spuma f foam; fizzy drink;
  spuma di tonno tuna mousse
spumante sparkling
spuntare to trim (*hair*)
spuntino m snack
sputare to spit
squadra f team; squad; **squadra
  mobile** flying squad
squillare to ring
S.r.l. Ltd
stabile stable; firm; m building
stabilimento m factory;
  stabilimento balneare bathing
  establishment
stabilire to establish
staccarsi to come off
stadio m stadium
stagionato(a) ripe; mature
stagione f season; **alta/bassa
  stagione** high/low season;
  stagione di prosa theatre season
stagno[1] m tin
stagno[2] m pond
stagnola f tin foil
stalla f stable

stampa f print; press
  (*newspapers, journalists*)
stampatello m block letters
stampigliatura f: **non è valido
  senza la stampigliatura** not
  valid unless stamped
stancarsi to get tired
stanco(a) tired
stanotte tonight; last night
stantio(a) stale
stanza f room; **stanza da bagno**
  bathroom; **stanza doppia/a due
  letti** double/twin-bedded room;
  stanza da letto bedroom; **stanza
  matrimoniale** double room;
  stanza degli ospiti guest room;
  stanza singola single room
stappare to uncork; to uncap
stare to stay; to be; to fit; **stare
  per fare** to be about to do; **stare
  in piedi** to stand
starnuto m sneeze
stasera tonight
Stati Uniti (d'America) mpl
  United States (of America),
  US(A)
stato m state
statura f height
stazione f station; resort;
  stazione autocorriere coach
  station; **stazione balneare**
  seaside resort; **stazione base di
  partenza bus** bus departure
  point; **stazione marittima**
  seaside town; **stazione di
  servizio** petrol station; **stazione
  termale** spa
stecca f splint; carton

stella f star
stelo m stem
stendere to stretch; to spread; to hang out; to lay down
stendersi to lie down
sterlina f sterling; pound
sterzo m steering wheel; steering
stesso(a) same; **io/lei** etc **stesso(a)** I myself/you yourself etc
stile m style
stima f estimate
stinco m shin
stipendio m salary
stirare to iron
stirarsi to strain (muscle); to stretch
stitichezza f constipation
stitico(a) constipated
stivale m boot
stivalone di gomma m wellington boot
stoccafisso m stockfish
stoffa f fabric
stomaco m stomach
storia f history; story
storico(a) historic(al)
storione m sturgeon
storto(a) crooked
stoviglie fpl crockery
stracchino m soft, creamy cheese
stracciatella f clear soup with eggs and cheese stirred in
straccio m rag; cloth
stracotto m beef stew
strada f road; street; **strada principale** main road; **strada** **secondaria** side road, side street; **strada sussidiaria** relief road; **strada statale** main road; **strada a doppia carreggiata** dual carriageway; **strada senza uscita** dead end
straniero(a) foreign; overseas; m/f foreigner
strano(a) strange; odd
straordinario(a) extraordinary
strappare to tear; to rip; to pull off
strapparsi to rip; to split
strappo m tear
strato m layer
stravagante extravagant; odd
strega f witch
stretto(a) narrow; tight
strillo m scream
stringa f shoelace
stringere to squeeze; **stringere** **la mano** to shake hands
striscia f strip; stripe; streak
strizzare to wring
strofinaccio m duster; dishcloth
strofinare to rub
strudel m: **strudel di mele** apple strudel
strumento m instrument
studiare to study
studio m study; studio
stufa f stove
stufato m stew
stufato(a) braised
stuoia f mat
stupore m amazement
stuzzicadenti m toothpick
stuzzichino m appetizer

su on; onto; over; about; up get over; to overtake

sua his; her; hers; its; your; yours

sub(acqueo) *m* skindiver

subacqueo(a) underwater

subire to suffer

subito at once

succedere to happen

succhiotto *m* dummy (*baby's*)

succo *m* juice; **succo di frutta** fruit juice; **succo di limone** lemon juice; **succo di pompelmo** grapefruit juice

succoso(a) juicy

succursale *f* branch

sud *m* south

sudare to sweat

suddito(a) *m/f* subject (*person*)

sudicio(a) filthy

sudore *m* sweat

sue his; her; hers; its; your; yours

suggerimento *m* suggestion

sughero *m* cork

sugli = su + gli

sugo *m* sauce; gravy; juice

sui = su + i

suino(a): carni suine *fpl* pork meats

suo his; her; hers; its; your; yours

suocera *f* mother-in-law

suocero *m* father-in-law

suoi his; her; hers; its; your; yours

suola *f* sole

suolo *m* ground; soil

suonare to ring; to play; to sound

suono *m* sound

superare to exceed; to pass; to

superficie *f* surface

superiore upper; senior; superior

supermercato *m* supermarket

supplementare extra

supplemento *m*: **supplemento singola** supplement for single room

supplente temporary; acting

supporre to suppose

supposta *f* suppository

surgelato(a): prodotti surgelati frozen foods

surriscaldarsi to overheat

susina *f* plum

sussidio *m* subsidy

svago *m* relaxation; pastime

svaligiare to rob

svalutazione *f* devaluation

svantaggio *m* disadvantage; handicap

sveglia *f* alarm (clock)

svegliare to wake

svegliarsi to wake up

sveglio(a) awake; smart

svelto(a) quick

svenire to faint

svestire to undress

svestirsi to undress

sviluppare to develop

sviluppo *m*: **sviluppo rapido** fast developing service (*photos*); **sviluppo e stampa** developing and printing

svincolo *m* slip road

svitare to unscrew

Svizzera *f* Switzerland

svizzero(a): (bistecca alla) svizzera f ≈ beefburger
svolta f turn
svuotare to empty; to drain

T

T ground floor; **T sali e tabacchi** tobacconist's (shop)
tabaccaio(a) m/f tobacconist
tabaccheria f tobacconist's (shop)
tabacco m tobacco; **tabacchi** tobacconist's (shop)
tabella f table (list)
tabellone m notice board
tacchino m turkey
tacco m heel; **tacchi a spillo** stiletto heels
taccole fpl mange-tout peas
tachimetro m speedometer
tafano m horsefly
taglia f size (of clothes); **taglie forti** larger sizes
tagliare to cut
tagliarsi to cut oneself
tagliatelle fpl flat strips of pasta
taglierini mpl thin soup noodles
taglio m cut
tailleur m (tailored) suit
tailleur-pantalone m trouser-suit
tale such
taleggio m mild, medium-hard cheese
talloncino m counterfoil
tallone m heel
tamburo m drum

tampone assorbente m tampon
tanti(e) so many
tanto(a) so much; so; **tanto(a) quanto(a)** as much/many as; **ogni tanto** now and then, now and again; **di tanto in tanto** from time to time
tappa f stop; stage
tappare to cork; to plug
tappetino m rug
tappeto m carpet
tappezzare to paper
tappo m top; cork; stopper; plug (for basin etc)
tardi late
targa d'immatricolazione f number plate
tariffa f tariff; rate; **tariffa doganale** customs tariff; **tariffa festiva** rate on holidays; **tariffa normale/ridotta** standard/reduced rate; **tariffa notturna** night rate; **tariffa ordinaria/a ore di punta** ordinary/peak rate
tartufo m truffle (fungus)
tasca f pocket
tassa f tax; **tassa d'ingresso** admission charge; **tassa di soggiorno** tourist tax; **tasse e percentuali di servizio** taxes and service charges
tassì m taxi
tasso m rate; **tasso di cambio** exchange rate
tasto m key
tattica f tactics
tavola f table; plank; board;

painting; **tavola calda** snack bar;
noleggio tavole surfboards/
windsurfing boards for hire;
tavola a vela windsurfing board
tavoletta f bar (of chocolate)
tazza f cup
te you
tè m tea; **tè al limone/al latte**
tea with lemon/milk; **tè freddo**
iced tea; **tè alla menta** mint tea
teatro m theatre; drama
tecnico(a) technical; m/f
technician
tedesco(a) German
tegame m (frying) pan; **patate in
tegame** potatoes with peppers,
onion, tomato and oregano
tegola f tile (on roof)
teiera f teapot
tela f cloth; canvas
telaio m chassis
telecamera f television camera
telecronaca f television report
telefonare to telephone
telefonata f phone-call;
telefonata con la R reversed
charge call
telefono m telephone
telegiornale m television news
teleobiettivo m telephoto lens
teleselezione f S.T.D.
televisione f television
televisore m television (set)
temere to fear
temperatura f: **temperatura
ambiente** room temperature;
temperatura di servizio: ...
temperature for serving: ...

temperino m penknife
tempio m temple (building)
tempo m weather; time
temporale m thunderstorm
tenda f curtain; tent; **tenda
canadese** ridge tent
tendere to stretch; to hold out;
to tend
tendina f blind
tenere to keep; to hold; **tenere
rigorosamente la destra** keep to
the right
tenero(a) tender
tenore m: **tenore alcolico**
alcohol content; **tenore di vita**
standard of living
tensione f voltage; tension
tentare to attempt; to tempt
tentativo m attempt
tenuta f estate (property)
teppista m vandal
tergicristallo m windscreen
wiper
terme fpl thermal baths
terminare to end
termine m term
terra f ground; earth; soil; land; **a
terra** ashore; **avere una gomma
a terra** to have a flat tyre
terrapieno m embankment
terrazza f terrace
terremoto m earthquake
terreno m ground
terzi mpl third party
terzo(a) third
teschio m skull
teso(a) tight; tense
tesoro m treasure

tessera f (membership) card; pass; season ticket; **tessera di credito** credit card; **tessera nominativa** card with named user

tessili mpl textiles

tessuto m fabric; **tessuti e filati** textiles

testa f head

testamento m will

testimone m witness

testimonianza f evidence (of witness)

testina f: **testina di abbacchio/vitello** lamb's/calf's head

testo m text

tettarella f teat (for bottle); dummy

tetto m roof

tettoia f shelter

Tevere m Tiber

TG abbreviation of **telegiornale**

ti you; to you; yourself

ticket m prescription charge

tifoso m fan

tigre f tiger

timballo m mixture of meat, fish etc cooked in a mould lined with pastry or potato

timbro m (rubber) stamp

timo m thyme

timone m rudder

tinca f tench

tinta f dye

tintoria f dry-cleaner's

tintura f dye; rinse (for hair); **tintura di iodio** tincture of iodine

tipo m type

tipografia f typography

tiramisù m sponge cake soaked in coffee and filled with a kind of cream cheese mixed with eggs, sugar, whipped cream and sprinkled with chocolate

tirare to pull

tiro m: **tiro con l'arco** archery

titoli mpl stocks

titolo m headline; title; qualification

toboga m toboggan

Tocai m dry white wine from Friuli

toccare to touch; to feel; to handle; **tocca a Lei** it's your turn; **vietato toccare la merce (esposta)** do not handle the merchandise

toeletta f dressing-table; toilet

togliere to remove; to take away

togliersi to take off

tomba f grave; tomb

tonfo m splash; thud

tonnellata f ton

tonno m tuna

tonsillite f tonsillitis

topo m mouse

torace m chest

torcere to twist

torcicollo m stiff neck

Torino f Turin

tornare to return; to come/go back

toro m bull

torre f tower

torrefazione f coffee shop

torrone m nougat

torta f cake; tart; pie; **torta di gelato** ice-cream cake; **torta di riso** rice mould; **torta salata** savoury tart; **torta di uova e asparagi** egg and asparagus flan

tortellini mpl pasta rings filled with seasoned meat; **tortellini in brodo** tortellini in broth

tortello m pasta ring filled with spinach and cream cheese

tortellone m pasta ring filled with cheese, egg, parsley and cream cheese

torto m wrong; **aver torto** to be wrong

Toscana f Tuscany

tosse f cough

tossicomane m/f drug addict

tostapane m toaster

tosti mpl toasted sandwiches

totip m similar to football pools, but for horse-racing

Totocalcio m football pools

tovaglia f tablecloth

tovagliolo m napkin

tra between; among(st); in

traccia f trace; track

tracciato m: **posteggio limitatamente entro i tracciati** parking only within area indicated

traduzione f translation

traghetto m ferry

traguardo m finishing line

trama f plot

tramezzino m sandwich

tramonto m sunset

trampolino m diving-board

tranne except (for)

tranquillante m tranquillizer

tranquillo(a) quiet; calm; peaceful

transito m: **transito voli nazionali/internazionali** domestic/international transit passengers

trapano m drill

trappola f trap

trapunta f quilt

trascorrere to pass; to spend

trasferibile transferable

trasferimento m transfer

trasferire to transfer

trasferirsi to move

trasgressore m: **i trasgressori saranno assoggettati alla penalità di ...** offenders will be subject to a fine of ...

trasloco m move (moving house)

trasmettere to transmit; to broadcast

trasmissione f broadcast; transmission

trasparente transparent; clear

traspirare to perspire

trasporto m transport; **trasporto consentito con biglietto preacquistato** bus tickets must be purchased before boarding

trasversale f: **(strada) trasversale** side street

trattamento m treatment

trattare to treat; to handle

trattative fpl talks; negotiations

trattenere to keep back; to detain

trattino m dash; hyphen

tratto m: **tratto di linea interrotto per lavori** section of the line closed due to maintenance work

trave f beam

traversata f crossing; flight

travestimento m disguise

tre three

treccia f plait

tredici thirteen

tremare to shake

treno m train; **treno merci** goods train; **treno navetta** alpine train for the transport of cars and their passengers; **treno periodico** train which operates only during certain periods; **treni in partenza** train departures

trenta thirty

tribù f tribe

tribunale m court (law)

triglia f mullet

trimestre m term

trinciare to cut up

trippa f tripe

triste sad

tritacarne m mincer

tritare to mince; to chop

trittico m triptych

tromba f trumpet

tronco m trunk

troppi(e) too many

troppo too much; too

troppo(a) too much

trota f trout

trovare to find

truccarsi to make (oneself) up

trucco m make-up; trick

truppa f troop

tu you

tua your; yours

tubo m pipe; tube; **il tubo di scappamento** exhaust

tue your; yours

tuffo m dive; **vietati i tuffi** no diving

tumulto m riot

tuo your; yours

tuoi your; yours

tuono m thunder

tuorlo m yoke

turista m/f tourist

turno m turn; shift; **di turno** on duty; **chiuso per turno (di riposo) il lunedì** closed on Mondays

tuta f overall; suit (astronaut, diver); track suit

tutore(trice) m/f guardian

tuttavia nevertheless

tutti(e) all; everybody

tutto everything

tutto(a) all; **tutta la giornata** all day

U

ubbidire to obey

ubicazione f location

ubriaco(a) drunk

uccello m bird

uccidere to kill

ufficiale[1] m officer; official

ufficiale[2] official

ufficio m bureau; office; service (*in church*); **ufficio informazioni** information office; **ufficio oggetti smarriti** lost property office; **ufficio del personale** personnel office; **ufficio postale** post office; **ufficio del registro** registry office; **ufficio turistico** tourist office

ufficioso(a) unofficial

uguale equal; even

ultimo(a) last

umano(a) human

umidi mpl stews

umido(a) wet, damp; **carne/ pesce in umido** meat/fish stew

umore m mood

un a; an; one

uncino m hook

undici eleven

unghia f nail

unguento m ointment

unico(a) only; unique

unire to join; to unite; to connect

unità sanitaria locale f local health centre

unito(a) united; plain; self-coloured

università f university

uno(a) a; an; one; **l'un l'altro** one another

uomo m (*pl* **uomini**) man; **uomo d'affari** businessman

uovo m egg; **uovo al burro** egg fried in butter; **uovo in camicia/ alla coque** poached/boiled egg; **uovo fritto/ripieno/sodo** fried/ stuffed/hard-boiled egg; **uovo di Pasqua** Easter egg; **uova affogate** poached eggs; **uova in frittata** omelette; **uova in strapazzata** scrambled eggs

uragano m hurricane

urlo m scream; howl

urtare to bump; to bump into

usare to use

usato(a): auto usate second-hand cars

uscire to come out; to go out; **vietato uscire dalla pista** follow the ski tracks

uscita f exit; **uscita operai** factory exit; **uscita di sicurezza** emergency exit; **uscita a vela** sailing trip

uscite fpl outgoings

USL abbreviation of **unità sanitaria locale**

uso m use

utero m womb; uterus

utile useful

utilitaria f runabout

uva f grapes; **uva passa** currants; raisins; **uva spina** gooseberry

V

va: Lei va you go; **lui va** he goes

vacanza f holiday(s)

vacca f cow

vado I go

vagabondo(a) m/f tramp

vaglia m postal order; money order; **vaglia estero** or **internazionale** international

postal order
vago(a) vague
vagone m carriage; wagon;
  vagone letto sleeping car;
  vagone ristorante restaurant car
vaiolo m smallpox
valanga f avalanche
valere to be worth; to be valid;
  vale la pena it's worth it
valico m pass; **valico di confine**
  border crossing
validare to make valid
valigeria f leather goods; leather
  goods shop
valigia f suitcase
valle f valley; **a valle**
  downstream; downhill
valore m value
Valpolicella m light, dry red
  wine with a trace of bitterness
valuta f currency
valutare to value
valvola f valve
valzer m waltz
vandalismo m: **atti di**
  vandalismo acts of vandalism
vaniglia f vanilla
vanno they/you go
vano m room
vantaggio m benefit; advantage
vantaggioso(a): a condizioni
  vantaggiose on favourable
  terms
vantarsi to boast
vapore m steam
variabile variable; changeable
variare to vary
varicella f chicken pox

vario(a) various
vasca da bagno f bath
vasellame m crockery, china
vaso m vase; pot
vassoio m tray
ve before lo, la, li, le, ne = **vi**
vecchio(a) old
vedere to see; **non vedere l'ora**
  di to look forward to
vedersi to meet; to show
vedova f widow
vedovo m widower
veduta f view
veicolo m vehicle
vela f sail; sailing; **vela d'altura**
  ocean sailing
veleno m poison
veliero m sail(ing) boat
velina f tissue paper
vellutato(a) velvety
velluto m velvet; **velluto a coste**
  corduroy
velo m veil
veloce fast
velocità f speed
vena f vein
venatura f grain (in wood)
vendemmia f grape harvest,
  vintage
vendere to sell; **qui si vende . . .**
  . . . sold here
vendita f sale; **in vendita** on
  sale; **vendita al minuto** retail;
  vendita promozionale special
  offer; **vendita a rate** hire
  purchase; **vendita di realizzo**
  per rinnovo locali clearance
  sale due to refurbishing

venerdì m Friday; **venerdì santo** Good Friday

Venezia f Venice

venire to come

ventaglio m fan (folding)

venti twenty

ventilatore m fan; ventilator

vento m wind

ventola f fan

ventuno m twenty-one; pontoon

veramente really

verbale m minutes; record

verde green; **il rispetto del verde è affidato al senso civico dei cittadini** look after your town's parks and gardens

Verdicchio m dry white wine from the Marche

verdura f vegetables

Verduzzo m dry white wine

vergogna f shame

vergognarsi (di) to be ashamed (of)

verificare to check

verità f truth

verme m worm

vermicelli mpl: **vermicelli alle vongole veraci** thin noodles with real clams

vermut m vermouth

Vernaccia m dry or sweet white wine

vernice f varnish; paint; **vernice fresca** wet paint

vero(a) true; real

versamento m payment; deposit

versare to pour; to deposit

verso toward(s)

vertigine f dizziness

vescica f bladder

vescovo m bishop

vespa f wasp

vestaglia f dressing gown

veste f dress

vestiario m wardrobe

vestibolo m hall

vestire to dress

vestirsi to dress (oneself)

vestiti mpl clothes

vestito m dress; suit (man's)

vetrata f glass door/window

vetrina f shop window

vetro m pane; glass

vettura f coach (of train)

vi you; to you; yourselves; each other; there; here

via¹ f street

via² via, by way of

viadotto m viaduct

viaggiare to travel

viaggiatore m traveller

viaggio m journey; trip; drive; **viaggi** travel; **buon viaggio!** enjoy your trip!; **viaggio di nozze** honeymoon; **viaggio organizzato** package holiday; **viaggi per studenti** student travel

viale m avenue

vicenda f event; **a vicenda** in turn

vicinato m neighbourhood

vicino near; close by

vicino(a) m/f neighbour

vicolo m alley; lane; **vicolo cieco**

dead end

vietare to forbid

vietato(a): vietato fumare no smoking; **vietato scendere** no exit

vigile m policeman; **vigili del fuoco** fire brigade; **vigile urbano** traffic warden

vigilia f eve

vigliacco m coward

vigna f vineyard

villaggio m: **villaggio vacanze** holiday village

villeggiante m/f holidaymaker

villeggiatura f: **in villeggiatura** on holiday; **luogo di villeggiatura** holiday resort

vimine m wicker

vincere to win; to defeat

vincitore(trice) m/f winner

vincolo m: **senza alcun vincolo** without obligation

vino m wine; **vino bianco/rosso/rosato** or **rosé** white/red/rosé wine; **vino in lattina** can of wine; **vino novello di pronta beva** new wine, ready for drinking; **vini da pasto** table wines; **vini pregiati** quality wines; **vini da taglio** blending wines

Vin Santo m dessert wine, gold in colour, from Tuscany

violenza f violence

violoncello m cello

viottolo m lane

vipera f adder

virare di bordo to tack

virgola f comma; decimal point

visiera f visor; peak (of cap)

visione f vision; **cinema di prima visione** cinema where new-release films are shown

visita f visit; medical examination; **visita guidata** guided tour; **visita in pullman** coach tour

viso m face

visone m mink

vista f eyesight; view; **camera con vista mare** room with sea view

visto m visa; **visto di ingresso/di transito** entry/transit visa

visualizzatore m: **nel visualizzatore si accenderà la lampadina rossa** the red light will show on the display

vita f life; waist; **vita notturna** night life

vite f vine; screw

vitello m veal; calf; **vitello tonnato** veal in tuna fish sauce, served cold

vitigno m vine

vittima f victim

vivace lively

vivande fpl food

vivere to live

vivo(a) to live; alive

viziare to spoil (child)

vocabolario m vocabulary; dictionary

voce f voice; **ad alta voce** aloud

voi you

volano m badminton

volante[1] *m* steering wheel
volante[2] *f* flying squad
volare to fly
volere to want
volo *m* flight; **volo di linea** scheduled flight; **volo provenienza ...** flight from ...
volpe *f* fox
volta *f* time; **una volta** once
voltare to turn
voltarsi to turn round; to turn over
vongola *f* clam
vortice *m* whirlpool
vostri(e) your; yours
vostro(a) your; yours
voto *m* vote; mark (*in school*)
vulcano *m* volcano
vuotare to empty
vuoto(a) empty

Z

zabaione *m* whipped egg yolks and sugar with Marsala wine
zafferano *m* saffron
zaino *m* rucksack
zampa *f* leg; paw; foot
zampone *m* pig's trotter stuffed with minced pork and spices
zanzara *f* mosquito
zanzariera *f* mosquito net
zenzero *m* ginger
zia *f* aunt(ie)
zingaro *m* gypsy
zio *m* uncle
zitto(a) quiet
zolletta *f* cube; lump
zona *f* zone; **zona pedonale** pedestrian precinct; **zona di produzione** area where produced; **zona residenziale** housing estate
zoppo(a) *m/f* cripple
zucca *f* pumpkin; marrow
zuccheriera *f* sugar bowl
zucchero *m* sugar
zucchini *mpl* courgettes; **zucchini in agrodolce** courgettes in a sweet and sour sauce; **zucchini in teglia** baked courgettes with onions and Parmesan cheese
zuccotto *m* ice-cream sponge
zuppa *f* soup; **zuppa di cipolle** onion soup; **zuppa di pesce** fish soup; **zuppa inglese** trifle

ENGLISH-ITALIAN

A

a un, una *oon, oona;* **a boy** un ragazzo *oon ragats-so;* **a girl** una ragazza *oona ragats-sa*

abbey l'abbazia (f) *ab-batsee-a*

AB negative AB negativo *abee nayga-teevo*

about: a book about Venice un libro su Venezia *oon leebro soo vaynayts-ya;* **about ten o'clock** circa le dieci *cheerka lay dee-echee*

above sopra *sohpra;* superiore *soopayr-yohray*

AB positive AB positivo *abee pohzee-teevo*

abroad all'estero *al-les-tayro*

abscess l'ascesso (m) *ashes-so*

accelerator un acceleratore *at-chaylay-ra-tohray*

accident l'incidente (m) *eenchee-dentay;* **by accident** per sbaglio *payr zbal-yo;* **road accident** incidente stradale *eenchee-dentay stra-dahlay*

accommodation l'alloggio (m)

al-*lod-jo*

account (at bank, in shop) il conto *kohnto;* **Giro account** il conto corrente postale *kohnto kor-rentay po-stahlay*

accountant (male) il ragioniere *rajohn-yeray;* (female) la ragioniera *rajohn-yera*

ache[1] n il dolore *doh-lohray*

ache[2] vb fare male *fahray mahlay;* **my head aches** mi fa male la testa *mee fa mahlay la testa*

acid l'acido (m) *a-cheedo*

across (crosswise) attraverso *at-tra-vayrso;* (on the other side of) dall'altra parte di *dal-laltra partay dee*

acrylic acrilico *akree-leeko*

act l'azione (f) *ats-yohnay*

actor l'attore (m) *at-tohray*

actress l'attrice (f) *at-treechay*

adaptor (electrical) il riduttore *reedoot-tohray*

add (count) sommare *sohm-*

mahray

address l'indirizzo (m) *eendee-reets-so*

adhesive tape il nastro adesivo *nastro aday-zeevo*

adjust aggiustare *adjoos-tahray*

admission charge il prezzo del biglietto d'ingresso *prets-so dayl beelyayt-to deengres-so*

adopted adottato *adoht-tahto*

adult l'adulto (m) *a-doolto*

advance: in advance in anticipo *een antee-cheepo*

advertisement la pubblicità *poob-bleechee-ta*

aerial l'antenna (f) *antayn-na*

afford: I can't afford it non posso permettermelo *nohn pos-so payrmayt-tayrmelo*

afraid: to be afraid avere paura *a-vayray pa-oora*

after dopo *dohpoh*

afternoon il pomeriggio *pomay-reed-jo*

aftershave il dopobarba *dopo-bahrba*

again ancora *an-kora*

against contro *kohntro*

age l'età (f) *ayta*

agent l'agente (m/f) *a-jentay*

ago: a week ago una settimana fa *oona sayt-tee-mahna fa*

agree essere d'accordo *es-sayray dak-kordo*; **I agree with you** sono d'accordo con te *sohnoh dak-kordo kohn tay*

air l'aria (f) *ahree-a*; **in the open air** all'aria aperta *al-lahree-a a-*

payrta

air-conditioning l'aria (f) condizionata *ahree-a kohndeets-yoh-nahta*

aircraft l'aeroplano (m) *la-ayro-plahno*

air filter il filtro dell'aria *feeltro dayl-lahree-a*

air hostess la hostess *hostess*

air line (*in garage*) il tubo dell'aria *eel toobo dayl-lahree-a*

air mail via aerea *vee-a-ayray-a*

air-mattress il materassino gonfiabile *matay-ras-seeno gonfee-ah-beelay*

airport l'aeroporto (m) *a-ay-ropor-to*

aisle il passaggio pas-*sad-jo*

à la carte alla carta *al-la karta*

alarm l'allarme (m) *al-lahrmay*

alarm clock la sveglia *zvayl-ya*

album (*record*) un disco *deesko*

alcohol l'alcool (m) *alko-ol*

alcoholic alcolico *alko-leeko*

alive vivo *veevo*

all tutto *toot-to*

allergic allergico *al-layr-jeeko*

allergy l'allergia (f) *al-layr-jee-a*

allow permettere *paymayt-tayray*

allowance (*customs*) la quantità permessa *kwantee-ta paymays-sa*

all right (*agreed*) va bene *va benay*; **are you all right?** stai bene? *sta-ee benay*

almond la mandorla *man-dorla*

almost quasi *kwahzee*

alone solo *sohloh;* **I'll do it
alone** lo faccio da solo *loh fatcho
da sohlo*

along lungo *loongo*

already già *ja*

also anche *ankay*

altar l'altare (m) *al-tahray*

alternator l'alternatore (m)
altayr-na-tohray

although sebbene *sayb-benay*

altitude l'altitudine (f) *altee-too-
deenay*

always sempre *saympray*

am: I am sono *sohno*

ambassador l'ambasciatore (m)
amba-sha-toray

ambulance l'ambulanza (f)
amboo-lantsa

America l'America (f) *amay-
reeka*

American americano *amay-ree-
kahno*

among fra *fra*

amount (quantity) la quantità
kwantee-ta; (of bill) il totale *to-
tahlay*

amusement arcade la sala
giochi *sahla jokee*

an un, una *oon, oona*

anaesthetic l'anestetico (m)
anay-ste-teeko

anchor l'ancora (f) *an-kora*

and e *ay*

A negative A negativo *ah
nayga-teevo*

angry arrabbiato *ar-rab-yahto*

animal l'animale (m) *anee-
mahlay*

ankle la caviglia *kaveel-ya*

anniversary l'anniversario (m)
an-neevayr-sahr-yo

anorak la giacca a vento *jak-ka a
vento*

another un altro *oon altro;*
another beer? ancora una birra?
an-kohra oona beer-ra

answer¹ n la risposta *ree-
spohsta*

answer² vb rispondere
reespohn-dayray

antibiotic l'antibiotico (m)
antee-bee-o-teeko

antifreeze l'antigelo (m) *antee-
jaylo*

antique il pezzo d'antiquariato
pets-so dantee-kwar-yahto

antiseptic l'antisettico (m)
antee-set-teeko

any: have you any apples?
avete delle mele? *a-vaytay dayl-
lay maylay;* **I haven't any money**
non ho soldi *nohn o soldee*

anybody: I can't see anybody
non vedo nessuno *nohn vaydo
nays-soono*

anything qualcosa *kwal-koza;* **I
don't want anything** non voglio
niente *nohn vol-yo nee-entay;*
anything else? nient'altro? *nee-
ental-tro*

anyway in ogni modo *een on-
yee modo*

anywhere da qualche parte *da
kwalkay partay*

apartment l'appartamento (m)
ap-parta-maynto

aperitif l'aperitivo (m) *a-payree-teevo*

A positive A positivo *a pozee-teevo*

appendicitis l'appendicite (f) *ap-payn dee-cheetay*

apple la mela *mayla;* **apples** le mele *maylay*

appointment l'appuntamento (m) *ap-poonta-maynto*

apricot l'albicocca (f) *albee-kok-ka*

April aprile (m) *a-preelay*

arch l'arco (m) *arko*

archeology l'archeologia (f) *arkay-olo-jee-a*

architecture l'architettura (f) *arkee-tayt-toora*

are: you are (polite) Lei è *le-ee e;* **we are** siamo *see-amo;* **they are** sono *sohno*

area l'area (f) *aray-a*

arm il braccio *brat-cho;* **arms** le braccia *brat-cha*

armbands (for swimming) i bracciali *brat-chahlee*

around: around ten o'clock verso le dieci *vayrso lay dee-echee;* **around 50** circa cinquanta *cheerka cheen-kwanta*

arrange sistemare *seestay-mahray*

arrivals gli arrivi *ar-reevee*

arrive arrivare *ar-ree-vahray*

art gallery la galleria d'arte *gal-layree-a dartay*

arthritis l'artrite (f) *ar-treetay*

artichoke il carciofo *kar-chohfo*

artificial artificiale *arte-fee-chahlay*

artist l'artista (m/f) *ar-teesta*

as (while) mentre *mayntray;* (way, manner) come *kohmay*

ash (from burning) la cenere *chay-nayray*

ashamed: I am ashamed mi vergogno *mee vayrgon-yo*

ashore a riva *a reeva*

ashtray il portacenere *porta-chay-nayray*

ask chiedere *kee-e-dayray*

asleep addormentato *ad-dormayn-tahto*

asparagus gli asparagi *aspa-rajee*

aspirin l'aspirina (f) *aspee-reena*

assistant (in shop: male) il commesso *kom-mays-so;* (female) la commessa *kom-mays-sa*

asthma l'asma *azma*

at a *a;* **at home** a casa *a kahsa;* **at 2 o'clock** alle due *al-lay doo-ay;* **at the bar** al bar *al bar*

athletics l'atletica (f) *atle-teeka*

attendant (in petrol station) il benzinaio *bayndzee-na-yo;* (in museum, toilet) il custode *koo-stoday*

aubergine la melanzana *maylant-sahna*

auction l'asta (f) *asta*

August agosto (m) *a-gohstoh*

aunt la zia *tsee-a*

au pair girl la ragazza alla pari *ragats-sa al-la paree*

Australia l'Australia (f) *a-oostrahl-ya*

Australian australiano/a *a-oostral-yahno/a*

author l'autore *a-ooto-ray*

automatic automatico *a-ootoma-teeko*

autumn autunno *a-ootoon-no*

avocado l'avocado *avo-kahdo*

avoid evitare *ayvee-tahray*

awake sveglio *zvayl-yo*

away via *vee-a;* **it's 10 kilometres away** è a dieci kilometres di distanza *e a dee-echee kee-lo-maytree dee dee-stantsa*

awful terribile *tayr-ree-beelay*

awkward scomodo *sko-modo*

axe l'ascia (f) *asha*

axle l'assale (m) *as-sahlay*

B

baby il bambino *bam-beeno*

baby food gli alimenti per bambini *alee-mayntee payr bam-beenee*

babysitter il/la baby-sitter *baby-sitter*

babysitting service il servizio di baby-sitter *sayrveets-yo dee baby-sitter*

baby wipes i fazzolettini per pulire i bambini *fats-solayt-teenee payr poo-leeray ee bam-beenee*

back[1] adj di dietro *dee dee-etro*

back[2] n (body) la schiena *skee-*

e-na

backpack lo zaino *dza-eeno*

backwards indietro *eendee-etro*

bacon la pancetta *panchayt-ta*

bad (food) guasto *gwasto;* (weather, news) brutto *broot-to*

badge il distintivo *deesteen-teevo*

bag la borsa *borsa;* (suitcase) la valigia *va-leeja*

baggage i bagagli *bagal-yee*

baggage reclaim il ritiro bagagli *ree-teero bagal-yee*

baker's la panetteria *panayt-tay-ree-a*

balcony il balcone *bal-kohnay*

bald (person) calvo *kalvo;* (tyre) liscio *leesho*

ball la palla *pal-la*

ballet il balletto *bal-layt-to*

ballpoint la biro *beero*

banana la banana *ba-nana*

band (musical) la banda *banda*

bandage la benda *benda*

bank la banca *banka*

bank holiday la festa nazionale *festa natsyo-nahlay*

baptism il battesimo *bat-tay-zeemo*

bar il bar *bar*

barber il barbiere *barb-yeray*

bargain l'occasione (f) *ok-kaz-yohnay*

barmaid la cameriera *kamayr-yera*

barman il barista *ba-reesta*

basket il cestino *chay-steeno*

bath il bagno *ban-yo;* **to take a bath** fare un bagno *fahray oon ban-yo*

bathe fare un bagno *fahray oon ban-yo*

bathing cap la cuffia *koof-ya*

bathing costume il costume da bagno *ko-stoomay da ban-yo*

bathroom il bagno *ban-yo*

battery la batteria *bat-tayree-a*

bay la baia *ba-ya*

be essere *es-sayray*

beach la spiaggia *spee-ad-ja*

beans i fagioli *fa-jolee*

beautiful bello *bel-lo*

because perché *payrkay*

bed il letto *let-to*

bedding la biancheria *bee-ankay-ree-a*

bedroom la camera da letto *ka-mayra da let-to*

bee l'ape (f) *ahpay*

beef il manzo *mandzo*

beer la birra *beer-ra*

beetroot la barbabietola *bahrbab-yay-tola*

before prima di *preema dee;* **before 7 o'clock** prima delle sette *preema dayl-lay set-tay*

begin cominciare *komeen-chahray*

behind dietro di *dee-etro dee*

beige beige *bej*

believe credere *kray-dayray*

bell la campana *kam-pahna;* (doorbell) il campanello *kampa-nel-lo*

below sotto *soht-to*

belt la cintura *cheen-toora*

bend la curva *koorva*

bent storto *storto*

berry la bacca *bak-ka*

berth la cuccetta *koot-chayt-ta*

beside accanto a *ak-kanto a*

best migliore *meel-yohray*

better meglio *mel-yo*

between fra *fra*

beyond al di là di *al dee la dee*

Bible la Bibbia *beeb-ya*

bicycle la bicicletta *beechee-klayt-ta*

big grande *granday*

bigger più grande *pee-oo granday*

biggest il/la più grande *pee-oo granday*

big stores i grandi magazzini *grandee magadz-zeenee*

bikini il bikini *bee-keenee*

bill il conto *kohntoh*

bin il bidone *bee-dohnay*

binoculars il binocolo *beeno-kolo*

bird l'uccello *oot-chel-lo*

biro la biro *beero*

birthday il compleanno *complay-an-no*

birthday card il biglietto di auguri di buon compleanno *beel-yayt-to dee a-oo-gooree dee bwon komplay-an-no*

bit il pezzo *pets-so;* **a bit of** un po' di *oon po dee*

bite mordere *mor-dayray;* (insect) pungere *poon-jayray*

bitten morso *morso;* (by insect)

punto *poonto*

bitter amaro *a-mahro*

black nero *nayro*

black coffee il caffè nero *kaf-fe nayro*

blackcurrant il ribes nero *reebes nayro*

black ice uno strato di ghiaccio *oono strahto dee gee-atcho*

bladder la vescica *vay-sheeka*

blame incolpare *eenkol-pahray*

blanket la coperta *ko-payrta*

bleach la candeggina *kanday-jeena*

bleeding sanguinante *sangwee-nantay*

blind cieco *cheko*

blister la vescica *vay-sheeka*

blocked bloccato *blok-kahto*

blood il sangue *sangwe*

blood group il gruppo sanguigno *groop-po sangween-yo*

blood pressure la pressione sanguigna *praysee-ohnay sangween-ya*

blouse la camicetta *kamee-chayt-ta*

blow soffiare *sof-yah-ray*

blow-dry asciugare con il föhn *ashoo-gahray kohn eel fon*

blue blu *bloo*

blusher il fard *far*

B negative B negativo *bee nayga-teevo*

board imbarcarsi su *eembar-karsee soo*

boarding card la carta

d'imbarco *karta deem-barko*

boarding house la pensione *paynsee-ohnay*

boat la barca *barka*

boat trip la gita in barca *jeeta een barka*

bobsleigh il bob *bob*

body il corpo *korpo*

boil bollire *bol-leeray*

boiled egg l'uovo (m) sodo *wovo sodo*

bomb la bomba *bomba*

bone l'osso (m) *os-so*

bonnet (of car) il cofano *ko-fano*

book[1] *n* il libro *leebro*

book[2] *vb* prenotare *prayno-tahray*

book of tickets il blocchetto di biglietti *blok-kayt-to dee beel-yayt-tee*

booking la prenotazione *prayno-tats-yohnay*

booking office la biglietteria *beel-yayt-tayree-a*

bookshop la libreria *leebray-ree-a*

boom (sailing) il boma *bohma*

boot (of car) il portabagagli *porta-bagal-yee*

boots (to wear) gli stivali *stee-vahlee*; **ski boots** gli scarponi da sci *skar-pohnee da shee*

border (frontier) la frontiera *front-yera*; (edge) l'orlo (m) *orlo*

bored annoiato *an-no-yahto*

boring noioso *no-yohzo*

born nascere *na-shayray*; **I was born in 1955** sono nato nel millenovecento cinquantacinque *sohnoh nahto nayl* **meel**-*lay-novay*-**chento** *cheen-kwanta-* **cheenk**way

both tutti e due *toot-tee ay doo-ay*

bottle la bottiglia *bot-**teel**-ya*

bottle opener l'apribottiglie (m) *apree-bot-**teel**-yay*

bottom il fondo *fohndoh*

bow (of ship) la prua *proo-a;* (knot) il fiocco *feeok-ko*

bowels l'intestino (m) *eentay-steeno*

bowl la scodella *skodel-la*

box la scatola *skah-tola*

box office il botteghino *bot-tay-geeno*

box of matches la scatola di fiammiferi *skah-tola dee feeam-mee-fayree*

boy il ragazzo *ragats-so*

boyfriend il ragazzo *ragats-so*

B positive B positivo *bee-pozee-teevo*

bra il reggiseno *rayd-jee-**sayno***

bracelet il braccialetto *brat-chalayt-to*

braces le bretelle *braytel-lay*

brake frenare *fray-nahray*

brake fluid l'olio per i freni *ol-yo payr ee fraynee*

brakes i freni *fraynee;* to put the brakes on azionare i freni *ats-yo-**nahray** ee fraynee*

branch (of tree) il ramo *rahmo;* (of bank etc) l'agenzia *ajaynt-seea*

brand la marca *marka*

brandy brandy *brandy*

brass l'ottone (m) *oht-**tohnay***

brave coraggioso *korad-johzo*

bread il pane *pahnay*

break rompere *rohm-payray*

breakable fragile *fra-jeelay*

breakdown il guasto *gwasto*

breakdown van il carro attrezzi *karro at-**trayts**-see*

breakfast la colazione *kola-tsyohnay*

breast il seno *sayno*

breathe respirare *rayspee-**rahray***

breeze la brezza *braydz-za*

bride la sposa *spoza*

bridegroom lo sposo *spozo*

bridge il ponte *pohntay*

briefcase la cartella *kartel-la*

briefs le mutandine *mootan-deenay*

bright luminoso *loomee-nohzo*

bring portare *por-**tahray***

Britain La Gran Bretagna *gran braytan-ya*

British britannico *breetan-neeko*

broad largo *largo*

brochure il dépliant *dayplee-**on***

broken rotto *roht-to*

broken down (machine, car) guasto *gwasto*

bronchitis la bronchite *bron-keetay*

bronze il bronzo *brohndzo*

brooch la spilla *speel-la*

broom la scopa *skohpa*

brother il fratello *fratel-lo*

brown marrone *mar-**rohnay**;*

(hair) castano ka-**stah**no

brown paper la carta da pacchi **kar**ta da pak-kee

brown sugar lo zucchero greggio tsook-**kay**ro grayd-jo

bruise n il livido lee-**vee**do

brush[1] vb (clothes, hair) spazzolare spats-so-**lah**ray; **to brush one's teeth** lavarsi i denti la-**var**see ee dentee

brush[2] n la spazzola spats-**so**la

Brussels sprouts i cavoletti di Bruxelles kahvo-**layt**-tee dee **brook**sel

bucket il secchiello sek-**yayl**-lo

buffet il buffet boo-**fe**

buffet car la carrozza ristorante kar-**rots**-sa reesto-**ran**tay

build costruire kostroo-**ee**ray

building l'edificio (m) aydee-**fee**cho

bulb la lampadina lampa-**dee**na

bull il toro **to**ro

bullet il proiettile prohyayt-**tee**lay

bumper il paraurti para-**oor**tee

bun il panino dolce pa-**nee**no **dohl**chay

bureau de change l'ufficio (m) di cambio oof-**fee**cho dee **kamb**-yo

burgle svaligiare zvalee-**jah**ray

burn bruciare broo-**chah**ray

burst[1] adj scoppiato skop-**yah**to

burst[2] vb scoppiare skop-**yah**ray

bus l'autobus (m) a-oo-**to**boos

bus depot il deposito degli autobus daypo-**zee**to dayl-lyee a-

oo-**to**boos

bush il cespuglio chay**spool**-yo

business gli affari af-**fah**ree

business card il biglietto da visita beel-**yayt**-to da **vee**-zeeta

business trip il viaggio d'affari vee**ad**-jo daf-**fah**ree

bus station la stazione delle autolinee stats-**yoh**nay dayl-lay a-ooto-**lee**nay-ay

bus stop la fermata (dell'autobus) fayr-**mah**ta (dayl-**la-oo-to**boos)

bus tour la gita in pullman jeeta een poolman

busy occupato ok-koo-**pah**to

but ma ma

butcher il macellaio machayl-**la**-yo

butter il burro **boor**-ro

butterfly la farfalla far**fal**-la

button il bottone bot-**toh**nay

buy comprare kom-**prah**ray

by (close to) vicino a vee-**chee**no a; (via) via vee-a; (past) davanti a da-**van**tee a; **a poem by Dante** un poema di Dante oon-**po**-e-ma di dantay

bypass la strada di circonvallazione strahda dee cheerkon-val-lats-**yoh**nay

C

cabaret il cabaret kaba-**re**

cabbage il cavolo **kah**-volo

cabin la cabina ka-**bee**na

cablecar la funivia foonee-**vee**-a

café il caffè *kaf-fe*

cagoule la giacca a vento *jak-ka a vento*

cake la torta *torta*

calculator il calcolatore *kalkola-tohray*

call[1] vb chiamare *keea-mahray*

call[2] n (shout) il grido *greedo*; (on telephone) la chiamata *keea-mahta*; **a long-distance call** una chiamata interurbana *keea-mahta eentayr-oor-bahna*

calm calmo *kalmo*

camera la macchina fotografica *mak-keena foto-gra-feeka*

camp campeggiare *kampayd-jahray*

camp-bed il lettino da campeggio *layt-teeno da kampayd-jo*

camp site il campeggio *kampayd-jo*

can[1] n il barattolo *barat-tolo*

can[2] vb (to be able) potere *po-tayray*

Canada il Canada *kana-da*

Canadian Canadese *kana-dayzay*

cancel cancellare *kanchayl-lahray*

cancer il cancro *kankro*

candle la candela *kan-dayla*

canoe la canoa *kano-a*

can opener l'apriscatole (m) *apree-ska-tohlay*

capital (of a country) la capitale *kapee-tahlay*

capsize rovesciare *rovay-shahray*

captain il capitano *kapee-tahno*

car la macchina *mak-keena*

carafe la caraffa *karaf-fa*

caravan la roulotte *roolot*

carburettor il carburatore *kahrboo-ra-tohray*

card (greetings) la cartolina *karto-leena*; (playing) la carta da gioco *karta da joko*

cardigan il cardigan *cardigan*

car documents i documenti per la macchina *dokoo-mayntee payr la mak-keena*

care preoccuparsi *pray-ok-koopar-see*

careful attento *at-taynto*

careless negligente *nayglee-jentay*

car ferry il traghetto *tragayt-to*

car keys le chiavi della macchina *kee-ahvee dayl-la mak-keena*

car number la targa *targa*

carol il canto di Natale *kanto dee na-tahlay*

car park il parcheggio *parkayd-jo*

carpet il tappeto *tap-payto*

carriage (railway) la carrozza *kar-rots-sa*

carrier bag la busta *boosta*

carrots le carote *ka-rotay*

carry portare *por-tahray*

cartridge il caricatore *karee-ka-tohray*

car wash il lavaggio auto *lavad-jo a-ooto*

case (suitcase) la valigia *va-leeja*

cash¹ vb (cheque) incassare eenkas-**sahray**

cash² n i contanti kon-**tantee**; (in) cash in contanti een kon-**tantee**

cash advance l'anticipo (m) in contanti antee-**cheepo** een kon-**tantee**

cash desk la cassa kas-sa

cashier il cassiere kas-**yeray**

casino il casinò kazee-**no**

cassette la cassetta kas-**sayt**-ta

castle il castello kastel-lo

cat il gatto gat-to

Catacombs le Catacombe kata-**kombay**

catalogue il catalogo katah-logo

catch prendere **pren**-dayray

cathedral il duomo dwomo

Catholic cattolico kat-to-leeko

cauliflower il cavolfiore kahvolf-**yohray**

cause la causa ka-**ooza**

cave la grotta grot-ta

ceiling il soffitto sof-feet-to

celeriac il sedano rapa se-dano rahpa

celery il sedano se-dano

cellar la cantina kan-teena

cello il violoncello vee-olon-**chel**-lo

cemetery il cimitero cheemee-**tayro**

centigrade centigrado chayntee-grado

centimetre il centimetro chayntee-maytro

central centrale chayn-**trahlay**

central heating il riscaldamento centrale reeskal-da-**maynto** chayn-**trahlay**

centre il centro chentro

cereal (for breakfast) i fiocchi di cereali fee-**ok**-kee dee chayray-**ahlee**

certain (sure) certo chayrto

certificate il certificato chayrtee-fee-**kahto**

chain la catena ka-**tayna**

chair la sedia sed-ya

chairlift la seggiovia sayd-jovee-a

chalet lo chalet sha-le

champagne lo champagne shang-**pan**-ye

change¹ n il cambio kamb-yo; (small coins) gli spiccioli speet-cholee; (money returned) il resto resto

change² vb cambiare kamb-**yahray**; to change one's clothes cambiarsi kamb-**yarsee**; to change trains cambiare kamb-**yahray**; to change one's mind cambiare idea kamb-**yahray** eeday-a

changing room lo spogliatoio spol-**yato**-yo

Channel: the Channel La Manica **mah**-neeka

chapel la cappella kap-pel-la

charge¹ vb (amount) farsi pagare farsee pa-**gahray**; (battery) caricare karee-**kahray**

charge² n la tariffa tareef-fa

chart la carta (nautica) karta (na-

oo-teeka)

charter flight il volo charter *vohloh charter*

chassis il telaio *tayla-yo*

chauffeur l'autista (m) *owteesta*

cheap economico *ayko-nomeeko*

cheaper più economico *pee-oo ayko-no-meeko*

cheat truffare *troof-fahray*

check controllare *kontrol-lahray*

check in (at airport) fare il check-in *fahray eel check-in;* (at hotel) firmare il registro *feermahray eel ray-jeestro*

check-in desk l'accettazione (f) bagagli *at-chayt-tats-yohnay bagal-yee*

check out (of hotel) lasciare libera la stanza *la-shahray leebayra la stantsa*

cheek la guancia *gwancha*

cheeky sfacciato *sfat-chahto*

cheerio ciao *chao*

cheers salute *sa-lootay*

cheese il formaggio *formad-jo*

chef lo chef *chef*

chemist il/la farmacista *farmacheesta*

chemist's la farmacia *farmachee-a*

cheque l'assegno (m) *as-sayn-yo*

cheque book il libretto degli assegni *leebrayt-to dayl-lyee assayn-nee*

cheque card la carta assegni *karta as-sayn-yee*

cherries le ciliegie *cheel-yejay*

chess gli scacchi *skak-kee*

chest il torace *to-rahchay*

chestnut la castagna *kastan-ya*

chewing gum la gomma da masticare *gohm-ma da masteekahray*

chicken il pollo *pohl-lo*

chickenpox la varicella *vareechel-la*

chilblains i geloni *jay-lohnee*

child (boy) il bambino *bambeeno;* (girl) la bambina *bambeena*

children's pool la piscina per bambini *pee-sheena payr bambeenee*

chili il peperoncino *paypay-roncheeno*

chilled: is the wine chilled? è freddo il vino? *e frayd-do eel veeno*

chimney il camino *ka-meeno*

chin il mento *maynto*

china la porcellane *porchayl-lahnay*

chips le patatine fritte *patateenay freet-tay*

chocolate la cioccolata *chok-kolahta*

chocolates i cioccolatini *chokkola-teenee*

choke (in car) l'aria *ahr-ya*

choose scegliere *shayl-yayray*

chop la costoletta *kosto-layt-ta*

christening il battesimo *bat-tayzeemo*

Christian name il nome di

battesimo *nohmay dee bat-tay-zeemo*

Christmas Natale (*m*) *na-tahlay*

church la chiesa *kee-e-za*

churchyard il cimitero di una chiesa *cheemee-tayro dee oona kee-e-za*

cider il sidro *seedro*

cigar il sigaro *see-garo*

cigarette papers le cartine per sigarette *kar-teenay payr seega-rayt-tay*

cigarettes le sigarette *seega-rayt-tay*

cine-camera la cinepresa *cheenay-prayza*

cinema il cinema *chee-nayma*

cinnamon la cannella *kan-nel-la*

circle il circolo *cheer-kolo*; (in theatre) la galleria *gal-lay-ree-a*

circular circolare *cheerko-lahray*

circus il circo *cheerko*

city la città *cheet-ta*

claim richiedere *reek-ye-dayray*

clams le vongole *von-golay*

clarinet il clarinetto *klaree-nayt-to*

class la classe *klas-say*

clean[1] *adj* pulito *poo-lee-to*

clean[2] *vb* pulire *poo-leeray*

cleaner l'addetto/a (*m/f*) alle pulizie *ad-dayt-to/a al-lay pooleet-tseeay*

cleansing cream la crema detergente *krema daytayr-jentay*

clear[1] *vb* sgomberare *sgom-bay-rahray*

clear[2] *adj* (obvious) ovvio *ov-*

veeo; (transparent) trasparente *traspa-rentay*

clerk l'impiegato/a (*m/f*) *eempye-gahto/a*

clever intelligente *eentayl-lee-jentay*

client il/la cliente *klee-entay*

cliff la scogliera *skol-ye-ra*

climate il clima *kleema*

climber l'alpinista (*m/f*) *alpee-neesta*

climbing l'alpinismo (*m*) *alpee-neezmo*

climbing boots gli scarponi da montagna *skar-pohnee da montan-ya*

clip (cut) tagliare *tal-yahray*

cloakroom il guardaroba *gwarda-roba*

clock l'orologio (*m*) *oro-lojo*

close[1] *adj* (near) vicino a *vee-cheeno a*

close[2] *vb* chiudere *keeoo-dayray*

closed chiuso *kee-oozo*

cloth lo straccio *stratcho*

clothes i vestiti *vay-steetee*

clothes peg la molletta *mol-layt-ta*

cloud la nuvola *noo-vola*

cloudy nuvoloso *noovo-lohzo*

clove il chiodo *kee-odo*

club il club *kloob*

clumsy goffo *gof-fo*

clutch (in car) la frizione *freets-yohnay*

coach (bus) il pullman *poolman*; (train) la carrozza *kar-rots-sa*

coach trip la gita in pullman

jeeta een poolman

coal il carbone *kar-bohnay*

coarse grezzo *graydz-zo*

coast la costa *kosta*

coastguard il guardacoste *gwarda-kostay*

coat il cappotto *kap-potto*

coat hanger la gruccia *grootcha*

cobweb la ragnatela *ran-ya-tayla*

cock il gallo *gal-lo*

cockle il cardio *kar-deeo*

cocktail il cocktail *cocktail*

cocoa il cacao *kaka-o*

coconut la noce di cocco *nohchay dee kok-ko*

cod il merluzzo *mayr-loots-so*

coffee il caffè *kaf-fe*

coin la moneta *mo-nayta*

colander lo scolapasta *skola-pasta*

cold[1] n il raffreddore *raf-frayd-dohray*

cold[2] adj freddo *frayd-do*; **I'm cold** ho freddo *o frayd-do*

Coliseum il Colosseo *kolos-sayo*

collar il collo *kol-lo*

colleague il/la collega *kol-lega*

collect raccogliere *rak-kol-yayray*

collection la collezione *col-layts-yohnay*

college l'istituto superiore *eestee-tooto soopayr-yohray*

colour il colore *ko-lohray*

colour-blind daltonico *dalto-neeko*

coloured pencils le matite colorate *ma-teetay koloh-rahtay*

colour film il rullino a colori

rool-leeno a kohlohree

colour slide la diapositiva a colori *deea-pozee-teeva a kohlohree*

comb il pettine *pet-teenay*

come venire *vay-neeray*; (arrive) arrivare *ar-ree-vahray*; **to come back** tornare *tor-nahray*; **to come in** entrare *ayn-trahray*; **come in!** avanti! *a-vantee*; **to come off** (button) staccarsi *stak-kahrsee*; (stain) venire via *vay-neeray vee-a*; **to come out** (stain) venire via *vay-neeray vee-a*; **to come to** (after faint) rinvenire *reenvay-neeray*

comedy la commedia *kom-med-ya*

comfortable comodo *ko-modo*

comic comico *ko-meekoh*

commercial[1] adj commerciale *kom-mayr-chahlay*

commercial[2] n (TV) la pubblicità *poob-bleechee-ta*

common comune *ko-moonay*; **the Common Market** il Mercato Comune *eel mayr-kahto ko-moonay*

communication cord il segnale d'allarme *sayn-yahlay dal-larmay*

communion la comunione *komoon-yohnay*

company la compagnia *kompan-yee-a*

compare paragonare *para-go-nahray*

compartment il compartimento

kompar-tee-maynto

compass la bussola *boos-sola*

competition la gara *gahra*

complain fare un reclamo *fahray oon ray-klahmo*

complaint il reclamo *ray-klahmo*

completely completamente *komplay-ta-mayntay*

complicated complicato *komplee-kahto*

comprehensive completo *kompleto;* **comprehensive insurance policy** la polizza casco *poleets-sa kasko*

compulsory obbligatorio *ob-bleega-tor-yo*

computer il computer *komputer*

concert il concerto *kon-chayrto*

concussion la commozione cerebrale *kom-mots-yohnay chayray-brahlay*

condensed milk il latte condensato *laht-tay kondayn-sahto*

condition la condizione *kondeets-yohnay;* (*medical*) la malattia *malat-tee-a*

conditioner il balsamo *bal-samo*

conductor (*on bus*) il bigliettaio *beel-yayt-ta-yo;* (*of orchestra*) il direttore *deerayt-tohray*

conference il congresso *kongres-so*

confession la confessione *konfays-yohnay*

confetti i coriandoli *koree-an-dolee*

confidential confidenziale *konfee-daynts-yahlay*

confirm confermare *konfayr-mahray*

confirmed confermato *konfayr-mahto*

congratulations le congratulazioni *kongra-toolats-yohnee*

conjunctivitis la congiuntivite *konjoon-tee-veetay*

connect collegare *kol-lay-gahray*

conscious cosciente *ko-shentay*

constipated stitico *stee-teeko*

consul il console *kon-solay*

consulate il consolato *konso-lahto*

contact mettersi in contatto con *mayt-tayrsee een kontat-to kohn*

contact lens cleaner il liquido per lenti a contatto *lee-kweedo payr lentee a kontat-to*

contact lenses le lenti a contatto *lentee a kontat-to*

Continental europeo *ay-ooro-pe-o*

Continental breakfast la colazione all'europea *kolats-yohnay al-lay-ooro-pe-a*

contraceptive il contraccettivo *kontrat-chayt-teevo*

contract il contratto *kontrat-to*

controls i controlli *kontrol-lee*

convenient (*place*) comodo *ko-modo;* (*time*) opportuno *op-por-toono*

convent il convento *kon-vento*

cook[1] vb cucinare *koochee-nahray*

cook[2] n il cuoco/la cuoca *kwoko/kwoka*

cooker la cucina *koo-cheena*

cool fresco *fraysko*

cooling system il sistema di raffreddamento *see-stema dee raf-frayda-maynto*

copper il rame *rahmay*

copy[1] n la copia *kop-ya*

copy[2] vb copiare *kop-yahray*

corduroy il velluto a coste *vayl-looto a kostay*

cork il sughero *soo-gayro*

corkscrew il cavatappi *kava-tap-pee*

corn il grano *grahno*

corner l'angolo (m) *an-golo*

cornflakes i cornflakes *cornflakes*

cornflour la fecola di patate *fe-kola dee pa-tahtay*

corn on the cob la pannocchia *pan-nok-ya*

correct corretto *kor-ret-to*

corridor il corridoio *kor-reedo-yo*

cortisone il cortisone *kortee-zohnay*

cosmetics i cosmetici *kozmay-teechee*

cost costare *kos-tahray*; **how much does it/do they cost?** quanto costa/costano? *kwanto kosta/ko-stano*

cot il lettino *layt-teeno*

cottage la casetta *kazayt-ta*

cottage cheese i fiocchi di latte *fee-ok-kee dee lat-tay*

cotton il cotone *ko-tohnay*

cotton wool il cotone idrofilo *ko-tohnay eedro-feelo*

couch il divano *dee-vahno*

couchette la cuccetta *koot-chayt-ta*

cough la tosse *tohs-say*

cough medicine lo sciroppo per la tosse *sheerop-po payr la tohs-say*

count contare *kon-tahray*

counter lo sportello *sportel-lo*

country (not town) la campagna *kampan-ya*; (nation) il paese *pa-ayzay*

couple (2 people) la coppia *kop-ya*; **a couple of times** un paio di volte *oon pa-yo dee voltay*

courgettes gli zucchini *tsook-keenee*

courier il corriere *kor-yeray*

course (of meal) il piatto *peeat-to*

courtyard il cortile *kor-teelay*

cousin (male) il cugino *koo-jeeno*; (female) la cugina *koo-jeena*

cover[1] n (of dish) il coperchio *kopayrk-yo*; (of book) la copertina *kopayr-teena*

cover[2] vb coprire *ko-preeray*

cover charge il coperto *ko-payrto*

cow la vacca *vak-ka*

crab il granchio *grank-yo*

crack[1] vb (break) incrinare

eenkree-nahray

crack[2] n (in glass etc) la crepa
krepa

crash[1] n lo scontro skohntro

crash[2] vb scontrarsi skon-
trahrsee

crash helmet il casco di
protezione kasko dee protayts-
yohnay

crawl (child) andare a gattoni
an-dahray a gat-tohnee

crayons i pastelli a cera pastel-
lee a chayra

cream (lotion) la crema kre-ma;
(on milk) la panna pan-na

creche l'asilo (m) nido a-zeelo
needo

credit il credito kray-deeto

credit card la carta di credito
karta dee kray-deeto

cress il crescione kray-shohnay

crevasse il crepaccio kraypat-
cho

crew l'equipaggio (m) aykwee-
pad-jo

crimson color cremisi kolohr
kray-meezee

crisp croccante krok-kantay

crisps le patatine pata-teenay

crochet lavorare all'uncinetto
lavo-rahray al-loonchee-nayt-to

crooked storto storto

croquette la crocchetta krok-
kayt-ta

cross[1] n la croce krohchay

cross[2] vb (road) attraversare at-
travayr-sahray; (cheque) sbarrare
zbar-rahray

crossed line l'interferenza (f)
eentayr-fay-rent-sa

crossing (by sea) la traversata
travayr-sahta; (road junction)
l'incrocio (m) een-krohcho

crossroads l'incrocio (m) een-
krohcho

crowded affollato af-fol-lahto

crown la corona ko-rohna

crucifix il Crocifisso krochee-
fees-so

cruel crudele kroo-daylay

cruise la crociera kro-chera

crush schiacciare skeeat-chahray

crust la crosta krosta

crutch la stampella stampel-la

cry[1] vb (call out) gridare gree-
dahray; (weep) piangere peean-
jayray

cry[2] n (shout) il grido greedo

crystal il cristallo kreestal-lo

cube il cubo koobo

cucumber il cetriolo chaytree-
olo

cuddle coccolare kok-ko-lahray

cuff il polsino pol-seeno

cup la tazza tats-sa

cupboard l'armadio armahd-yo

cure[1] n la cura koora

cure[2] vb guarire gwa-reeray

curl il ricciolo reet-cholo

curler il bigodino beego-deeno

curly ricciuto reet-chooto

currant la sultanina soolta-
neena

currency la valuta va-loota

current la corrente kor-rayntay

curtain la tenda tenda

curve[1] n la curva *koorva*

curve[2] vb curvare *koor-vahray*

cushion il cuscino *koo-sheeno*

custard la crema pasticcera *krema pasteet-chera*

customs la dogana *do-gahna*

customs officer l'agente (m) doganale *a-jentay doga-nahlay*

cut[1] n il taglio *tal-yo*

cut[2] vb tagliare *tal-yahray*; **to cut off** tagliare *tal-yahray*; **we've been cut off** è caduta la linea *e ka-doota la leenay-a*

cutlery le posate *po-zahtay*

cycle la bicicletta *beechee-klayt-ta*

cycling il ciclismo *chee-kleezmo*

cyclist il/la ciclista *chee-kleesta*

D

daily (each day) ogni giorno *on-yee jorno*

damage[1] n il danno *dan-no*

damage[2] vb danneggiare *dan-nayd-jahray*

damp umido *oo-meedo*

damson la prugna selvatica *proon-ya saylva-teeka*

dance[1] n il ballo *bal-lo*

dance[2] vb ballare *bal-lahray*

dangerous pericoloso *payree-ko-lohzo*

dark scuro *skooro*

darling tesoro *tay-zohro*

darn rammendare *ram-mayn-dahray*

darts le freccette *frayt-chayt-tay*

dashboard il cruscotto *krooskot-to*

data i dati *dahtee*

date la data *dahta*; **what's the date today?** quanti ne abbiamo oggi? *kwantee nay ab-yahmo od-jee*

date of birth la data di nascita *dahta dee na-sheeta*

daughter la figlia *feel-ya*

day il giorno *jorno*

dead morto *morto*

deaf sordo *sordo*

dealer il/la commerciante *kom-mayr-chantay*

dear caro *kahro*; **Dear Mary** Cara Maria *kahra maree-a*; **Dear Sir** Egregio Signore *ay-grejo seen-yohray*

debt il debito *day-beeto*

decaffeinated coffee il caffè decaffeinato *kaf-fe daykaf-fay-ee-nahto*

December dicembre (m) *dee-chembray*

decide decidere *daychee-dayray*

decimal decimale *daychee-mahlay*

deck il ponte *pohntay*

deck chair la sedia a sdraio *sed-ya a zdra-yo*

declare dichiarare *deek-ya-rahray*

deep profondo *pro-fohndo*

deep freeze il surgelatore *soorjay-la-tohray*

deer il cervo *chayrvo*

defrost sgelare *zjay-lahray*

degree (on scale) il grado
grahdo; (from university) la
laurea la-ooray-a

de-ice liberare dal ghiaccio
leebay-rahray dayl gee-at-cho

delay¹ n il ritardo ree-tahrdo

delay² vb (postpone) rimandare
reeman-dahray; (hold up)
ritardare reetahr-dahray

delicate delicato daylee-kato

delicious delizioso dayleets-
yohzo

demonstration (showing) la
dimostrazione deemos-trats-
yohnay; (political) la
manifestazione manee-faystats-
yohnay

denim il tessuto di jeans tays-
sooto dee jeans

dent¹ n l'ammaccatura (f) am-
mak-ka-toora

dent² vb ammaccare am-mak-
kahray

dentist il/la dentista dayn-teesta

dentures la dentiera daynt-yera

deodorant il deodorante day-
oh-dohrantay

department il reparto ray-
pahrto

department store il grande
magazzino granday magadz-
zeeno

departure lounge la sala
d'attesa sahla dat-tayza

departures le partenze par-
tentsay

deposit il deposito daypo-zeeto

describe descrivere dayskree-

vayray

description la descrizione
dayskreets-yohnay

design¹ n il disegno deezayn-yo

design² vb disegnare deezayn-
yahray

desk (in hotel) la reception
reception; (in office) la scrivania
skreeva-neea

dessert il dolce dohlchay

dessertspoon il cucchiaino da
dessert kook-keea-eeno da
daysayr

details i dettagli dayt-tal-yee

detective l'investigatore (m)
eenvay-steega-tohray

detergent il detersivo daytayr-
seevo

detour la deviazione dayvee-ats-
yohnay

develop sviluppare sveeloop-
pahray

diabetic diabetico deea-be-
teeko

dial: to dial a number fare un
numero fahray oon noo-mayro

dialling code il prefisso
telefonico prayfees-so taylay-fo-
neeko

dialling tone il segnale di linea
libera sayn-yahlay dee leenay-a
lee-bayra

diamond il diamante dee-a-
mantay

diarrhoea la diarrea deear-ray-a

diary l'agenda (f) a-jenda

dice i dadi dahdee

dictionary il dizionario deets-

yonahr-yo

did: I did it l'ho fatto io *lo faht-to ee-o;* **did you buy it?** l'hai comprato? *la-ee kom-prahto*

didn't: I didn't do it non l'ho fatto *nohn lo faht-to*

die morire *mo-reeray*

diesel il gasolio *gazol-yo*

diet la dieta *dee-eta*

different diverso *dee-vayrso*

difficult difficile *deef-fee-cheelay*

dinghy il canotto *kanot-to*

dining room la sala da pranzo *sahla da prantso*

dinner la cena *chayna*

dinner jacket lo smoking *smoking*

diplomat il diplomatico *deeplo-ma-teeko*

dipped headlights le luci anabbaglianti *loochee anab-bal-yantee*

direct (*train etc*) diretto *deeret-to*

directory l'elenco (m) telefonico *ay-lenko taylay-fo-neeko*

dirty sporco *sporko*

disabled handicappato *andee-kap-pahto*

disappointed deluso *day-loozo*

disappointing deludente *dayloo-dentay*

disco la discoteca *deesko-teka*

discount lo sconto *skohntoh*

dish il piatto *peeat-to*

dishcloth lo strofinaccio *strofee-nat-cho*

dishtowel lo strofinaccio

strofee-nat-cho

dishwasher la lavastoviglie *lahva-stoveel-yay*

disinfectant il disinfettante *deezeen-fayt-tantay*

dislocate slogare *zlo-gahray*

disposable nappies i pannolini per bambini usa e getta *pan-no-leenee payr bam-beenee*

distance la distanza *dee-stantsa*

distilled water l'acqua distillata *akwa deesteel-lahta*

distributor il distributore *deestree-boo-tohray*

district (*of country*) la regione *rayj-yohnay;* (*of town*) il quartiere *kwart-yeray*

disturb disturbare *deestoor-bahray*

dive tuffarsi *toof-fahrsee*

diver (*male*) il tuffatore *toof-fa-tohray;* (*female*) la tuffatrice *toof-fa-treechay*

divorced divorziato *deevorts-yahto*

dizzy stordito *stor-deeto*

do fare *fahray;* **I do** faccio *fat-cho;* **you do** Lei fa *le-ee fa;* **he does** fa *fa*

doctor il medico *me-deeko*

documents i documenti *dokoo-mayntee*

dog il cane *kahnay*

doll la bambola *bam-bola*

dollars i dollari *dol-laree*

dome la cupola *koo-pola*

dominoes il domino *do-meeno*

done: I've done it l'ho fatto lo

faht-to
donkey l'asino (m) a-zeeno
door la porta porta
double doppio dop-yo
double bed letto matrimoniale
let-to matree-mon-yahlay
double room la camera
matrimoniale ka-mayra matree-
mon-yahlay
double whisky il whisky
doppio whisky dop-yo
dough l'impasto (m) eem-pasto
doughnut il krapfen krapfen
down giù joo; **to go down**
(downstairs) scendere shayn-
dayray; (sun) tramontare tramon-
tahray; **down the road** lungo la
strada loongo la strahda
downstairs giù joo
drain[1] la fogna fohn-ya
drain[2] vb (vegetables) scolare
sko-lahray; (tank) vuotare vwo-
tahray
draught la corrente (d'aria) kor-
rentay (dahr-ya)
draughts la dama dahma
draw (picture) disegnare
deezayn-yahray; (money)
prelevare praylay-vahray
drawer il cassetto kas-sayt-to
drawing book l'album (m) di
disegno alboom dee deezayn-yo
dreadful terribile tayr-reebee-
lay
dress[1] n il vestito vay-steeto
dress[2] vb: **to get dressed** vestirsi
vay-steersee
dressing (for food) il

drier (for hair) il föhn fon; (for
clothes) l'asciugabiancheria (m)
ashoo-gabee-ankay-ree-a
drink[1] n la bibita bee-beeta
drink[2] vb bere bayray
drinking water l'acqua (f)
potabile akwa potah-beelay
drip sgocciolare sgot-cholah-ray
drive guidare gwee-dahray
driver (of car) l'autista (m/f)
a-oo-teesta; (of train) il
macchinista mak-kee-neesta
driving la guida gweeda
driving licence la patente
pa-tentay
drown annegare an-nay-gahray
drug[1] n la droga droga
drug[2] vb drogare dro-gahray
drum il tamburo tam-booro
drunk ubriaco oobree-ako
dry[1] adj secco sayk-ko
dry[2] vb asciugare ashoo-gahray
dry cleaner's la tintoria teento-
reea
duck l'anatra (f) a-natra
due: when is the train due?
quando dovrebbe arrivare il
treno? kwando dovrayb-bay
ar-ree-vahray eel treno
dufflecoat il montgomery
montgomery
dull (day, weather) nuvoloso
noovo-lohzo
dumb (unable to speak) muto
mooto
dummy la tettarella tayt-ta-rel-la
dune la duna doona

during durante *doo-rantay*
dust la polvere *pohl-vayray*
dusty polveroso *polvay-rohzo*
duty (*tax*) l'imposta (*f*) *eem-posta*
duty-free esente da dogana *ay-zentay da do-gahna*
duty-free shop il duty free *duty free*
duvet il piumino *peeoo-meeno*
dynamo la dinamo *dee-namo*

E

each ogni *on-yee*
ear un orecchio *orayk-yo*
earache mal d'orecchi *mal dorayk-yee*
earlier più presto *pee-oo presto*
early presto *presto*
earn guadagnare *gwadan-yahray*
earphones le cuffie *koof-yay*
earplugs i tappi *tap-pee*
earrings gli orecchini *orayk-keenee*
earth (*world*) il mondo *mondo*; (*soil*) la terra *ter-ra*
east l'est (*m*) *est*
Easter La Pasqua *paskwa*
easy facile *fa-cheelay*
eat mangiare *man-jahray*
economic economico *ayko-no-meeko*
eczema l'eczema (*m*) *ayk-dzema*
edge l'orlo (*m*) *orlo*
editor il direttore (*m*) *deerayt-tohray*
eel l'anguilla (*f*) *angweel-la*

efficient efficiente *ayf-fee-chentay*
egg l'uovo (*m*) *wovo;* **eggs** le uova *wova;* **fried egg** uovo fritto *wovo freet-to;* **hard-boiled egg** uovo sodo *wovo sodo;* **scrambled eggs** uova strapazzate *wova strapats-sahtay*
eight otto *ot-to*
eighteen diciotto *deechot-to*
eighth ottavo *ot-tahvo*
eighty ottanta *ot-tanta*
either: either one l'uno o l'altro *loono o laltro*
elastic l'elastico (*m*) *aylas-teeko*
elastic band l'elastico (*m*) *aylas-teeko*
elbow il gomito *goh-meeto*
election l'elezione (*f*) *aylayts-yohnay*
electric elettrico *aylet-treeko*
electric blanket la termocoperta *tayrmo-ko-payrta*
electric fire la stufa elettrica *stoofa aylet-treeka*
electrician l'elettricista (*m*) *aylayt-tree-cheesta*
electricity l'elettricità (*f*) *aylayt-treechee-ta*
electricity meter il contatore della luce *konta-tohray dayl-la loochay*
electrics l'impianto elettrico (*m*) *emp-yanto aylet-treeko*
electronic elettronico *aylet-tro-neeko*
element (*electrical*) l'elemento (*m*) *aylay-maynto*

eleven undici *oon-deechee*

eleventh undicesimo *oondee-che-zeemo*

embarrassed imbarazzato *eemba-rats-sahto*

embarrassing imbarazzante *eemba-rats-santay*

embassy l'ambasciata (f) *amba-shahta*

embroidered ricamato *reeka-mahto*

emerald lo smeraldo *zmay-raldo*

emergency l'emergenza (f) *aymayr-jentsa*

emery boards le limette di carta smerigliata *leemayt-tay dee kahrta zmayreel-lyahta*

empty[1] *adj* vuoto *vwoto*

empty[2] *vb* vuotare *vwo-tahray*

enamel lo smalto *zmalto*

encyclopedia l'enciclopedia (f) *aynchee-klopay-deea*

end la fine *feenay*

energetic energico *aynayr-jeeko*

engaged (to be married) fidanzato *feedant-sahto*; (toilet) occupato *ok-koo-pahto*

engine il motore *moh-tohray*

engineer l'ingegnere (m) *eenjayn-yeray*

England L'Inghilterra (f) *eengeel-ter-ra*

English inglese *een-glayzay*

enjoy: I enjoyed the tour la visita mi è piaciuta *la vee-zeeta mee e peea-choota*; **I enjoy swimming** mi piace nuotare *mee pee-achay nwo-tahray*

enough abbastanza *ab-bas-tantsa*

enquiry desk il banco delle informazioni *banko dayl-lay eenfor-mats-yohnay*

entertainment il divertimento *deevayr-tee-maynto*

enthusiastic entusiastico *ayntoo-zeea-steeko*

entrance l'entrata (f) *ayn-trahta*

entrance fee il prezzo d'ingresso *prets-so deengres-so*

envelopes le buste *boostay*

epilepsy l'epilessia *aypee-lay-seea*

equal uguale *oo-gwahlay*

equipment l'attrezzatura (f) *at-trayts-sa-toora*

escalator la scala mobile *skahla mo-beelay*

especially specialmente *spaychal-mayntay*

essential essenziale *ays-saynts-yahlay*

estate (land) la tenuta (f) *tay-noota*

estate agent l'agente (m) immobiliare *a-jentay eem-mobeel-yahray*

Eurocheque l'eurocheque (m) *e-ooro-chek*

Europe L'Europa (f) *ay-oo-ropa*

European europeo *ay-ooro-pay-o*

evaporated milk il latte concentrato *lat-tay konchayn-trahto*

even (speed) uniforme *oonee-*

formay; (smooth) regolare *raygo-*
lahray; (numbers) pari *pahree;*
even on Sundays perfino la
domenica *payr-feeno la domay-*
neeka
evening la sera *sayra;* **in the**
evening la sera *la sayra*
evening dress l'abito (m) da
sera *a-beeto da sayra*
evening meal la cena *chayna*
every ogni *on-yee*
everyone tutti *toot-tee*
everything tutto *toot-to*
everywhere dappertutto *dap-*
payrtoot-to
evidence la prova *prova*
examination l'esame (m) *ay-*
zahmay
example l'esempio (m)
ayzemp-yo
excellent ottimo *ot-teemo*
except eccetto *ayt-chet-to*
excess luggage il bagaglio in
eccedenza *bagal-yo een ayt-*
chay-dentsa
exchange[1] n lo scambio
skamb-yo
exchange[2] vb cambiare *kamb-*
yahray
exchange rate il cambio
kamb-yo
excited eccitato *ayt-chee-tahto*
exciting emozionante *aymots-*
yo-nantay
excursion l'escursione (f)
ayskoors-yohnay
excuse scusare *skoo-zahray;*
excuse me! (sorry) mi scusi!

mee skoozee; (when passing)
permesso! *payrmays-so*
exercise l'esercizio (m) *ayzayr-*
cheets-yo
exhaust pipe il tubo di
scappamento *toobo dee skap-*
pa-maynto
exhibition la mostra *mostra*
exit l'uscita (f) *o-sheeta*
expect aspettare *aspayt-tahray*
expensive costoso *kohs-tohzo*
expert l'esperto (m) *ay-spayrto*
expire (ticket, passport) scadere
ska-dayray
explain spiegare *speeay-gahray*
explosion l'esplosione (f)
aysploz-yohnay
exposure meter l'esposimetro
(m) *ayspo-zee-maytro*
express[1] n (train) l'espresso (m)
aysprays-so
express[2] adj (parcel etc)
espresso *aysprays-so*
extension (electrical) la
prolunga *pro-loonga;* **extension**
37 interno 37 *een-tayrno tray*
set-tay
extra (spare) in più *een pee-oo;*
(more) supplementare *soop-*
playmayn-tahray
eye l'occhio (m) *ok-yo*
eyebrow il sopracciglio *soprat-*
cheel-yo
eyelash il ciglio *cheel-yo*
eye liner la matita per occhi
ma-teeta payr ok-kee
eye shadow l'ombretto
ombrayt-to

F

fabric la stoffa *stof-fa*
face la faccia *fat-cha*
face cloth la spugnetta per il viso *spoon-yayt-ta payr eel veezo*
face cream la crema per il viso *krema payr eel veezo*
face powder la cipria *cheepreea*
facilities i servizi *sayr-veetsee*
fact il fatto *fat-to*
factory la fabbrica *fab-breeka*
faeces gli escrementi *ayskraymayntee*
failure il fallimento *fal-lee-maynto*
faint svenire *zvay-neeray*
fair¹ *adj* (hair) biondo *beeohndo*; (weather) bello *bel-lo*
fair² *n* (fun fair) il luna-park *loona-park*
faithfully: Yours faithfully distinti saluti *dee-steentee salootee*
fake l'imitazione (*f*) *eemee-tatsyohnay*
fall cadere *ka-dayray*
false teeth la dentiera *dayntyera*
family la famiglia *fameel-ya*
famous famoso *fa-mohzo*
fan (electric) il ventilatore *vayntee-la-tohray*; (supporter) il tifoso *tee-fohzo*
fan belt la cinghia del ventilatore *cheeng-ya dayl vayntee-la-tohray*

fancy dress il costume *kostoomay*
far lontano *lon-tahno*; **is it far?** è lontano? *e lon-tahno*
fare la tariffa *tareef-fa*
farm la fattoria *fat-toree-a*
farmer l'agricoltore (*m*) *agree-kol-tohray*
farmhouse la cascina *ka-sheena*
farther più lontano *pee-oo lontahno*
fast veloce *vay-lohchay*
fasten attaccare *at-tak-kahray*
fat grasso *gras-so*
father il padre *pahdray*
father-in-law il suocero *swochayro*
fatty (greasy) grasso *gras-so*
fault (defect) il difetto *deefet-to*; **it's not my fault** non è colpa mia *nohn e kohlpa mee-a*
favourite preferito *prayfay-reeto*
fawn fulvo *foolvo*
feather la piuma *pee-ooma*
February febbraio (*m*) *faybbra-yo*
feed dare da mangiare *dahray da man-jahray*
feel sentirsi *sayn-teersee*; **I don't feel well** non mi sento bene *nohn mee saynto benay*; **to feel sick** sentirsi male *sayn-teersee mahlay*
felt-tip pen il pennarello *paynnarel-lo*
female femmina *faym-meena*
fence il recinto *ray-cheento*
fern la felce *faylchay*

ferry il traghetto *tra-gayt-to*

festival la festa *festa*

fetch (bring) portare *por-tahray*; (go and get) andare a prendere *an-dahray a pren-dayray*

fever la febbre *feb-bray*

few pochi/e *pokee/ay*; **a few** alcuni/e *al-koonee/ay*

fiancé(e) il/la fidanzato/a *feedant-sahto/a*

fibreglass la lana di vetro *lahna dee vaytro*

field il campo *kampo*

fifteen quindici *kween-deechee*

fifth quinto *kweento*

fifty cinquanta *cheen-kwanta*

fight¹ vb (physically) combattere *kombat-tayray*; (verbally) litigare *leetee-gahray*

fight² n (physical) il combattimento *kombat-tee-maynto*; (verbal) il litigio *leeteed-jo*

fill riempire *ree-aym-peeray*; **to fill in** (form) riempire *ree-aym-peeray*; **to fill up** (container) riempire *ree-aym-peeray*; **fill it up!** faccia il pieno! *fat-cha eel pee-ayno*

fillet il filetto *feelayt-to*

fillet steak la bisteca di filetto *beestek-ka dee feelayt-to*

filling (in tooth) l'otturazione (f) *ot-toorats-yohnay*

film (in cinema) il film *feelm*; (for camera) la pellicola *payl-lee-kola*

film show la rappresentazione cinematografica *rap-prayzayn-*

tats-yohnay cheenay-mato-gra-feeka

filter il filtro *feeltro*

filter-tipped con filtro *kohn feeltro*

fine¹ adj (delicate) delicato *daylee-kahto*; (weather) bello *bel-lo*

fine² n la multa *moolta*

finger il dito *deeto*

finish finire *fee-neeray*

fire il fuoco *fwoko*; **fire!** al fuoco! *al fwoko*

fire brigade i vigili del fuoco *vee-jeelee dayl fwoko*

fire extinguisher l'estintore (m) *aysteen-tohray*

fireworks i fuochi d'artificio *fwokee dahrtee-feecho*

first primo *preemo*

first aid il pronto soccorso *pronto sok-korso*

first class la prima classe *preema klas-say*

first floor il primo piano *preemo pee-ahno*

first name il nome di battesimo *nohmay dee bat-tay-zeemo*

fish¹ n il pesce *payshay*

fish² vb pescare *pay-skahray*

fishing la pesca *payska*

fishing rod la canna da pesca *kan-na da payska*

fit¹ adj (strong and healthy) in forma *een forma*

fit² vb (clothes) andare bene *an-dahray be-nay*; (go in) entrare *ayn-trahray*; **this shirt doesn't**

fit me questa camicia non mi va bene *kwaysta ka-meecha non mee va benay*

fit³ n (medical) l'attacco (m) *at-tak-ko*

five cinque *cheenkway*

fix riparare *reepa-rahray*

fizzy frizzante *freedz-zantay*

flag la bandiera (f) *band-yera*

flannel (for face) la spugnetta per il viso *spoon-yayt-ta payr eel veezo*

flash il flash *flash*

flash bulb la lampadina per il flash *lampa-deena payr eel flash*

flash cubes i flash *flash*

flask il thermos *termos*

flat¹ n (apartment) l'appartamento (m) *ap-pahrta-maynto*

flat² adj piatto *pee-at-to*

flavour il sapore *sa-pohray*

flaw il difetto *deefet-to*

flea la pulce *poolchay*

flight il volo *vohloh*

flight bag la borsa da viaggio *borsa da vee-ad-jo*

flippers le pinne *peen-nay*

float galleggiare *gal-layd-jahray*

flood l'inondazione (f) *eenon-dats-yohnay*

floodlight il riflettore *reeflayt-tohray*

floodlit illuminato a giorno *eel-loomee-nahto a jorno*

floor (of building) il piano *pee-ahno*; (of room) il pavimento *pavee-maynto*

flour la farina *fa-reena*

flow scorrere *skohr-rayray*

flowers i fiori *feeo-ree*

flu l'influenza (f) *eenfloo-entsa*

fluent: he is fluent in Italian parla l'italiano correntemente *parla leetal-yahno kor-rayntay-mayntay*

flush: to flush the toilet tirare l'acqua *tee-rahray lakwa*

fly¹ vb volare *vo-lahray*

fly² n la mosca *moska*

fly sheet il soprattetto *soprat-taytto*

fog la nebbia *nayb-ya*

foggy nebbioso *nayb-yohzo*

foil la carta stagnola *karta stan-yola*

fold piegare *pee-e-gahray*

follow seguire *say-gweeray*

food il cibo *cheebo*

food poisoning l'intossicazione (f) alimentare *eentos-seekats-yohnay alee-mayn-tahray*

foot il piede *pee-e-day*; (measure) = 30.48 cm

football il calcio *kalcho*

for (in exchange for) per *payr*; for you per lei *payr le-ee*

forbidden vietato *vee-ay-tahto*

foreign straniero *stran-yero*

foreigner lo straniero/la straniera *stran-yero/a*

forest la foresta *fo-resta*

forget dimenticare *dee-mayntee-kahray*

forgive perdonare *payrdo-nahray*

fork la forchetta *forkayt-ta*; (in

road) la biforcazione *beefor-kats-yohnay*

form (shape) la forma *forma*;
(document) il modulo *mo-doolo*

fortnight quindici giorni *kween-deechee jornee*

forty quaranta *kwa-ranta*

foundation cream il fondo tinta *fondo teenta*

fountain la fontana *fon-tahna*

four quattro *kwat-tro*

fourteen quattordici *kwat-tor-deechee*

fourth quarto *kwarto*

France la Francia *francha*

free (not occupied) libero *lee-bayro*; (costing nothing) gratis *gratees*

freezer il congelatore *konjay-la-tohray*

French francese *fran-chayzay*

French beans i fagiolini *fajo-leenee*

frequent frequente *fray-kwentay*

fresh fresco *fresko*

Friday venerdi (m) *vaynayr-dee*

fridge il frigorifero *freego-ree-fayro*

fried fritto *freet-to*

friend l'amico/a (m/f) *a-meeko/a*

frill (dress) il fronzolo *frohnd-zolo*

fringe la frangia *franja*

frog la rana *rahna*

from da *da*

front davanti *da-vantee*

front door la porta d'ingresso

porta deengres-so

frost la brina *breena*

frostbite il congelamento *konjay-la-maynto*

frozen (food) surgelato *soorjay-lahto*

fruit la frutta *froot-ta*

fruit juice il succo di frutta *sook-ko dee froot-ta*

fruit salad la macedonia *machay-don-ya*

frying-pan la padella *padel-la*

fuel il combustibile *komboo-stee-beelay*

fuel gauge l'indicatore (m) della benzina *eendee-ka-tohray dayl-la bend-zeena*

fuel pump la pompa del carburante *pompa dayl karboo-rantay*

full pieno *pee-e-no*

full board la pensione completa *paynsee-ohnay komple-ta*

fumes i vapori *va-pohree*

fun il divertimento *deevayr-tee-maynto*

funeral il funerale *foonay-rahlay*

funny (amusing) divertente *deevayr-tentay*; (strange) strano *strahno*

fur la pelliccia *payl-leet-cha*

furniture i mobili *mo-beelee*

fuse il fusibile *foozee-beelay*

fuss: to make a fuss fare storie *fahray stor-yay*

fussy pignolo *peen-yolo*

future il futuro *foo-tooro*

G

gale la bufera *boo-fera*

gallery la galleria *gal-layree-a;* (in theatre) il loggione *lod-johnay*

gallon = 4.54 litres

gallstone il calcolo biliare *kal-kolo beel-yahray*

gambling il gioco d'azzardo *joko dadz-zardo*

game il gioco *joko*

garage l'autorimessa (f) *a-ooto-reemays-sa*

garden il giardino *jar-deeno*

garlic l'aglio (m) *al-yo*

gas il gas *gas*

gas cylinder la bombola di gas *bohm-bola dee gas*

gasket la guarnizione *gwarneets-yohnay*

gas refill la bomboletta di gas *bombo-layt-ta dee gas*

gate il cancello *kanchel-lo*

gear la marcia *marcha*

gearbox la scatola del cambio *skah-tola dayl kamb-yo*

gear lever la leva del cambio *leva dayl kamb-yo*

gears le marce *mahrchay*

general generale *jaynay-rahlay*

generous generoso *jaynay-rohzo*

Genoa Genova *je-nova*

gentle dolce *dohlchay*

gentleman il signore *seen-yohray*

gents' la toilette (per uomini) *twalet (payr wo-meenee)*

genuine (leather, silver) vero *vayro;* (antique, picture) autentico *a-ooten-teeko*

germ il microbo *meek-robo*

German tedesco *tay-daysko*

German measles la rosolia *rozo-leea*

Germany la Germania *jayrmahn-ya*

get (obtain) ottenere *ot-tay-nayray;* (receive) ricevere *reechay-vayray;* (fetch) prendere *pren-dayray;* **to get in** (arrive) arrivare *ar-ree-vahray;* **to get into** (house, clothes) entrare in *ayn-trahray een;* (vehicle) salire in *sa-leeray een;* **to get off** (bus etc) scendere da *shayn-dayray da;* **to get on to** (mount) montare *mon-tahray;* **to get through** (pass through) passare per *pas-sahray payr*

gherkin il cetriolino *chaytree-o-leeno*

ghost il fantasma *fan-tazma*

gift il regalo *ray-gahlo*

gin il gin *gin*

gin and tonic il gin tonic *gin tonic*

ginger lo zenzero *dzaynd-zayro*

girl la ragazza *ragats-sa*

girlfriend la ragazza *ragats-sa*

give dare *dahray;* **to give back** restituire *raystee-too-eeray*

glad contento *kon-tento*

glass (for drinking) il bicchiere *beek-yeray;* (substance) il vetro *vaytro*

glasses gli occhiali *ok-yahlee*

gloves i guanti *gwantee*

glow[1] n il bagliore *bal-yohray*

glow[2] vb ardere *ar-dayray*

glucose il glucosio *glookoz-yo*

glue la colla *kol-la*

go andare *an-dahray*; **I go** vado *vahdo*; **you go** Lei va *le-ee va*; **he goes** va *va*; **to go back** ritornare *reetor-nahray*; **to go down** (sun) calare *ka-lahray*; (downstairs etc) scendere *shayn-dayray*; **to go in** entrare *ayn-trahray*; **to go out** (leave) uscire *oo-sheeray*; (fire, light) spegnersi *spen-yayrsee*

goal (football) il goal *goal*

goat la capra *kapra*

God Dio *dee-o*

goggles gli occhiali *ok-yahlee*; (for skiing) gli occhiali da sci *ok-yahlee da shee*

gold[1] adj d'oro *doroh*

gold[2] n l'oro (m) *oro*

golf il golf *golf*

golf course il campo di golf *kampo dee golf*

gone: she's gone to the beach è andata alla spiaggia *e an-dahta al-la spee-ad-ja*

good buono *bwono*; (pleasant) bello *bel-lo*

good afternoon buona sera! *bwona sayra*

goodbye arrivederci *ar-reevay-dayrchee*

good evening buona sera! *bwona sayra*

Good Friday il Venerdì Santo *vaynayr-dee santo*

good morning buon giorno *bwon jorno*

good night buona notte *bwona not-tay*

goose l'oca (f) *oka*

gooseberry l'uva spina (f) *oova speena*

grammar la grammatica *gram-ma-teeka*

gramme il grammo *gram-mo*; **100 grammes of** un etto di *oon et-to dee*

grandchildren i nipoti *nee-pohtee*

granddaughter la nipote *nee-pohiay*

grandfather il nonno *non-no*

grandmother la nonna *non-na*

grandson il nipote *nee-pohtay*

grapefruit il pompelmo *pom-pelmo*

grapefruit juice il succo di pompelmo *sook-ko dee pom-pelmo*

grapes l'uva (f) *oova*

grass l'erba (f) *ayrba*

grateful grato *grahto*

grave (tomb) la tomba *tomba*

gravy il sugo *soogo*

greasy grasso *gras-so*

great grande *granday*

greedy goloso *go-lohzo*

green verde *vayrday*

green card la carta verde *karta vayrday*

greeting il saluto *sa-looto*

grey grigio *greejo*

grilled alla griglia *al-la greel-ya*

grocer's il negozio di alimentari *naygots-yo dee alee-mayn-tahree*

ground la terra *ter-ra*

ground floor il pianterreno *peean-ter-rayno*

groundsheet il telone impermeabile *tay-lohnay eempayr-may-ah-beelay*

group il gruppo *groop-po*; (*musical*) il complesso *komples-so*

group passport il passaporto collettivo *pas-sa-porto kol-layt-teevo*

grow crescere *kray-shayray*

guarantee¹ *vb* garantire *garanteeray*

guarantee² *n* la garanzia (*f*) *garant-see-a*

guard (*on train*) il capotreno *kapo-trayno*

guess indovinare *eendo-veenahray*

guest (*house guest*) l'ospite (*m/f*) *os-peetay*; (*in hotel*) il/la cliente *klee-entay*

guesthouse la pensione familiare *paynsee-ohnay fameel-yahray*

guide¹ *n* la guida *gweeda*

guide² *vb* fare da guida *fahray da gweeda*

guide book la guida *gweeda*

guided tour la visita guidata *vee-zeeta gwee-dahta*

guilty colpevole *kolpay-volay*

gums le gengive *jayn-jeevay*

gun la pistola *peesto-la*

guy rope il tirante *tee-rantay*

gymnasium la palestra *palestra*

gym shoes le scarpe da ginnastica *skarpay da jeen-nasteeka*

H

had: he had two cameras aveva due macchine fotografiche *avayva doo-ay mak-keenay foto-gra-feekay*

haddock l'eglefino (*m*) *ayglay-feeno*

haemorrhoids le emorroidi *aymor-ro-eedee*

hail la grandine *gran-deenay*

hair i capelli *kapayl-lee*

hairbrush la spazzola per capelli *spats-sola payr kapayl-lee*

haircut il taglio di capelli *tal-yo dee kapayl-lee*

hairdresser (*male*) il parrucchiere *parrook-yeray*; (*female*) la parrucchiera *parrook-yera*

hairdryer il föhn *fon*

hairgrip il fermacapelli *fayrma-kapayl-lee*

hair spray la lacca per capelli *lak-ka payr kapayl-lee*

half la metà *mayta*; **a half bottle of . . .** una mezza bottiglia di . . . *oona medz-ya bot-teel-ya dee . . .*; **half past 2** le due e mezza *lay doo-ay ay medz-za*

half-board la mezza pensione

medz-za paynsee-ohnay

half fare metà prezzo *mayta prets-so*

halibut l'ippoglosso (*m*) *eep-glos-so*

hall (*in house*) l'ingresso (*m*) *eengres-so*; (*for concerts etc*) la sala dei concerti *sahla day-ee kon-chayrtee*

halyard la drizza *dreets-sa*

ham il prosciutto *proshoot-to*

hammer il martello *martel-lo*

hand la mano *mahno*

handbag la borsa *borsa*

handbrake il freno a mano *frayno a mahno*

hand cream la crema per le mani *krema payr lay mahnee*

handicapped handicappato *andee-kap-pahto*

handkerchief il fazzoletto *fats-solayt-to*

handle (*of door, drawer*) la maniglia *maneel-ya*; (*of brush, basket, knife*) il manico *mahneeko*

hand luggage il bagaglio a mano *bagal-yo a mahno*

hand-made fatto a mano *fat-to a mahno*

hang appendere *ap-pen-dayray*; **to hang up** (*phone*) riattaccare *reeat-tak-kahray*

hangover i postumi d'una sbornia *po-stoomee doona zborn-ya*

happen succedere *soot-che-dayray*; **what happened?** cos'è

successo? *ko-ze soot-ches-so*

happy felice *fay-leechay*

harbour il porto *porto*

hard duro *dooro*

hard shoulder la corsia di emergenza *korsee-a dee aymayr-jentsa*

hare la lepre *lepray*

harmonica l'armonica (*f*) a bocca *armo-neeka a bok-ka*

harp l'arpa (*f*) *arpa*

harvest (*of cereal*) il raccolto *rak-kolto*; (*of grapes*) la vendemmia *vayndaym-ya*

hat il cappello *kap-pel-lo*

hate odiare *od-yahray*

have avere *a-vayray*; **I have** ho *o*; **you have** Lei ha *le-ee a*; **he/she has** ha *a*

hay il fieno *fee-eno*

hay fever la febbre da fieno *feb-bray da fee-eno*

hazard il pericolo *payree-kolo*

hazard lights le luci d'emergenza *loochee daymayr-jentsa*

hazelnut la nocciola *not-chola*

hazy (*weather*) caliginoso *kalee-jee-nohzo*

he lui *loo-ee*

head la testa *testa*

headache il mal di testa *mal dee testa*

heading il titolo *tee-tolo*

headlights i fari *fahree*

head waiter il capocameriere *kapo-kamayr-yeray*

heal guarire *gwa-reeray*

healthy sano *sahno*

hear sentire *sayn-teeray*

hearing aid l'apparecchio (m) acustico *ap-parayk-yo akoo-steeko*

heart il cuore *kworay*

heart attack l'infarto (m) *een-farto*

heat il calore *ka-lohray*

heater il termosifone *tayrmo-see-fohnay*

heather l'erica (f) *e-reeka*

heating il riscaldamento *reeskal-da-maynto*

heatstroke il colpo di calore *kolpo dee ka-lohray*

heavy pesante *pay-zantay*

hedge la siepe *see-epay*

heel (of person) il tallone *tal-lohnay*; (of shoe) il tacco *tak-ko*

height l'altezza (f) al*tets-sa*

helicopter l'elicottero *aylee-kot-tayro*

hello ciao *chao*; (on telephone) pronto *prohnto*

help[1] n l'aiuto (m) *a-yooto*; **help!** aiuto! *a-yooto*

help[2] vb aiutare *a-yoo-tahray*; **can you help me?** può aiutarmi? *pwo a-yoo-tahrmee*

hem l'orlo (m) *orlo*

hen la gallina *gal-leena*

her[1] pers pron la *la*; **I give it to her** gliel'ho dato *lyay-lo dahto*; **before her** prima di lei *preema dee le-ee*

her[2] poss adj il suo *eel soo-o*; **this is her room** questa è la sua

stanza *kwaysta e la soo-a stantsa*

herb l'erba (f) aromatica *ayrba aro-mahtee-ka*

here qui *kwee*

heroin l'eroina (f) *ayro-eena*

herring l'aringa (f) *a-reenga*

hers il suo *eel soo-o*; **this bag is hers** questa borsa è la sua *kwaysta borsa e la soo-a*

hide nascondere *naskohn-dayray*

high (price, number, temperature) alto *alto*; (speed) forte *fortay*

high blood pressure la pressione alta *pray-see-ohnay alta*

high chair il seggiolone *sayd-jo-lohnay*

higher più alto *pee-oo alto*

high season l'alta stagione (f) *alta sta-johnay*

high tide l'alta marea (f) *alta ma-ray-a*

hijack dirottare *deerot-tahray*

hill la collina *kol-leena*

hill-walking l'escursionismo (m) *ayskoors-yo-neezmo*

him lo *loh*; **I shall send it to him** glielo spedirò *lyay-lo spaydee-ro*; **with him** con lui *kohn loo-ee*

hip l'anca (f) *anka*

hire noleggiare *nolayd-jahray*; **for hire** a noleggio *a nolayd-jo*

his[1] poss adj il suo *eel soo-o*; **his friend** il suo amico *eel soo-o a-meeko*; **these are his tickets** questi sono i suoi biglietti *kwaystee sohno ee swo-ee* beelyayt-tee

his² poss pron il suo *eel soo-o*; is this one his? è questo il suo? *e kwaysto eel soo-o*

history la storia *stor-ya*

hit colpire *kol-peeray*

hitchhike fare l'autostop *fahray la-ooto-stop*

hitchhiker l'autostoppista (m/f) *a-ooto-stop-peesta*

hoarse rauco *ra-ooko*

hobby l'hobby (m) *hobby*

hold tenere *tay-nayray*; (contain) contenere *kontay-nayray*

hold-up (robbery) la rapina *ra-peena*; (traffic jam) l'ingorgo (m) *een-gorgo*

hole il buco *booko*

holiday la festa *festa*; **on holiday** in vacanza *een va-kantsa*

holiday-maker il/la villeggiante *veel-layd-jantay*

hollow vuoto *vwoto*

holly l'agrifoglio (m) *agree-fol-yo*

holy santo *santo*

home la casa *kasa*

homesick: to be homesick avere nostalgia di casa *a-vayray nostal-jeea dee kasa*

honest onesto *o-nesto*

honey il miele *mee-elay*

honeymoon la luna di miele *loona dee mee-elay*

hood il cappuccio *kap-poot-cho*

hook (for fishing) l'amo (m) *ahmo*; (for coats) il gancio *gancho*

hop saltellare *saltayl-lahray*

hope sperare *spay-rahray*; **I hope so** spero di sì *spayro dee see*; **I hope not** spero di no *spayro dee no*

horn (of car) il clacson *klakson*; (musical) il corno *korno*

horrible orribile *or-ree-beelay*

hors d'oeuvre l'antipasto (m) *antee-pasto*

horse il cavallo *kaval-lo*

hose il manicotto *manee-kot-to*

hospital l'ospedale (m) *ospay-dahlay*

host l'ospite (m) *os-peetay*

hostess l'ospite (f) *os-peetay*; (on plane) la hostess *hostess*

hot caldo *kaldo*; **I'm hot** ho caldo *o kaldo*; **it's hot** (weather) fa caldo *fa kaldo*

hotel l'albergo (m) *al-bayrgo*

hotplate la piastra *pee-astra*

hot water l'acqua (f) calda *akwa kalda*

hot-water bottle la borsa dell'acqua calda *borsa dayl-lakwa kalda*

hour l'ora (f) *ohra*

house la casa *kasa*

housewife la casalinga *kasa-leenga*

house wine il vino della casa *veeno dayl-la kasa*

hovercraft l'hovercraft (m) *hovercraft*

how (in what way) come *kohmay*; **how much?** quanto/a? *kwanto/a*; **how many?** quanti/e? *kwantee/e* *kwantee/ay;* **how are you?** come sta? *kohmay sta;* **how long are you staying?** quanto tempo si ferma? *kwanto tempo see fayrma*

hull lo scafo *skahfo*

human umano *oo-mahno*

hundred cento *chento*

hungry: I am hungry ho fame *o fahmay*

hurry: I'm in a hurry ho fretta *o frayt-ta*

hurt fare male *fahray mahlay;* **my back hurts** mi fa male la schiena *mee fa mahlay la skee-ena*

husband il marito *ma-reeto*

hut la capanna *kapan-na*

hydroelectric idroelettrico *eedro-aylet-treeko*

hydrofoil l'aliscafo (m) *alee-skahfo*

I

I io *eeoh*

ice il ghiaccio *geeat-cho*

ice cream il gelato *jay-lahto*

iced (drink) ghiacciato *geeat-chahto;* (coffee, tea) freddo *frayd-do*

ice lolly il ghiacciolo *geeat-cholo*

ice rink la pista di pattinaggio su ghiaccio *peesta dee pat-teenad-jo soo geeat-cho*

icing la glassa *glas-sa*

idea l'idea (f) *eeday-a*

if se *say*

ignition l'accensione (f) *at-*

chayns-yohnay

ignition key la chiave dell'accensione *kee-ahvay dayl-lat-chayns-yohnay*

ill malato *ma-lahto*

illness la malattia *malat-tee-a*

imagine immaginare *eem-majee-nahray*

immediately subito *soo-beeto*

impatient impaziente *eempats-yentay*

important importante *eempor-tantay*

impossible impossibile *eempos-see-beelay*

in in *een*

inch = 2.5 cm

included compreso *kom-prayzo*

income il reddito *red-deeto*

independent indipendente *eendee-payn-dentay*

indicator (of car) l'indicatore (m) *eendee-ka-tohray*

indigestion la dispepsia *deespep-see-a*

indoors dentro *dayntro;* (at home) a casa *a kasa*

industry l'industria (f) *eendoo-streea*

infection l'infezione (f) *eenfayts-yohnay*

infectious contagioso *konta-johzo*

inflamed infiammato *eenf-yam-mahto*

inflatable (boat) gonfiabile *gonf-yah-beelay*

informal informale *eenfor-*

mahlay

information le informazioni *eenfor-mats-yohnee*

information office l'ufficio (m) informazioni *oof-feecho eenfor-mats-yohnee*

initials le iniziali *eeneets-yahlee*; (abbreviation) la sigla *seegla*

injection l'iniezione (f) *een-yayts-yohnay*

injured ferito *fay-reeto*

ink l'inchiostro (m) *eenk-yostro*

ink cartridge la cartuccia *kartoot-cha*

innocent innocente *een-no-chentay*

insect l'insetto (m) *eenset-to*

insect bite la puntura d'insetto *poon-toora deenset-to*

insect repellent l'insettifugo (m) *eensayt-tee-foogo*

inside dentro *dayntro*; **inside the car** dentro la macchina *dayntro la mak-keena*; **it's inside** è dentro *e dayntro*

insist insistere *eensee-stayray*

instant coffee il caffè solubile *kaf-fe soloo-beelay*

instead invece *een-vaychay*; **instead of** invece di *een-vaychay dee*

instructor l'istruttore (m) *eestroot-tohray*

insulin l'insulina (f) *eensoo-leena*

insult insultare *eensool-tahray*

insurance l'assicurazione (f) *as-seekoo-rats-yohnay*

insurance certificate il certificato di assicurazione *chaytee-fee-kahto dee as-seekoo-rats-yohnay*

insurance company la compagnia di assicurazione *kompan-yee-a dee as-seekoo-rats-yohnay*

insurance cover l'assicurazione (f) *as-seekoo-rats-yohnay*

insure assicurare *as-seekoo-rahray*

intelligent intelligente *eentayl-lee-jentay*

interested interessato *eentay-ray-sahto*

interesting interessante *eentay-ray-santay*

international internazionale *eentayr-nats-yo-nahlay*

interpreter l'interprete (m/f) *eentayr-praytay*

interval l'intervallo (m) *eentayr-val-lo*

interview l'intervista (f) *eentayr-veesta*

into in *een*

introduce presentare *prayzayn-tahray*

invalid l'infermo (m) *een-fayrmo*

invitation l'invito (m) *een-veeto*

invite invitare *eenvee-tahray*

invoice la fattura *fat-toora*

Ireland l'Irlanda (f) *eer-landa*

Irish irlandese *eerlan-dayzay*

iron[1] n (metal) il ferro *ferro*; (for clothes) il ferro (da stiro) *ferro (da steero)*

iron² vb stirare stee-rahray

ironmonger's il negozio di ferramenta naygots-yo dee ferra-maynta

is è e

island l'isola (f) ee-zola

it lo, la; loh, la; **I've sent it** l'ho spedito lo spay-deeto; **where's the book? — it's here** dov'è il libro? — è qui dohve eel leebro — e kwee; **give it to me** me lo dia may loh dee-a

Italian italiano eetal-yahno

Italy l'Italia (f) eetal-ya

itch il prurito proo-reeto

itemized bill il conto dettagliato kohnto dayt-tal-yahto

ivory l'avorio (m) avor-yo

J

jack (for car) il cricco kreek-ko

jacket la giacca jak-ka

jam (food) la marmellata mahrmayl-lahta; (traffic jam) l'ingorgo (m) een-gorgo

jammed bloccato blok-kahto

January gennaio (m) jayn-na-yo

jar (container) il vasetto vazayt-to

jaundice l'itterizia (f) eet-tay-reets-ya

jaw la mascella mashel-la

jazz il jazz jazz

jeans i jeans jeans

jelly (dessert) la gelatina jayla-teena

jellyfish la medusa may-dooza

jersey la maglia mal-ya

jet (plane) il jet jet

jeweller's la gioielleria jo-yayl-lay-reea

jewellery i gioielli jo-yel-lee

Jewish ebreo ay-bre-o

jib (of boat) il fiocco feeok-ko

job il lavoro la-vohro

jog: to go jogging fare footing fahray footing

join (things together) collegare kol-lay-gahray; (club etc) iscriversi eeskree-vayrsee

joint (on body) l'articolazione (f) artee-kolats-yohnay; (of meat) il pezzo di carne pets-so dee karnay; (technical) lo snodo znodo

joke lo scherzo skayrtso

journalist il/la giornalista (m/f) jorna-leesta

journey il viaggio veead-jo

judge il giudice joo-deechay

jug la brocca brok-ka

juice il succo sook-ko

July luglio (m) lool-yo

jumbo jet il jumbo joombo

jump saltare sal-tahray

jump leads i cavi per far partire la macchina kahvee payr fahr par-teeray la mak-keena

June giugno (m) joon-yo

junction (road) l'incrocio (m) een-krohcho

just: just two solamente due sola-mayntay doo-ay; **just there** proprio lì propree-o lee; **I've just arrived** sono appena arrivato sohnoh ap-payna ar-ree-vahto

K

keep (*retain*) tenere *tay-nayray;* (*continue*) continuare *kontee-noo-ahray*

key la chiave *kee-ahvay*

key ring il portachiavi *porta-kee-ahvee*

khaki cachi *kakee*

kick[1] *vb* dare un calcio a *dahray oon kalcho a*

kick[2] *n* il calcio *kalcho*

kidney il rene *renay*

kidneys (*as food*) i rognoni *ron-yohnee*

kill uccidere *oot-chee-dayray*

kilo il chilo *keelo;* **a kilo of** un chilo di *oon keelo dee*

kilometre il chilometro *keelo-maytro*

kind[1] *n* (*sort, type*) il tipo *teepo*

kind[2] *adj* (*person*) gentile *jayn-teelay*

king il re *re*

kiosk il chiosco *kee-osko*

kiss baciare *ba-chahray*

kitchen la cucina *koo-cheena*

knee il ginocchio *jeenok-yo*

knife il coltello *koltel-lo*

knit fare a maglia *fahray a mal-ya*

knitting needle il ferro da calza *fer-ro da kaltsa*

knock (*strike*) colpire *kol-peeray;* (*bump into*) sbattere contro **sbat**-*tayray kohntro;* (*on door*) bussare *boos-sahray*

knot il nodo *nodo*

know (*facts*) sapere *sa-payray;* (*be acquainted with*) conoscere *kono-shayray*

L

label l'etichetta (*f*) *aytee-kayt-ta*

lace (*fabric*) il pizzo *peets-so;* (*of shoe*) il laccio *lat-cho*

ladder la scala *skahla*

ladies' la toilette (*per signore*) *la twalet (payr seen-yohray)*

ladle il mestolo *may-stolo*

lady la signora *seen-yohra*

lager la birra bionda *beer-ra bee-onda*

lake il lago *lahgo*

lamb l'agnello (*m*) *an-yel-lo*

lamp la lampada *lam-pada*

lamp-post il lampione *lamp-yohnay*

lampshade il paralume *para-loomay*

land[1] *vb* (*plane*) atterrare *at-ter-rahray*

land[2] *n* la terra *ter-ra;* (*country*) il paese *pa-ayzay*

landlady (*of pub*) la proprietaria *propree-aytahr-ya;* (*of boarding house*) la padrona *pa-drohna*

landlord (*of pub*) il proprietario *propree-aytahr-yo;* (*of boarding house*) il padrone *pa-drohnay*

lane la stradina *stra-deena;* (*of motorway*) la corsia *korsee-a*

language il linguaggio *leengwad-jo*

large grande *granday*

larger più grande *pee-oo granday*

last[1] vb durare *doo-rahray*

last[2] adj scorso *skorso*; (final) ultimo *ool-teemo*; **last week** la settimana scorsa *la sayt-tee-mahna skorsa*

late tardi *tardee*; **the train is late** il treno è in ritardo *eel trayno e een ree-tardo*; **sorry we are late** scusi il ritardo *skoozee eel ree-tardo*

later più tardi *pee-oo tardee*

laugh ridere *ree-dayray*

launderette la lavanderia automatica *lavan-dayree-a a-ooto-ma-teeka*

laundry (clothes) la biancheria *bee-ankay-ree-a*

laundry room la lavanderia *lavan-dayree-a*

laundry service il servizio di biancheria *sayrveets-yo dee bee-ankay-ree-a*

lavatory il gabinetto *gabee-nayt-to*

law la legge *layd-jay*

lawyer l'avvocato (m) *av-vo-kahto*

laxative il lassativo *las-sa-teevo*

layby la piazzola di sosta *pee-ats-sola dee sosta*

layered (hair) scalati *ska-lahtee*

lazy pigro *peegro*

lead[1] vb (conduct) condurre *kondoor-ray*; (be leader) dirigere *deeree-jayray*

lead[2] n (metal) il piombo *pee-*

ombo

lead[3] n (electric) il filo *feelo*; (for dog) il guinzaglio *gweentsal-yo*

leader il capo *kapo*; (guide) la guida *gweeda*

leaf la foglia *fol-ya*

leak (of gas, liquid) la perdita *payr-deeta*; (in roof) il buco *booko*

learn imparare *eempa-rahray*

least (slightest) il minimo *eel mee-neemo*; (smallest) il più piccolo *eel pee-oo peek-kolo*; **at least** almeno *al-mayno*

leather il cuoio *kwo-yo*

leave (leave behind) lasciare *la-shahray*; **to leave the room** uscire dalla stanza *oo-sheeray dal-la stantsa*; **when does the train leave?** quando parte il treno? *kwando partay eel treno*

leeks i porri *por-ree*

left: (on/to the) left a sinistra *a see-neestra*

left-handed mancino *man-cheeno*

left luggage il deposito bagagli *daypo-zeeto bagal-yee*

leg la gamba *gamba*

legal legale *lay-gahlay*

lemon il limone *lee-mohnay*

lemonade la limonata *leemo-nahta*

lemon juice il succo di limone *sook-ko dee lee-mohnay*

lemon tea il tè al limone *te al lee-mohnay*

lend prestare *pray-stahray*

length (size) la lunghezza *loongayts-sa*; (duration) la durata *doo-rahta*

lens l'obiettivo (m) *ob-yayt-teevo*

lens cover il copri-obiettivo *kopree-ob-yayt-teevo*

lentils le lenticchie *laynteek-yay*

less meno *mayno*

lesson la lezione *layts-yohnay*

let (allow) permettere *payrmayt-tayray*; (hire out) affittare *af-feet-tahray*; '**to let**' 'affittasi' *af-feet-tasee*

letter la lettera *let-tayra*

letterbox la cassetta delle lettere *kas-sayt-ta dayl-lay let-tayray*

lettuce la lattuga *lat-tooga*

leukemia la leucemia *lay-oochay-meea*

level (flat) piano *pee-ahno*; (steady) costante *ko-stantay*; (equal) alla pari *al-la pahree*

level-crossing il passaggio a livello *pas-sad-jo a leevel-lo*

library la biblioteca *beeblee-o-teka*

licence il permesso *payrmes-so*

lick leccare *layk-kahray*

lid il coperchio *kopayrk-yo*

lie down sdraiarsi *zdra-yahrsee*

life la vita *veeta*

lifebelt il salvagente *salva-jentay*

lifeboat la scialuppa di salvataggio *shaloop-pa dee salva-tad-jo*

lifeguard il bagnino *ban-yeeno*

life jacket il giubbotto salvagente *joob-bot-to salva-jentay*

lift l'ascensore (m) *ashayn-sohray*

lift pass (on ski slopes) la tessera per gli impianti di risalita *tes-sayra payr lyee eempee-ahntee dee reesa-leeta*

light[1] adj (bright) chiaro *kee-aro*; (not heavy) leggero *layd-jero*

light[2] n la luce *loochay*; **have you got a light?** ha da accendere? *a da at-chen-dayray*

light bulb la lampadina *lampa-deena*

lighter l'accendino (m) *at-chayn-deeno*

light meter l'esposimetro (m) *ayspo-zee-maytro*

lightning (flash) il lampo *lampo*; (bolt) il fulmine *fool-meenay*

like[1] prep come *kohmay*; **like you** come lei *kohmay le-ee*; **like this** così *kozee*

like[2] vb piacere *pee-a-chayray*; **I like coffee** mi piace il caffè *mee pee-achay eel kaf-fe*; **I would like to go** vorrei andare *vor-re-ee an-dahray*; **I would like a newspaper** vorrei un giornale *vor-re-ee oon jor-nahlay*

likely probabile *probah-beelay*

lily il giglio *jeel-yo*

lime (fruit) la limetta *leemayt-ta*

limejuice il succo di limetta *sook-ko dee leemayt-ta*

line (row, queue) la fila *feela*; (railway) la linea *leenay-a*

linen il lino *leeno*

lip il labbro *lab-bro;* **lips** le labbra *lab-bra*

lip salve il burro di cacao *boor-ro dee kaka-o*

lipstick il rossetto *ros-sayt-to*

liqueur il liquore *lee-kwohray*

liquid il liquido *lee-kweedo*

list l'elenco (m) *ay-lenko*

listen (to) ascoltare *askol-tahray*

litre il litro *leetro*

litter (rubbish) i rifiuti *reef-yootee*

little: a little milk un po' di latte *oon po dee lat-tay*

live vivere *vee-vayray;* **I live in Edinburgh** abito ad Edimburgo *ah-beeto ad aydeem-boorgo*

liver il fegato *fay-gato*

living room la sala *sahla*

lizard la lucertola *loochayr-tola*

loaf il pane *pahnay*

loan il prestito *pre-steeto*

lobster l'aragosta (f) *ara-gosta*

local (wine, speciality) locale *lo-kahlay*

local anaesthetic l'anestesia (f) locale *anay-stayzee-a lo-kahlay*

lock¹ vb (door) chiudere a chiave *keeoo-dayray a kee-ahvay*

lock² n (on door, box) la serratura *sayr-ra-toora;* (on steering wheel) il bloccasterzo *blok-ka-stayrtso*

locker l'armadietto (m) *ahrmad-yayt-to*

log il ceppo *chayp-po*

logbook (of car) il libretto di circolazione *leebrayt-to dee*

cheerko-lats-yohnay

lollipop il lecca lecca *layk-ka layk-ka;* (iced) il ghiacciolo *geeat-cholo*

London Londra *lohndra*

lonely solitario *solee-tar-yo*

long lungo *loongo;* **for a long time** molto tempo *mohlto tempo;* **how long is it?** quant'è lungo? *kwante lyongo*

look guardare *gwar-dahray;* (seem) sembrare *saym-brahray;* **to look after** badare *ba-dahray;* **to look at** guardare *gwar-dahray;* **to look for** cercare *chayr-kahray*

loose (not firm) allentato *al-layn-tahto;* (clothes) ampio *amp-yo*

loosen allentare *al-layn-tahray*

lorry il camion *kam-yon*

lorry driver il camionista *kamyo-neesta*

lose perdere *payr-dayray*

lost (object) perso *payrso;* **I have lost my wallet** ho perso il portafoglio *o payrso eel porta-fol-yo;* **I am lost** ho perso la strada *o payrso la strahda*

lost property office l'ufficio (m) oggetti smarriti *oof-feecho od-jet-tee zmar-reetee*

lot: I like it a lot mi piace molto *mee pee-achay mohlto;* **a lot of oil** molto olio *mohlto ol-yo;* **a lot of tourists** molti turisti *mohltee too-reestee*

lotion la lozione *lohts-yohnay*

lottery la lotteria *lot-tayree-a*

loud forte *fortay*

lounge (at airport) la sala d'attesa *sahla dat-tayza*; (in hotel) il salone *sa-lohnay*

love (person) amare *a-mahray*; I love swimming mi piace molto nuotare *mee pee-achay mohlto nwo-tahray*; he loves Italian food gli piace molto la cucina italiana *lyee pee-achay mohlto la koo-cheena eetal-yahna*

lovely bellissimo *bayl-lees-seemo*

low basso *bas-so*; (standard, quality) scadente *ska-dentay*

low tide la bassa marea *bas-sa ma-ray-a*

luck la fortuna *for-toona*

lucky fortunato *fortoo-nahto*

luggage i bagagli *bagal-yee*

luggage allowance il bagaglio permesso *bagal-yo payrmays-so*

luggage hold il bagagliaio *bagal-ya-yo*

luggage rack (on car, in train) il portabagagli *porta-bagal-yee*

luggage tag l'etichetta (f) *aytee-kayt-ta*

luggage trolley il carrello *kar-rel-lo*

lump (of earth) la zolla *dzol-la*; (swelling) il nodulo *no-dooloh*

lunch il pranzo *prantso*

lung il polmone *pol-mohnay*

luxury di lusso *dee loos-so*

M

macaroni i maccheroni *mak-kay-rohnee*

machine la macchina *mak-keena*

mackerel lo sgombro *sgombro*

mad matto *mat-to*

madam signora *seen-yohra*; Dear Madam Gentile Signora *jayn-teelay seen-yohra*

made-to-measure su misura *soo mee-zoora*

magazine la rivista *ree-veesta*

magnetic magnetico *man-yetee-ko*

maid (in hotel) la cameriera *kamayr-yera*

maiden name il nome da ragazza *nohmay da ragats-sa*

main principale *preenchee-pahlay*

main road la strada principale *strahda preenchee-pahlay*

mains (electric) la linea principale *leenay-a preenchee-pahlay*

main square la piazza maggiore *peeats-sa mad-johray*

maize il granturco *gran-toorko*

major road la strada principale *strahda preenchee-pahlay*

make (generally) fare *fahray*; (manufacture) fabbricare *fab-bree-kahray*; (meal) preparare *praypa-rahray*

make-up il trucco *trook-ko*

male maschio *mask-yo*

mallet la mazza *mats-sa*

man l'uomo (m) *womo*

manager il direttore *deerayt-*

tohray

managing director
l'amministratore (m) delegato
am-meenee-stra-tohray daylay-gahto

manicure la manicure *manee-kooray*

Mantua Mantova *man-tova*

many molti *mohltee*

map la carta *karta*

marathon la maratona *maratohna*

marble il marmo *marmo*

March marzo (m) *martso*

margarine la margarina *mahrga-reena*

marina la marina *ma-reena*

mark (stain) la macchia *mak-ya*

market il mercato *mayr-kahto*

marmalade la marmellata di arance *marmayl-lahta dee a-ranchay*

married sposato *spo-zahto*

marrow la zucca *tsook-ka*

marry sposarsi *spo-zarsee*

marsh la palude *pa-looday*

marzipan il marzapane *martsa-pahnay*

mascara il mascara *ma-skara*

mashed potatoes il purè di patate *poo-re dee pa-tatay*

mass (in church) la messa *mays-sa*

mast l'albero (m) *albay-ro*

match (sport) la partita *par-teeta*

matches i fiammiferi *fee-am-mee-fayree*

material (cloth) il tessuto *tays-*

sooto; (substance) il materiale *matayr-yahlay*

matter: it doesn't matter non importa *nohn eem-porta*; **what's the matter?** cosa c'è? *kosa che*

mauve color malva *kolor malva*

May maggio (m) *mad-jo*

mayonnaise la maionese *ma-yo-nayzay*

me mi *mee*; **give it to me** me lo dia *may loh dee-a*; **with me** con me *kohn may*

meal il pasto *pasto*

mean (signify) voler dire *volayr deeray*; **what does this mean?** cosa vuol dire questo? *koza vwol deeray kwaysto*

meaning il significato *seen-yeefee-kahto*

meanwhile nel frattempo *nayl frat-tempo*

measles il morbillo *morbeel-lo*

measure misurare *meezoo-rahray*

meat la carne *karnay*

mechanic il meccanico *mayk-kaneeko*

mechanism il meccanismo *mayk-ka-neezmo*

medicine la medicina *maydee-cheena*

medieval medievale *mayd-yay-vahlay*

medium medio *med-yo*

medium rare poco cotto *poko kot-to*

meet incontrare *eenkon-trahray*

meeting (accidental) l'incontro

(m) *een-kontro;* (arranged) la riunione *reeoon-yohnay*

melon il melone *may-lohnay*

melt sciogliere *shol-yayray*

member (of family) il membro *membro;* (of club etc) il socio *socho*

men gli uomini *wo-meenee*

menu il menu *maynoo*

meringue la meringa *may-reenga*

mess la confusione *konfooz-yohnay;* **to make a mess** sporcare *spor-kahray*

message il messaggio *mays-sad-jo*

metal il metallo *maytal-lo*

meter il contatore *konta-tohray*

metre il metro *metro*

microwave oven il forno a microonde *forno a meekro-onday*

midday il mezzogiorno *maydz-zo-jorno*

middle il mezzo *medz-zo*

middle-aged di mezza età *dee medz-za ayta*

might: I might go forse vado *forsay vahdo*

migraine l'emicrania (f) *aymee-kran-ya*

Milan Milano *mee-lahno*

mild (weather) mite *meetay;* (flavour) delicato *daylee-kahto*

mile = 1609 metres

milk il latte *laht-tay*

milk chocolate il cioccolato al latte *chok-ko-lahto al laht-tay*

milkshake il frappé *frap-pay*

millimetre il millimetro *meel-lee-maytro*

million il milione *meel-yohnay*

mince la carne macinata *kahrnay machee-nahta*

mind: do you mind if I ...? Le dà fastidio se ...? *lay da fas-teed-yo say*

mine il mio *eel mee-o;* **this glass is mine** questo bicchiere è il mio *kwaysto beek-yeray e eel mee-o*

mineral water l'acqua (f) minerale *akwa meenay-rahlay*

minimum il minimo *mee-neemo*

minor road la strada secondaria *strahda saykon-dar-ya*

mint (herb) la menta *maynta;* (sweet) la mentina *mayn-teena*

minute il minuto *mee-nooto*

mirror lo specchio *spek-yo*

miss (train etc) perdere *payr-dayray;* **I miss him** mi manca *mee manka*

Miss Signorina *seenyo-reena*

missing: my son is missing manca mio figlio *manka mee-o feel-yo;* **there is a ... missing** manca un ... *manka oon ...*

mist la foschia *foskee-a*

mistake l'errore (m) *ayr-rohray*

misty nebbioso *nayb-yohzo*

misunderstanding: there's been a misunderstanding c'è stato un malinteso *che stahto oon maleen-tayzo*

mix mescolare *maysko-lahray*

mixture la mescolanza *maysko-lantsa*

model (of car etc) il modello *model-lo*

modern moderno *mo-dayrno*

mohair il mohair *mohair*

moisturizer l'idratante (m) *eedra-tantay*

monastery il monastero *mona-stayro*

Monday il lunedì *loonay-dee*

money i soldi *soldee*

money order il vaglia *val-ya*

monk il frate *frahtay*

monkey la scimmia *sheem-ya*

month il mese *mayzay*

monument il monumento *monoo-maynto*

moon la luna *loona*

moor[1] *n* la brughiera *broog-yera*

moor[2] *vb* ormeggiare *ormayd-jahray*

mooring line il cavo d'ormeggio *kahvo dormayd-jo*

mop[1] *n* (for floor) il lavapavimenti *lahva-pavee-mayntay*; (for dishes) lo spazzolino per i piatti *spats-so-leeno payr ee pee-at-tee*

mop[2] *vb* lavare *la-vahray*

more più *pee-oo*; **more than 3** più di tre *pee-oo dee tray*; **more wine please** ancora un po' di vino per favore *an-kora oon po dee veeno payr fa-vohray*

morning la mattina *mat-teena*

mosquito la zanzara *dzan-dzahra*

most: the most popular discotheque la discoteca più frequentata *la deesko-teka pee-oo fraykwayn-tahta*; **most of the town** la maggior parte della città *la mad-jor partay dayl-la cheet-ta*

motel il motel *motel*

moth la farfalla *farfal-la*

mother la madre *mahdray*

mother-in-law la suocera *swo-chayra*

motor il motore *mo-tohray*

motor boat il motoscafo *moto-skahfo*

motor cycle la moto *mohto*

motorway l'autostrada (f) *a-ooto-strahda*

mountain la montagna *montan-ya*

mountaineer l'alpinista (m/f) *alpee-neesta*

mouse il topo *topo*

mousse la mousse *mousse*

moustache i baffi *baf-fee*

mouth la bocca *bok-ka*

move: it isn't moving non si muove *nohn see mwovay*; **he can't move his leg** non riesce a muovere la gamba *nohn ree-eshay a mwo-vayray la gamba*

movie camera la cinepresa *cheenay-prayza*

Mr Signor *seen-yohr*

Mrs Signora *seen-yohra*

much molto *mohlto*; **much hotter** molto più caldo *mohlto pee-oo kaldo*; **it costs too much** costa troppo *kohsta trop-po*; **thank you very much** grazie molte *grats-yay mohltay*

mud il fango *fango*

mug il tazzone *tats-sohnay*

mumps gli orecchioni *orayk-yohnee*

municipal municipale *moonee-chee-pahlay*

murder l'omicidio (*m*) *omee-cheed-yo*

muscle il muscolo *moo-skolo*

museum il museo *moozay-o*

mushrooms i funghi *foongee*

music la musica *moo-zeeka*

musician il musicista *moozee-cheesta*

mussel la cozza *kots-sa*

must dovere *do-vayray*; **I must go** devo andare *dayvo an-dahray*; **you must go** lei deve andare *le-ee dayvay an-dahray*; **he must go** deve andare *dayvay an-dahray*

mustard la senape *se-napay*

mutton il montone *mon-tohnay*

my il mio *eel mee-o*; **my room** la mia camera *la mee-a ka-mayra*; **my friends** i miei amici *ee mee-e-ee a-meechee*

mystery il mistero *mee-stayro*

N

nail (*metal*) il chiodo *kee-odo*; (*fingernail*) l'unghia (*f*) *oong-ya*

nail file la lima per unghie *leema payr oong-yay*

nail polish lo smalto per le unghie *zmalto payr lay oong-yay*

nail polish remover l'acetone

(*m*) *achay-tohnay*

nailbrush lo spazzolino per le unghie *spats-solee-no payr lay oong-yay*

naked nudo *noodo*

name il nome *nohmay*; **what is your name?** come si chiama? *kohmay see kee-ahma*; **my name is ...** mi chiamo ... *mee kee-ahmo ...*

napkin il tovagliolo *toval-yolo*

Naples Napoli *nah-polee*

nappies i pannolini per bambini *pan-no-leenee payr bam-beenee*

narrow stretto *strayt-to*

national nazionale *nats-yo-nahlay*

nationality la nazionalità *nats-yona-leeta*

native: native land la patria *patree-a*; **native language** la madrelingua *mahdray-leengwa*

natural naturale *natoo-rahlay*

naughty (*child*) birichino *beeree-keeno*

navy blue il blu marino *bloo ma-reeno*

near: is it near? è vicino? *e vee-cheeno*; **near the station** vicino alla stazione *vee-cheeno al-la stats-yohnay*; **near here** qui vicino *kwee vee-cheeno*; **where's the nearest bar?** dov'è il bar più vicino? *dohve eel bar pee-oo vee-cheeno*

neat ordinato *ordee-nahto*

necessary necessario *naychayss-saryo*

neck il collo *kol-lo*

necklace la collana *kol-lahna*

need: I need an aspirin ho bisogno di un'aspirina *o beezon-yo dee oon as-pee-reena*; **I need to go** devo andare *dayvo an-dahray*; **you need to go** lei deve andare *le-ee dayvay an-dahray*; **he needs to go** deve andare *dayvay an-dahray*

needle l'ago (m) *ahgo*; **a needle and thread** un ago e del filo *oon ahgo ay dayl feelo*

negative (photography) il negativo *nayga-teevo*

neighbour il vicino *vee-cheeno*

nephew il nipote *nee-pohtay*

nervous nervoso *nayr-vohzo*

nest il nido *needo*

net la rete *ray-tay*

nettle l'ortica (f) *or-teeka*

never mai *ma-ee*; **I never drink wine** non bevo mai il vino *nohn bayvo ma-ee eel veeno*

new nuovo *nwovo*

news le notizie *no-teets-yay*

newsagent il giornalaio *jorna-la-yo*

newspaper il giornale *jor-nahlay*

New Year l'Anno (m) Nuovo *an-no nwovo*

New Zealand la Nuova Zelanda *nwova dzay-landa*

next: the next stop la prossima fermata *la pros-seema fayr-mahta*; **next week** la settimana prossima *la sayt-tee-mahna pros-seema*; **next year** l'anno prossimo *lan-no pros-seemo*; **what happened next?** poi cos'è successo? *po-ee koze soot-ches-so*; **next to the station** accanto alla stazione *ak-kanto al-la stats-yohnay*

nice piacevole *pee-achay-volay*

niece la nipote *nee-pohtay*

night la notte *not-tay*; **last night** stanotte *stanot-tay*; **at night** di notte *dee not-tay*

night club il night *night*

nightdress la camicia da notte *ka-meecha da not-tay*

night porter il portiere di notte *port-yeray dee not-tay*

nine nove *novay*

nineteen diciannove *deechan-novay*

ninety novanta *no-vanta*

ninth nono *nono*

no no *no*; **no thank you** no grazie *no grats-yay*; **no smoking** vietato fumare *vee-ay-tahto foo-mahray*

nobody nessuno *nays-soono*

noise il rumore *roo-mohray*

noisy rumoroso *roomo-rohzo*

non-alcoholic analcolico *anal-ko-leeko*

none nessuno; **there's none left** non ce n'è più *nohn chay ne pee-oo*

non-smoking (compartment) per non-fumatori *payr nohn fooma-tohree*

noodles le tagliatelle *tal-yatel-lay*

normal normale *nor-mahlay*

north il nord *nord*
Northern Ireland L'Irlanda (f) del Nord *eer-landa dayl nord*
nose il naso *nahzo*
nosebleed l'emorragia (f) nasale *aymor-raja na-zahlay*
not non *nohn*; **I don't know** non lo so *nohn loh so*; **not me** io no *ee-o no*
note (bank note) la banconota *banko-nota*; (letter) il biglietto *beel-yayt-to*
note pad il bloc-notes *blok-not*
nothing niente *nee-entay*; **I've eaten nothing** non ho mangiato niente *nohn o man-jahto nee-entay*
notice (sign) il cartello *kartel-lo*
novel il romanzo *ro-mandzo*
November novembre (m) *no-vembray*
now adesso *ades-so*
nowhere da nessuna parte *da nays-soona partay*
nuclear nucleare *nooklay-ahray*
nuisance la seccatura *sayk-ka-toora*
numb intorpidito *eentor-pee-deeto*
number il numero *noo-mayro*
number plate la targa *targa*
nurse l'infermiera (f) *eenfayrm-yera*
nursery l'asilo (m) *a-zeelo*
nursery slope la pista per principianti *peesta payr preencheep-yantee*
nut (to eat) la noce *nohchay*; (for

bolt) il dado *dahdo*
nutmeg la noce moscata *nohchay mos-kahta*
nylon il nylon *nylon*

O

oar il remo *remo*
oats l'avena (f) *a-vayna*
object l'oggetto (m) *od-jet-to*
oblong oblungo *ob-loongo*
obvious ovvio *ov-yo*
occasionally ogni tanto *on-yee tanto*
October ottobre (m) *ot-tohbray*
odd (strange) strano *strahno*
of di *dee*; **of course** naturalmente *natoo-ral-mayntay*
off (machine etc) spento *spento*; **this meat is off** questa carne è andata a male *kwaysta karnay e an-dahta a mahlay*
offence l'infrazione (f) *eenfrats-yohnay*
offer offrire *of-freeray*
office l'ufficio (m) *oof-feecho*
officer (police) il poliziotto *poleets-yot-to*
official ufficiale *oof-fee-chahlay*
often spesso *spes-so*; **how often do you go?** ogni quanto ci vai? *on-yee kwanto chee va-ee*
oil l'olio (m) *ol-yo*
oil filter il filtro dell'olio *feeltro dayl-lol-yo*
ointment l'unguento (m) *oon-gwento*
O.K. va bene *va benay*
old vecchio *vayk-yo*; **old man** il

vecchio *vayk-yo;* **old woman** la vecchia *vayk-ya;* **how old are you?** quanti anni ha? *kwantee an-nee a*

olive oil l'olio (m) d'oliva *ol-yo do-leeva*

olives le olive *o-leevay*

omelette l'omelette (f) *omay-let*

on (light, engine) acceso *at-chayzo;* (tap) aperto *a-payrto;* **on the table** sulla tavola *sool-la tah-vola;* **on board** a bordo *a bordo;* **on Friday** venerdì *vaynayr-dee*

once una volta *oona volta*

one uno, una *oono, oona*

O negative O negativo *o nayga-teevo*

one-way (street) a senso unico *a senso oo-neeko*

onions le cipolle *cheepohl-lay*

only solo *solo*

open[1] adj aperto *a-payrto*

open[2] vb aprire *a-preeray*

opera l'opera (f) *o-payra*

opera house il teatro lirico *tay-ahtro leeree-ko*

operate (surgically) operare *opay-rahray*

operation l'operazione (f) *opay-rats-yohnay*

operator il/la centralinista *chayntra-lee-neesta*

O positive O positivo *o pozee-teevo*

opposite: opposite the hotel di fronte all'albergo *dee frontay al-lal-bayrgo*

optician l'ottico (m) *ot-teeko*

or o *oh*

orange[1] adj arancione *aran-chohnay*

orange[2] n l'arancia (f) *a-rancha*

orange juice il succo d'arancia *sook-ko da-rancha*

orchestra l'orchestra (f) *or-kaystra*

order[1] vb ordinare *ordee-nahray*

order[2] n l'ordine (m) *or-deenay*

ordinary comune *ko-moonay*

oregano l'origano (m) *oree-gano*

organ l'organo (m) *or-gano*

organized organizzato *orga-needz-zahto*

original originale *oree-jee-nahlay*

ornament l'ornamento (m) *orna-maynto*

other: the other one l'altro *laltro;* **do you have any others?** ce ne sono altri? *chay nay sohno altree*

ought: I ought to go dovrei andare *dovre-ee an-dahray;* **you ought to go** lei dovrebbe andare *le-ee dovrayb-bay an-dahray;* **he ought to go** dovrebbe andare *dovrayb-bay an-dahray*

ounce = 28.35 grams

our il nostro *eel nostro;* **our car** la nostra macchina *la nostra mak-keena;* **our photographs** le nostre foto *lay nostray foto*

ours il nostro *eel nostro;* **this case is ours** questa valigia è la nostra *kwaysta valee-ja e la nostra*

out (light) spento *spento;* **she's**

out è fuori e fwooee; **out of the room** fuori dalla stanza fwooree dal-la stantsa

outdoor (pool etc) all'aperto al-la-payr-to

outside fuori fwooee

outside line la linea con l'esterno leenay-a kohn lay-stayrno

oval ovale o-vahlay

oven il forno forno

over (on top of) sopra sohpra; **the film is over** il film è finito eel feelm e fee-neeto; **over there** laggiù lad-joo

overcharge far pagare troppo far pa-gahray trop-po

overheat surriscaldare soor-reeskal-dahray

overnight (travel) di notte dee not-tay; **we're staying overnight** ci fermiamo a dormire chee fayrm-yahmo a dor-meeray

overtake sorpassare sorpas-sahray

owe dovere do-vayray; **I owe you ...** le devo ... lay dayvo ...

owner il proprietario propree-aytar-yo

oxygen l'ossigeno (m) os-see-jayno

oyster l'ostrica (f) os-treeka

P

pack (gift) impacchettare eempak-kayt-tahray; **I must pack** devo fare le valigie dayvo

fahray lay va-leejay

package il pacco pak-ko

package tour il viaggio organizzato veead-jo orga-needz-zahto

packed lunch il cestino con il pranzo chay-steeno kohn eel prantso

packet il pacchetto pak-kayt-to

paddling pool la piscina per bambini pee-sheena payr bam-beenee

padlock il lucchetto look-kayt-to

Padua Padova pah-dova

page la pagina pa-jeena

paid pagato pa-gahto

pail il secchio sayk-yo

pain il dolore do-lohray

painful doloroso dolo-rohzo

painkiller il calmante kal-mantay

paint[1] n la vernice vayr-neechay; **paints** i colori koh-lohree

paint[2] vb dipingere deepeen-jayray

painter (artist) il pittore peet-tohray

painting il quadro kwadro

pair il paio pa-yo

palace il palazzo palats-so

pale pallido pal-leedo

pan la pentola payn-tola

pancake la crêpe krep

pane il vetro vaytro

panties le mutandine mootan-deenay

pants le mutande moo-tanday

paper la carta karta

paper bag il sacchetto di carta *sak-kayt-to dee karta*

paperback il tascabile *taskah-beelay*

paperclip la clip *kleep*

paprika la paprica *pa-preeka*

paraffin il cherosene *kayro-zenay*

paralysed paralizzato *para-leedz-zahto*

parcel il pacco *pak-ko*

pardon (*I didn't understand*) scusi? *skoozee*; **I beg your pardon!** mi scusi! *mee skoozee*

parents i genitori *jaynee-tohree*

park¹ *n* il parco *parko*

park² *vb* parcheggiare *parkayd-jahray*

parking disc il disco orario *deesko orar-yo*

parking meter il parchimetro *par-keemaytro*

parking ticket la contravvenzione per sosta vietata *kontrav-vaynts-yohnay payr sosta veeay-tahta*

parsley il prezzemolo *prayts-se-molo*

part la parte *partay*

parting (*in hair*) la riga *reega*

partly in parte *een partay*

partner (*in firm*) il socio *socho*; (*in sport, for dance*) il/la partner *partner*

party (*group*) il gruppo *groop-po*; (*celebration*) la festa *festa*

pass passare *pas-sahray*

passenger il passeggero *pas-*

sayd-jayro

passport il passaporto *pas-sa-porto*

passport control il controllo passaporti *kontrol-lo pas-sa portee*

pasta la pasta *pasta*

pastry la pasta *pasta*; (*cake*) il pasticcino *pasteet-cheeno*

patch (*of material*) il pezzo *pets-so*

pâté il pâté *patay*

path il sentiero *saynt-yero*

patient il paziente *pats-yentay*

pattern il disegno *deezayn-yo*

patterned: a patterned shirt una camicia fantasia *oona ka-meecha fanta-zee-a*

pavement il marciapiede *marcha-pee-eday*

pay pagare *pa-gahray*; **can I pay by cheque?** si può pagare con un assegno? *see pwo pa-gahray kohn oon as-sayn-yo*; **can I pay by credit card?** si può pagare con una carta di credito? *see pwo pa-gahray kohn oona karta dee kray-deeto*

payment il pagamento *paga-maynto*

peaches le pesche *peskay*

peanuts le arachidi *ara-keedee*

pearl la perla *payrla*

pears le pere *payray*

peas i piselli *peezel-lee*

pebbles i ciottoli *chot-tolee*

pedal il pedale *pay-dahlay*

pedestrian il pedone *pay-*

dohnay

peel[1] *vb (fruit)* sbucciare *sboot-chahray*; **my face is peeling** mi si spella il viso *mee see spayl-la eel veezo*

peel[2] *n* la buccia *boot-cha*

peg *(for clothes)* la molletta *mol-layt-ta*; *(for tent)* il picchetto *peek-kayt-to*

pen la penna *payn-na*

pencil la matita *ma-teeta*

pencil sharpener il temperamatite *taympay-rama-teetay*

penicillin la penicillina *paynee-cheel-leena*

penknife il temperino *taympay-reeno*

pensioner il pensionato *paynsee-o-nahto*

people la gente *jentay*

pepper *(spice)* il pepe *paypay*; *(vegetable)* il peperone *paypay-rohnay*

peppermint la menta *maynta*; **a peppermint** una menta *oona maynta*

per: **per hour** all'ora *al-lohra*; **per week** alla settimana *al-la sayt-tee-mahna*; **per person** per persona *payr payr-sohna*

perfect perfetto *payrfayt-to*

performance: **what time is the performance?** a che ora comincia lo spettacolo? *a kay ohra ko-meencha loh spayt-tah-kolo*

perfume il profumo *pro-foomo*

perhaps forse *forsay*

period *(menstruation)* le mestruazioni *maystroo-ats-yohnee*

perm la permanente *payrma-nentay*; **to have a perm** farsi fare la permanente *farsee fahray la payrma-nentay*

permit il permesso *payrmes-so*

person la persona *payr-sohna*

pet l'animale *(m)* domestico *anee-mahlay domay-steeko*

petrol la benzina *baynd-zeena*

petrol can la latta di benzina *lat-ta dee baynd-zeena*

petrol gauge la spia della benzina *spee-a dayl-la baynd-zeena*

petrol pump il distributore di benzina *deestree-boo-tohray dee baynd-zeena*

petrol station la stazione di servizio *stats-yohnay dee sayrveets-yo*

petrol tank il serbatoio *sayrba-to-yo*

petticoat la sottogonna *sot-togon-na*

phone[1] *n* il telefono *tayle-fono*

phone[2] *vb* telefonare *taylay-fo-nahray*

phone box la cabina telefonica *ka-beena taylay-fo-neeka*

phone call la telefonata *taylay-fo-nahta*

photocopy fotocopiare *foto-kop-yahray*

photograph la fotografia *foto-*

gra-fee-a

phrase book il vocabolarietto *voka-bolar-yayt-to*

piano il pianoforte *pee-ano-fortay*

pick (*flowers*) cogliere *kol-yeray*; (*fruit*) raccogliere *rak-kol-yeray*; **can you pick me up?** mi può venire a prendere? *mee pwo vay-neeray a pren-dayray*

picnic il picnic *peekneek*

picture (*painting*) il quadro *kwadro*; (*photo*) la foto *foto*

pie la torta *torta*

piece il pezzo *pets-so*

pier il molo *molo*

pig il maiale *ma-yahlay*

pigeon il piccione *peet-chohnay*

pigskin il cinghiale *cheeng-yahlay*

pile la pila *peela*

pill la pillola *peel-lola*

pillar la colonna *kolon-na*

pillow il guanciale *gwan-chahlay*

pillowcase la federa *fe-dayra*

pilot il pilota *pee-lota*

pilot light la fiammella di sicurezza *fee-am-mayl-la dee seekoo-rayts-sa*

pin lo spillo *speel-lo*

pine il pino *peeno*

pineapple l'ananas (*m*) *a-nanas*

pingpong il ping-pong *ping pong*

pink rosa *roza*

pint = .47 litres; **a pint of beer** una mezza birra *oona medz-za beer-ra*

pipe la pipa *peepa*

pipe cleaners gli scovolini *skovo-leenee*

pipe tobacco il tabacco per la pipa *tabak-ko payr la peepa*

piston il pistone *pee-stohnay*

place il posto *pohsto*

plain (*food*) alla buona *al-la bwona*; (*material*) in tinta unita *een teenta oo-neeta*

plan il progetto *projet-to*

plane l'aereo (*m*) *a-e-ray-o*

plant la pianta *pee-anta*

plaster (*sticking plaster*) il cerotto *chayrot-to*

plastic di plastica *dee pla-steeka*

plastic bag il sacchetto di plastica *sak-kayt-to dee pla-steeka*

plate il piatto *pee-at-to*

platform il binario *beenar-yo*

play[1] *n* la commedia *kom-med-ya*

play[2] *vb* (*games*) giocare *jo-kahray*; (*instrument*) suonare *swo-nahray*; **he plays tennis** gioca a tennis *joka a ten-nis*

playroom la stanza dei giochi *stantsa dayee jokee*

pleasant gradevole *graday-volay*

please: could you please ...? per piacere potrebbe ...? *payr pee-a-chayray potrayb-bay ...*

pleased contento *kon-tento*

plenty: plenty of water abbastanza acqua *ab-ba-stantsa akwa*

pliers le pinze *peentsay*

plug (*electrical*) la spina *speena;* (*for sink*) il tappo *tap-po*

plum la susina *soo-seena*

plumber l'idraulico (*m*) *eedra-oo-leeko*

pneumonia la polmonite *polmo-neetay*

poached egg l'uovo (*m*) affogato *wovo af-fo-gahto*

pocket la tasca *taska*

point *n* (*of knife, pencil*) la punta *poonta*

pointed appunito *ap-poon-teeto*

points (*in car*) le puntine *poon-teenay*

poisoning l'intossicazione (*f*) *eentos-seekats-yohnay*

poisonous velenoso *vaylay-nohzo*

police la polizia *poleet-see-a;* **police!** polizia! *poleet-see-a*

police car la macchina della polizia *mak-keena dayl-la poleet-see-a*

policeman il poliziotto *poleets-yot-to*

police station il commissariato *kom-mees-sar-yahto*

polio la polio *pol-yo*

polish[1] *n* (*for shoes*) il lucido *loo-cheedo;* (*for floor*) la cera *chayra*

polish[2] *vb* lucidare *loochee-dahray*

polite educato *aydoo-kahto*

political politico *polee-teeko*

polluted inquinato *eenkwee-nahto*

polo neck (*jumper*) il maglione a collo alto *mal-yohnay a kol-lo alto*

polyester il poliestere *polee-e-stayray*

polystyrene il polistirolo *polee-stee-rolo*

polythene bag il sacchetto di plastica *sak-kayt-to dee plas-teeka*

pond (*in park*) il laghetto *lagayt-to*

pony-trekking l'escursione (*f*) a cavallo *ayskoors-yohnay a kaval-lo*

pool (*swimming*) la piscina *pee-sheena*

poor povero *po-vayro;* **poor quality** di pessima qualità *dee pes-seema kwalee-ta*

Pope il papa *papa*

popular popolare *popo-lahray*

population la popolazione *popo-lats-yohnay*

porcelain la porcellana *porchayl-lahna*

pork il maiale *ma-yahlay*

port (*seaport*) il porto *porto;* (*on ship*) il babordo *ba-bordo;* (*wine*) il porto *porto*

portable portabile *portah-beelay*

porter (*in hotel*) il portiere *port-yeray;* (*in station*) il facchino *fak-keeno*

porthole l'oblò (*m*) *oblo*

portrait il ritratto *reetrat-to*

possible possibile *pos-see-beelay*

post[1] n il palo *pahlo*

post[2] vb spedire *spay-deeray*

postage l'affrancatura (f) *af-franka-toora*

postbox la cassetta delle lettere *kas-sayt-ta dayl-lay let-tayray*

postcard la cartolina *karto-leena*

postcode il codice postale *ko-deechay po-stahlay*

poster il poster *postayr*

postman il postino *po-steeno*

post office l'ufficio (m) postale *oof-feecho po-stahlay*

pot (for cooking) la pentola *payn-tola*; (for jam) il vasetto *vazayt-to*

potatoes le patate *pa-tahtay*

pottery la terracotta *tayr-rakot-ta*

potty (for baby) il vasino *va-zeeno*

poultry il pollame *pol-lahmay*

pound (weight) il mezzo chilo *medz-zo keelo*; (money) la sterlina *stayr-leena*

pour versare *vayr-sahray*

powder la polvere *pohl-vayray*

powdered milk il latte in polvere *laht-tay een pohl-vayray*

power (electricity) l'energia (f) elettrica *aynayr-jee-a aylet-treeka*

power cut l'interruzione (f) di corrente *eentayr-roots-yohnay dee kor-rentay*

power point la presa *prayza*

pram la carrozzina *kar-rots-seena*

prawn il gambero *gam-bayro*

prayer la preghiera *prayg-yera*

prefer preferire *prayfay-reeray*

pregnant incinta *een-cheenta*

prepare preparare *praypa-rahray*

present (gift) il regalo *ray-gahlo*

pretty carino *ka-reeno*

price il prezzo *prets-so*

price list il listino dei prezzi *lee-steeno dayee prets-see*

priest il prete *pretay*

primary school la scuola elementare *skwola aylay-mayn-tahray*

print[1] vb (photo) stampare *stam-pahray*

print[2] n (picture) la stampa *stampa*

prison la prigione *pree-johnay*

private privato *pree-vahto*

prize il premio *prem-yo*

probably probabilmente *proba-beel-mayntay*

problem il problema *pro-blema*

profit il profitto *profeet-to*

programme il programma *program-ma*

promise promettere *promayt-tayray*

pronounce pronunciare *pronoon-chahray*; **how do you pronounce it?** come si pronuncia? *kohmay see pro-nooncha*

propeller l'elica (f) *e-leeka*

properly correttamente *kor-rayt-ta-mayntay*

protein la proteina *protay-eena*

Protestant protestante *protay-stantay*

prunes le prugne *proon-yay*

psychiatrist lo psichiatra *pseekee-atra*

public pubblico *poob-bleeko*

public holiday la festa nazionale *festa nats-yo-nahlay*

pudding il dolce *dohlchay*

pull tirare *tee-rahray*

pullover il pullover *pullover*

pump¹ *n* la pompa *pompa*

pump² *vb*: **to pump up** (*tyre*) gonfiare *gonf-yahray*

puncture la foratura *fora-toora*

pupil (*at school*) l'allievo/a (*m/f*) *al-yevo/a;* (*of eye*) la pupilla *poopeel-la*

pure puro *pooro*

purple viola *vee-ola*

purse il borsellino *borsayl-leeno*

purser il commissario di bordo *komees-sahr-yo dee bordo*

push spingere *speen-jayray*

pushchair il passeggino *passayd-jeeno*

put (*insert*) mettere *mayt-tayray;* (*put down*) posare *po-zahray;* **put it there** lo metta lì *loh mayt-ta lee;* **put it on my account** me lo addebiti *may loh ad-day-beetee*

puzzle il rompicapo *rompee-kapo*

pyjamas i pigiama *pee-jama*

Q

quarantine la quarantena *kwaran-tayna*

quarter: quarter past two le due e un quarto *lay doo-ay ay oon kwarto;* **quarter to two** le due meno un quarto *lay doo-ay mayno oon kwarto*

quay il molo *molo*

question la domanda *do-manda*

queue¹ *n* la coda *koda*

queue² *vb* fare la coda *fahray la koda*

quick veloce *vay-lohchay*

quickly velocemente *vaylochay-mayntay*

quiet (*place*) tranquillo *trankweel-lo;* (*person*) taciturno *tachee-toorno*

quilt il piumino *pee-oo-meeno*

quite: it's quite good è abbastanza buono *e ab-bastantsa bwono;* **it's quite expensive** è piuttosto caro *e pee-oot-tosto kahro;* **quite perfect** proprio perfetto *propree-o payr-fayt-to*

R

rabbi il rabbino *rab-beeno*

rabbit il coniglio *koneel-yo*

rabies la rabbia *rab-ya*

race la corsa *korsa*

racket la racchetta *rak-kayt-ta*

radiator il radiatore *rad-ya-tohray*

radio la radio *rahd-yo*

radio-cassette la radio-cassetta *rahd-yo kas-sayt-ta*

radishes i ravanelli *rava-nayl-lee*
raft la zattera *dzat-tayra*
railway la ferrovia *fer-ro-veea*
railway station la stazione *stats-yohnay*
rain la pioggia *peeod-ja*
rainbow l'arcobaleno (m) *arkoba-layno*
raincoat l'impermeabile (m) *eempayr-may-ah-beelay*
raining: it's raining piove *peeovay*
raisin l'uvetta (f) *oovayt-ta*
rally il rally *rally*
ramp (on road) la rampa *rampa*
rare (unique) raro *rahro*; (steak) al sangue *al sangwe*
rash lo sfogo *sfogo*
raspberries i lamponi *lampohnee*
rat il ratto *rat-to*
rate la tariffa *tareef-fa*; **rate of exchange** il cambio *kamb-yo*
rather (quite) piuttosto *pee-oottosto*; **I'd rather do that** preferirei fare quello *prayfay-ree-re-ee fahray kwayl-lo*
raw crudo *kroodo*
razor il rasoio *razo-yo*
razor blades le lamette *lamayt-tay*
reach raggiungere *rad-joon-jayray*
read leggere *led-jayray*
ready pronto *prohnto*
real vero *vayro*
realize rendersi conto **ren-**dayrsee kohnto*

really: really good veramente buono *vayra-mayntay bwono*
reason la ragione *ra-johnay*
receipt la ricevuta *reechay-voota*
receiver il ricevitore *reechay-vee-tohray*
recently recentemente *raychayn-tay-mayntay*
reception (desk) la reception *reception*
receptionist il/la receptionist *receptionist*
recipe la ricetta *reechet-ta*
reclining seats i sedili ribaltabili *se-deelee reebal-tah-beelee*
recognize riconoscere *reeko-no-shayray*
recommend consigliare *konseel-yahray*
record (music etc) il disco *deesko*; (sport) il record *rekord*
recover ricuperare *reekoo-pay-rahray*
red rosso *ros-so*
redcurrant il ribes *ree-bes*
reduction la riduzione *reedoots-yohnay*
reel il rotolino *roto-leeno*
refill (for pen) il ricambio *reekamb-yo*; (for lighter) la bomboletta di gas *bombo-layt-ta dee gas*
refund il rimborso *reem-borso*
regional regionale *rayjo-nahlay*
registered raccomandata *rak-koman-dahta*
regulations il regolamento

raygo-la-**maynto**

reheel rifare i tacchi ree-**fahray** ee tak-kee

reimburse rimborsare reembor-**sahray**

relation (family) il parente pa-**rentay**

relax rilassarsi reelas-**sahrsee**

relaxing rilassante reelas-**santay**

reliable (company, service) sicuro see-**kooro**

religion la religione raylee-**johnay**

remain restare ray-**stahray**

remember ricordare reekor-**dahray**

remove togliere tol-**yayray**

rent (house) affittare af-feet-**tahray**; (car) noleggiare noled-**jahray**

rental (house) l'affitto (m) af-**feet**-to; (car) il nolo nolo

repair riparare reepa-**rahray**

repeat ripetere ree-**petay**-ray

reply[1] n la risposta ree-**sposta**

reply[2] vb rispondere reespon-**dayray**

reply coupon la ricevuta di ritorno reechay-**voota** dee ree-**torno**

rescue salvare sal-**vahray**

reservation la prenotazione prayno-tats-**yohnay**

reserve prenotare prayno-**tahray**

reserved prenotato prayno-**tahto**

rest[1] n (repose) il riposo ree-**pozo**; **the rest of the wine** il resto del vino eel resto dayl

veeno

rest[2] vb riposarsi reepo-**zahrsee**

restaurant il ristorante reesto-**rantay**

restaurant car il vagone ristorante va-**gohnay** reesto-**rantay**

retail price il prezzo al minuto prets-so al mee-**nooto**

retired in pensione een paynsee-**ohnay**

return (go back) ritornare reetor-**nahray**; (give back) restituire raystee-too-**eeray**

return ticket il biglietto di andata e ritorno beelyayt-to dee an-**dahta** ay ree-**torno**

reverse fare marcia indietro fahray marcha eendee-**etro**

reverse charge call la chiamata a carico del destinatario kee-a-**mahta** a ka-**reeko** dayl daystee-na-**tar**-yo

reverse (gear) la marcia indietro marcha eendee-**etro**; **in reverse** in retromarcia een raytro-**marcha**

reversing lights le luci di retromarcia loochee dee raytro-**marcha**

rheumatism il reumatismo ray-**ooma-teezmo**

rhubarb il rabarbaro (m) rabar-baro

rib (body) la costola ko-**stola**

ribbon il nastro nastro

rice il riso reezo

rich (person) ricco reek-ko;

(food) sostanzioso *sostants-yohzo*

ride (in car) andare in macchina *andah-ray een mak-keena*; **to go for a ride** andare a fare un giro in macchina *an-dahray a fahray oon jeero een mak-keena*

riding l'equitazione (f) *aykwee-tats-yohnay*; **to go riding** andare a cavallo *andah-ray a kaval-lo*

rigging l'attrezzatura (f) *at-trayts-sa-toora*

right¹ adj (correct) giusto *joosto*

right² adv: (on/to the) **right** a destra *a destra*

ring l'anello (m) *a-nel-lo*

rink la pista di pattinaggio *peesta dee pat-teenad-jo*

ripe maturo *ma-tooro*

river il fiume *fee-oomay*

road la strada *strahda*

road conditions le condizioni stradali *kondeets-yohnee stra-dahlee*

road map la carta stradale *karta stra-dahlay*

road sign il segnale stradale *sayn-yahlay stra-dahlay*

road works i lavori stradali *la-vohree stra-dahlee*

roast arrosto *ar-rosto*

roll (bread) il panino *pa-neeno*

Rome Roma *rohma*

roof il tetto *tayt-to*

roof-rack il portabagagli *porta-bagal-yee*

room (in house, hotel) la stanza *stantsa*; (space) lo spazio

spats-yo

room service il servizio da camera *sayrveets-yo da ka-mayra*

rope il cavo *kahvo*

rose la rosa *rosa*

rosé rosato *ro-zahto*

rotten marcio *marcho*

rough (surface) ruvido *roo-veedo*; (sea) mosso *mos-so*

round rotondo *ro-tohndo*; **round the house** intorno alla casa *een-torno al-la kasa*; **round the corner** dietro l'angolo *dee-etro lan-golo*

roundabout (at fair) la giostra *jostra*; (traffic junction) la rotatoria *rotat-tor-ya*

route l'itinerario (m) *eetee-nayrar-yo*

row¹ vb (boat) remare *ray-mahray*

row² n (of people) la fila *feela*

rowing boat la barca a remi *barka a raymee*

royal reale *ray-ahlay*

rub fregare *fray-gahray*

rubber la gomma *gohm-ma*

rubber band l'elastico *aylas-teeko*

rubbish la spazzatura *spats-sa-toora*

ruby il rubino *roo-beeno*

rucksack lo zaino *dza-eeno*

rudder il timone *tee-mohnay*

rude maleducato *malay-doo-kahto*

rug il tappeto *tap-payto*

ruin rovinare *rovee-nahray*

ruins le rovine *ro-veenay*

ruler (for measuring) il righello *reegayl-lo*

rum il rum *rum*

run[1] n (skiing) la pista *peesta*; (outing) il giro *jeero*

run[2] vb correre *kor-rayray*; (manage) dirigere *deeree-jayray*; (function) andare *an-dahray*; **I've run out of petrol** sono rimasto senza benzina *sohno ree-masto sentsa baynd-zeena*

rush hour l'ora (f) di punta *ohra dee poonta*

rusty rugginoso *rood-jee-nohzo*

rye bread il pane di segala *pahnay dee say-gala*

S

saccharin la saccarina *sak-ka-reena*

sad triste *treestay*

saddle la sella *sel-la*

safe[1] n la cassaforte *kas-sa-fortay*

safe[2] adj (beach, medicine) non pericoloso *non payree-ko-loh-zo*

safety pin la spilla di sicurezza *speel-la dee seekoo-rayts-sa*

sage (herb) la salvia *salv-ya*

sail la vela *vayla*

sailing (sport) la vela *vayla*

sailing boat la barca a vela *barka a vayla*

sailor il marinaio *maree-na-yo*

salad l'insalata (f) mista *eensa-lahta meesta*

salad dressing il condimento per l'insalata *kondee-maynto payr leensa-lahta*

sale (selling) la vendita *vayn-deeta*; (of bargains) il saldo *saldo*

salmon il salmone *sal-mohnay*

salt il sale *sahlay*

salty salato *sa-lahto*

same stesso *stays-so*

sample il campione *kamp-yohnay*

sand la sabbia *sab-ya*

sandals i sandali *san-dalee*

sandwich il panino *pa-neeno*

sandy (beach) sabbioso *sab-yohzo*

sanitary towels gli assorbenti *as-sor-bayntee*

sapphire lo zaffiro *dzaf-feero*

sardine la sardina *sar-deena*

Sardinia la Sardegna *sardayn-ya*

satin il raso *raso*

Saturday sabato (m) *sah-bato*

sauce la salsa *salsa*

saucepan la pentola *payn-tola*

saucer il piattino *peeat-teeno*

sauna la sauna *sa-oona*

sausage la salsiccia *salseet-cha*

sauté saltato *sal-tahto*

save (rescue) salvare *sal-vahray*; (money) risparmiare *reesparm-yahray*

savoury (not sweet) salato *sa-lahto*

say dire *deeray*

scales la bilancia *bee-lancha*

scallop il pettine *pet-teenay*

scampi gli scampi *skampee*

scarf la sciarpa *shahrpa*
scenery il paesaggio *pa-ayzad-jo*
scheduled flight il volo di linea *vohlo dee leenay-a*
school la scuola *skwola*
science la scienza *shentsa*
scientific scientifico *shayntee-feeko*
scientist il/la scienziato/a *shaynts-yahto*
scissors le forbici *forbee-chee*
Scotland la Scozia *skots-ya*
Scottish scozzese *skots-sayzay*
scrambled eggs le uova strapazzate *wova strapats-sahtay*
scrape scorticare *skortee-kahray*
scratch[1] n il graffio *graf-yo*
scratch[2] vb graffiare *graf-yahray*
screen (TV etc) lo schermo *skayrmo*
screw la vite *veetay*
screwdriver il cacciavite *katcha-veetay*
sculpture (object) la scultura *skool-toora*
sea il mare *mahray*
sea level il livello del mare *leevayl-lo dayl mahray*
seafood i frutti di mare *froot-tee dee mahray*
seafront il lungomare *loongo-mahray*
seaside: at the seaside al mare *al mahray*
season la stagione *sta-johnay*
season ticket l'abbonamento (m) *ab-bona-maynto*
seat (chair) la sedia *sed-ya*; (in

train, theatre) il posto *pohstoh*; (in toilet) il cerchio del water *chayrk-yo dayl vatayr;* **are there any seats left?** ci sono posti? *chee sohnoh pohstee*
seat belt la cintura di sicurezza *cheen-toora dee seekoo-rayts-sa*
seat reservation la prenotazione posto *prayno-tats-yohnay pohstoh*
seaweed le alghe *algay*
second[1] adj secondo *say-kohndo*
second[2] n (of time) il secondo *say-kohndo*
second class la seconda classe *say-kohnda klas-say;* **to travel second class** viaggiare in seconda classe *veead-jahray een say-kohnda klas-say*
second-hand di seconda mano *dee say-kohnda mahno*
secret il segreto *say-grayto*
secretary la segretaria *saygray-tar-ya*
sedative il calmante *kal-mantay*
see vedere *vay-dayray*
seem sembrare *saym-brahray*
self-service self-service *self service*
sell vendere *ven-dayray*
Sellotape lo scotch *scotch*
send mandare *man-dahray*
senior citizen l'anziano/a (m/f) *ants-yahno/a*
sensible (act) ragionevole *rajonay-volay;* (person) di buon senso *dee bwon senso*
sentence la frase *frahzay*

separate separato *saypa-rahto*

September settembre *sayt-taymbray*

serious grave *grahvay*

serve servire *sayr-veeray*

service (in restaurant) il servizio *sayrveets-yo*; (in church) la funzione *foonts-yohnay*

service charge il servizio *sayrveets-yo*

set menu il menù turistico *maynoo tooree-steeko*

settle (bill) saldare *sal-dahray*

seven sette *set-tay*

seventeen diciassette *deechas-set-tay*

seventh settimo *set-teemo*

seventy settanta *sayt-tanta*

several parecchi/parecchie *parayk-kee/parayk-yay*

sew cucire *koo-cheeray*

sex (gender) il sesso *ses-so*; (intercourse) i rapporti sessuali *rap-portee says-soo-ahlee*

shade (of colour) tonalità *tona-leeta*

shadow l'ombra (f) *ohmbra*

shake scuotere *skwo-tayray*; to shake hands stringersi la mano *streen-jayrsee la mahno*

shallow poco profondo *poko pro-fohndo*

shampoo lo shampoo *shampoo*

shampoo and set shampoo e messa in piega *shampoo ay may-sa een pee-ega*

shandy la birra con gassosa *beer-ra kohn gas-sohza*

shape la forma *forma*

share dividere *deevee-dayray*

sharp (edge, point) affilato *af-fee-lahto*; (pain) acuto *a-kooto*

shattered (windscreen) frantumato *frantoo-mahto*

shave farsi la barba *farsee la barba*

shaver il rasoio elettrico *razo-yo aylayt-treeko*

shaving cream la crema da barba *krema da barba*

shaving point la presa per i rasoi elettrici *prayza payr ee razoh-ee aylayt-treechee*

she lei *le-ee*

sheet il lenzuolo *laynt-swolo*

shelf lo scaffale *skaf-fahlay*

shell (seashell) la conchiglia *konkeel-ya*; (of egg, nut) il guscio *goosho*

shellfish i frutti di mare *froot-tee dee mahray*

shelter: to take shelter mettersi al riparo *mayt-tayrsee al ree-pahro*

sherry lo sherry *sherry*

shin lo stinco *steenko*

shiny lucido *loo-cheedo*

ship la nave *nahvay*

shirt la camicia *ka-meecha*

shiver tremare dal freddo *tray-mahray dal frayd-do*

shock (emotional) lo shock *shock*; (electric) la scossa *skos-sa*; it was a shock! è stata una brutta sorpresa! *e stahta oona broot-ta sor-prayza*

shock absorber
l'ammortizzatore (m)
am-morteedz-za-tohray

shoe la scarpa *skarpa*

shoot sparare *spa-rahray*

shop il negozio *naygots-yo*

shopping: to go shopping fare
compere *fahray kom-payray*

**shopping area: where's the
main shopping area?** dove sono
i negozi principali? *dohvay
sohnoh ee nay-gotsee
preenchee-pahlee*

shopping bag la borsa per la
spesa *borsa payr la spayza*

shore la riva *reeva*

short corto *korto*

short cut la scorciatoia *skorcha-
toh-ya*

shorts i calzoncini corti *kaltson-
cheenee kortee*

should: I should go dovrei
andare *dovre-ee an-dahray;* **you
should go** dovresti andare *dov-
raystee an-dahray;* **he should go**
dovrebbe andare *dovrayb-bay
an-dahray;* **he should be there
by now** dovrebbe essere già
arrivato *dovrayb-bay es-sayray ja
ar-ree-vahto*

shoulder la spalla *spal-la*

shout[1] vb urlare *oor-lahray*

shout[2] n il grido *greedo*

shovel la pala *pahla*

show[1] n lo spettacolo *spayt-tah-
kolo*

show[2] vb mostrare *mo-strahray*

shower la doccia *dot-cha*

shrimp il gamberetto *gambay-
rayt-to*

shrink restringersi *raystreen-
jayrsee*

shut[1] vb chiudere *kee-oo-dayray*

shut[2] adj chiuso *kee-oozo*

shutter l'otturatore (m) *ot-toora-
tohray*

Sicily la Sicilia *seecheel-ya*

sick (ill) malato *ma-lahto;*
I feel sick ho la nausea *o la
na-oozay-a*

side (of person) il fianco *fee-
anko;* (of object) il lato *lahto*

sidelights (of car) le luci di
posizione *loochee dee poseets-
yohnay*

side street la traversa *tra-vayrsa*

sieve (for liquids) il colino
ko-leeno; (for flour) il setaccio
saytat-cho

sightseeing il turismo *too-
reezmo*

sign il segnale *sayn-yahlay*

signal il segnale *sayn-yahlay*

signature la firma *feerma*

silencer la marmitta *marmeet-ta*

silent silenzioso *seelaynts-yohzo*

silk la seta *seta*

silver (colour) color argento
kolor ar-jaynto; (made of silver)
fatto d'argento *faht-to dar-jaynto*

similar simile *see-meelay*

simple semplice *saym-pleechay*

since: since he arrived da
quando è arrivato lui *da kwando
e ar-ree-vahto loo-ee;* **since he's
away** dato che lui non c'è *dahto*

kay loo-ee nohn che
sincerely: Yours sincerely
distinti saluti *dee-steentee
sa-lootee*
sing cantare *kan-tahray*
single (unmarried) non sposato
nohn spo-zahto; (not double)
singolo *seen-golo*
single bed il letto a una piazza
let-to a oona pee-ats-sa
single room la camera singola
ka-mayra seen-gola
sink[1] *n* il lavandino *lavan-deeno*
sink[2] *vb* affondare *af-fon-dahray*
sir signore *seen-yohray*; **Dear Sir**
Egregio Signore *ay-grejo seen-
yohray*
sister la sorella *sorel-la*
sister-in-law la cognata *kon-
yahta*
sit: to sit down sedersi *say-
dayrsee*; **I am sitting** sono
seduto *sohno say-dooto*
site (of town, building)
l'ubicazione (f) *oobee-kats-
yohnay*; (archeological) la località
loka-leeta
six sei *se-ee*
sixteen sedici *say-deechee*
sixth sesto *sesto*
sixty sessanta *says-santa*
size la misura *mee-zoora*
skate[1] *vb* pattinare *pat-tee-
nahray*
skate[2] *n* il pattino *pat-teeno*
skating rink la pista di
pattinaggio *peesta dee pat-
teenad-jo*

skewer lo spiedo *spee-edo*
ski[1] *vb* sciare *shee-ahray*
ski[2] *n* lo sci *shee*
ski boots gli scarponi da sci
skar-pohnee da shee
skid lo slittamento *zleet-ta-
maynto*
skimmed milk il latte scremato
laht-tay skray-mahto
skin la pelle *pel-lay*
skindiving le attività subacquee
at-teevee-ta soobak-way-ay
ski pants i pantaloni da sci
panta-lohnee da shee
ski pole la racchetta da sci
rak-kayt-ta da shee
skirt la gonna *gon-na*
ski run la pista *peesta*
ski suit il completo da sci
kom-pleto da shee
skull il cranio *krahn-yo*
sky il cielo *chelo*
slack lento *lento*
sledge la slitta *zleet-ta*
sleep dormire *dor-meeray*
sleeper (in train) la cuccetta
koot-chayt-ta
sleeping bag il sacco a pelo
sak-ko a paylo
sleeping car il vagone letto *va-
gohnay let-to*
sleeping pill il sonnifero *son-
nee-fayro*
sleeve la manica *mah-neeka*
slide[1] *vb* scivolare *sheevo-lahray*
slide[2] *n* (in park) lo scivolo *shee-
volo*; (for hair) il fermacapelli
fayrma-kapayl-lee; (photograph)

la diapositiva *deea-pozee-teeva*

sling (*bandage*) la fascia *fasha*

slip scivolare *sheevo-lahray*

slippers le pantofole *panto-folay*

slippery scivoloso *sheevo-lohzo*

slope (*for skiing*) la pista *peesta*

slow lento *laynto*

small piccolo *peek-kolo*

smaller più piccolo *pee-oo peek-kolo*

smash rompere *rohm-payray*

smell[1] *vb*: **I smell wine** sento odore di vino *saynto o-dohray dee veeno*; **that smells of wine** sa di vino *sa dee veeno*

smell[2] *n* (*pleasant*) il profumo *pro-foomo*; (*unpleasant*) il puzzo *poots-so*

smile[1] *vb* sorridere *sor-ree-dayray*

smile[2] *n* il sorriso *sor-reeso*

smoke[1] *n* il fumo *foomo*

smoke[2] *vb* fumare *foo-mahray*

smoked affumicato *af-foomee-kahto*

smooth (*surface*) liscio *leesho*

smuggle portare di contrabbando *por-tahray dee kontrab-bando*

snack bar la tavola calda *tah-vola kalda*

snail la lumaca *loo-mahka*

snake il serpente *ser-pentay*

sneeze starnutire *starnoo-teeray*

snore russare *roos-sahray*

snorkel il boccaglio *bok-kal-lyo*

snow la neve *nayvay*

snowed up isolato a causa della neve *eezo-lahto a ka-ooza dayl-la nayvay*

snowing: it's snowing nevica *nay-veeka*

snowplough lo spazzaneve *spats-sa-nayvay*

so dunque *doonkway*; **and so I went there** così ci sono andato *kozee chee sohnoh an-dahto*; **so much sun** tanto sole *tanto sohlay*

soap la saponetta *sapo-nayt-ta*

soap powder il detersivo *daytayr-seevo*

soapflakes il sapone in scaglie *sa-pohnay een skalyay*

sober sobrio *sobree-o*

socket la presa *prayza*

socks i calzini *kalt-seenee*

soda la soda *soda*; **a whisky and soda** un whisky con soda *oon whisky kohn soda*

sodawater l'acqua di selz *akwa dee selts*

soft soffice *sof-feechay*

soft drink l'analcolico (*m*) *anal-ko-leekoh*

soft-boiled egg l'uovo (*m*) alla coque *wovo al-la kok*

sole (*of foot*) la pianta *pee-anta*; (*of shoe*) la suola *swola*; (*fish*) la sogliola *sol-yola*

solid solido *so-leedo*

soluble solubile *soloo-beelay*

some del, della *dayl, dayl-la*; (*plural*) alcuni, alcune *al-koonee, alkoonay*; **some wine** del vino *dayl veeno*; **some friends** alcuni

amici *al-koonee a-meechee*
somehow in qualche modo *een kwalkay modo*
someone qualcuno *kwal-koono*
something qualcosa *kwal-kosa*
sometimes qualche volta *kwalkay volta*
somewhere da qualche parte *da kwalkay partay*
son il figlio *feel-yo*
son-in-law il genero *je-nayro*
song la canzone *kant-sohnay*
soon presto *presto*
sooner prima *preema*
sore: my back is sore mi fa male la schiena *mee fa mahlay la skee-ena*
sorry: I'm sorry! mi scusi! *mee skoozee*
sort: what sort of cheese? che tipo di formaggio? *kay teepo dee formad-jo*
soufflé il soufflé *sooflay*
sound *n* il suono *swono*
soup la minestra *mee-nestra*
sour aspro *aspro*
south il sud *sood*
souvenir il souvenir *soovneer*
space lo spazio *spats-yo*;
parking space il posto *pohstoh*
spade la paletta *palayt-ta*
spanner la chiave *kee-ahvay*
spare: a spare battery una batteria di riserva *bat-tayree-a dee reeserva*
spare part il pezzo di ricambio *pet-tso dee ree-kambyo*
spare wheel la ruota di scorta

rwota dee skorta
spark plug la candela *kan-dayla*
sparkling frizzante *freets-santay*
speak parlare *par-lahray*
special speciale *spay-chahlay*
special menu il menù speciale *maynoo spay-chahlay*
special rate la tariffa speciale *tareef-fa spay-chahlay*
speciality la specialità *spaycha-leeta*
speed la velocità *vaylo-cheeta*
speed limit il limite di velocità *lee-meetay dee vaylo-cheeta*
speedometer il tachimetro *takee-maytro*
spell: how do you spell it? come si scrive? *komay see skreevay*
spend (time) passare *pas-sahray*; (money) spendere *spen-dayray*
spices le spezie *le spets-yay*
spicy piccante *peek-kantay*
spill rovesciare *rovay-shahray*
spinach gli spinaci *spee-nachee*
spin-dryer la centrifuga *chayntree-fooga*
spine (backbone) la spina dorsale *speena dor-sahlay*
spirits i liquori *lee-kwohree*
spit sputare *spoo-tahray*
splint la stecca *stayk-ka*
splinter la scheggia *sked-ja*
split spaccare *spak-kahray*
spoil rovinare *rovee-nahray*
sponge la spugna *spoon-ya*
sponge bag la borsa per oggetti da toilette *borsa payr od-jet-tee*

da twalet

spoon il cucchiaio *kook-ya-yo*

sport lo sport *sport*

sprain la storta *storta*

spring (season) la primavera *preema-ve-ra*; (coiled metal etc) la molla *mol-la*

sprinkle spruzzare *sproots-sahray*

square (shape) il quadrato *kwa-drahto*; (in town) la piazza *pee-ats-sa*

squash (game) lo squash *squash*; (drink) la spremuta *spray-moota*

squeeze spremere *spre-mayray*

stage (in theatre) il palcoscenico *palko-shay-neeko*; (phase) la fase *fahzay*

stain la macchia *mak-ya*

stainless steel l'acciaio (m) inossidabile *at-cha-yo eenos-seedah-beelay*

stairs le scale *skahlay*

stalls (theatre) la platea *platay-a*

stamp il francobollo (m) *franko-bohl-lo*

stand[1] vb stare in piedi *stahray een pee-edee*; **to stand up** alzarsi *alt-sahrsee*

stand[2] n (at exhibition) il banco *banko*

standard standard *standard*

stapler la cucitrice *koochee-treechay*

staples la graffetta *graf-fayt-ta*

star (in sky) la stella *stayl-la*; (person) il/la divo/a *deevo/a*

starboard il tribordo *tree-bordo*

start[1] n l'inizio (m) *eeneets-yo*

start[2] vb cominciare *komeen-chahray*

starter (in meal) l'antipasto (m) *antee-pasto*; (in car) il motorino d'avviamento *moto-reeno dav-vee-a-maynto*

station la stazione *stats-yohnay*

stationer's la cartoleria *karto-lay-reea*

statue la statua *statoo-a*

stay[1] n la permanenza *payrma-nentsa*

stay[2] vb (remain) restare *ray-stahray*; **I'm staying at a hotel** sto in un albergo *sto een oon al-bayrgo*

steak la bistecca *beestayk-ka*

steamer il piroscafo *peero-skahfo*

steel l'acciaio (m) *at-cha-yo*

steep ripido *ree-peedo*

steeple il campanile *kampa-neelay*

steering lo sterzo *stayrtso*

steering column il piantone dello sterzo *peean-tohnay dayl-lo stayrtso*

steering wheel il volante *vo-lantay*

step il gradino *gra-deeno*

stepdaughter la figliastra *feel-yastra*

stepfather il patrigno *patreen-yo*

stepmother la matrigna *matreen-ya*

stepson il figliastro *feel-yastro*

stereo lo stereo *ste-ray-o*

sterling la sterlina *stayr-leena*

stew lo stufato *stoo-fahto*

steward lo steward *steward*

stewardess la hostess *hostess*

stick[1] *n* il bastone *ba-stohnay*

stick[2] *vb* incollare *eenkol-lahray*

sticking plaster il cerotto *chayrot-to*

sticky appiccicoso *ap-peet-chee-kohzo*

stiff rigido *ree-jeedo*

still (motionless) fermo *fayrmo;* **I'm still here** sono ancora qui *sohnoh an-kohra kwee*

sting la puntura *poon-toora*

stir mescolare *maysko-lahray*

stitching la cucitura *koochee-toora*

stock (for soup) il brodo *brodo;* **in stock** in magazzino *een magad-dzeeno*

stockings le calze *kaltsay*

stolen rubato *roo-bahto*

stomach la pancia *pancha*

stomach upset il mal di pancia *mal dee pancha*

stone la pietra *pee-etra*

stop[1] *vb* fermarsi *fayr-mahrsee*

stop[2] *n* (for bus etc) la fermata *fayr-mahta*

stop light la luce d'arresto *loochay dar-resto*

stopover la sosta *sosta*

stopping train l'accelerato (m) *at-chaylay-rahto*

storm la tempesta *taym-pesta*

stormy tempestoso *taympay-stohzo*

story la storia *sto-ree-a*

straight diritto *deereet-to*

straight on diritto *deereet-to*

strange strano *strahno*

stranger lo/la sconosciuto/a *skono-shooto/a*

strap la cinghia *cheeng-ya*

straw (for drinking) la cannuccia *kan-noot-cha*

strawberries le fragole *frahgolay*

stream il ruscello *rooshel-lo*

street la strada *strahda*

street plan la piantina *pee-an-teena*

stretch (clothes) allargarsi *al-lar-gahrsee*

stretcher la barella *barel-la*

strike lo sciopero *sho-payro;* **on strike** in sciopero *een sho-payro*

string lo spago *spahgo*

strip (of paper etc) la striscia *streesha*

striped a strisce *a streeshay*

strong forte *fortay*

stuck bloccato *blok-kahto*

student (male) lo studente *stoo-dayntay;* (female) la studentessa *stoodayn-tes-sa*

stuffing (for meat) il ripieno *reep-yeno*

stung punto *poonto*

stupid stupido *stoo-peedo*

style lo stile *steelay*

styling mousse il fissatore *fees-sa-tohray*

suburb la periferia *payree-fayree-a*

subway il sottopassaggio *sottopas-sad-jo*

success il successo *soot-chays-so*

suck succhiare *sook-yahray*

suddenly improvvisamente *eempro-veeza-mayntay*

suede il camoscio *ka-mosho*

sugar lo zucchero **tsook**-*kayro*

suit (man's) l'abito (m) **a**-*beeto*; (woman's) il tailleur *ta-yer*

suitable adatto *adat-to*

suitcase la valigia *va-leeja*

summer l'estate (f) *ay-stahtay*

sun il sole *sohlay*

sunbathe prendere il sole **prayn**-*dayray eel sohlay*

sunburn la scottatura solare *skot-ta-toora so-lahray*

Sunday domenica *domay-neeka*

sunglasses gli occhiali da sole *ok-yahlee da sohlay*

sunhat il cappello da sole *kap-pel-lo da sohlay*

sunny assolato *as-so-lahto*; it's sunny c'è il sole *che eel sohlay*

sunshade l'ombrellone (m) *ombrayl-lohnay*

sunstroke l'insolazione (f) *eenso-lats-yohnay*

suntan l'abbronzatura (f) *ab-brond-za-toora*

suntan oil l'olio solare (m) *ol-yo so-lahray*

supermarket il supermercato *soopayr-mayr-kahto*

supper (dinner) la cena *chayna*

supplement il supplemento *soop-play-**maynto***

suppose supporre *soop-por-ray*; I suppose so credo di sì *kraydo dee see*

suppository la supposta *soop-posta*

sure sicuro *see-kooro*

surface la superficie *soopayr-feechay*

surface mail la posta ordinaria *posta ordee-nar-ya*

surfboard la tavola per surfing *tah-vola payr surfing*

surfing il surfing *surfing*

surname il cognome *kon-yohmay*

surprised sorpreso *sor-**prayzo***

suspension la sospensione *sospayn-see-**ohnay***

suspicious (causing suspicion) sospetto *sospet-to*

sweat sudare *soo-dahray*

sweater il maglione *mal-yohnay*

sweep spazzare *spats-sahray*

sweet dolce *dohlchay*

sweets le caramelle *kara-mel-lay*

swelling il gonfiore *gonf-yohray*

swerve sterzare *stayr-tsahray*

swim nuotare *nwo-tahray*

swimming il nuoto *nwoto*

swimming pool la piscina *pee-sheena*

swimsuit il costume da bagno *ko-**stoomay** da ban-yo*

swing (in park) l'altalena (f) *alta-layna*

Swiss svizzero *zveet-sayro*
switch l'interruttore (*m*) *eentayr-root-tohray*
switch off spegnere *spen-yayray*
switch on accendere *at-chen-dayray*
Switzerland Svizzera *zveet-sayra*
swollen gonfio *gonf-yo*
symptom il sintomo *seen-tomo*
synagogue la sinagoga *seena-goga*
system il sistema *see-stema*

T

table la tavola *tah-vola*
tablecloth la tovaglia *toval-ya*
table d'hôte il menù a prezzo fisso *maynoo a prets-so fees-so*
tablespoon il cucchiaio *kook-ya-yo*
tablet la pastiglia *pasteel-ya*
table tennis il ping-pong *ping pong*
table wine il vino da pasto *veeno da pasto*
tail la coda *kohda*
tailback la coda *kohda*
tailor il sarto *sarto*
take (carry) portare *por-tahray*; (grab, seize) prendere *pren-dayray*; **how long does it take?** quanto tempo ci vuole? *kwanto tempo chee vwolay*; **to take out** (tooth) togliere *tol-yeray*; **can I take you out to lunch?** posso invitarti a pranzo fuori? *pos-*

so eenvee-*tahrtee* a prantso *fworee*
talc il borotalco *boro-talko*
talk[1] vb parlare *par-lahray*
talk[2] n la conversazione *konvayr-sats-yohnay*
tall alto *alto*
tame addomesticato *ad-domay-stee-kahto*
tampons i tamponi *tam-pohnee*
tap il rubinetto *roobee-nayt-to*
tape il nastro *nastro*
tape-measure il metro a nastro *metro a nastro*
tape-recorder il registratore *rayjee-stra-tohray*
tapestry l'arazzo *arats-so*
target il bersaglio *bayrsal-yo*
tarmac il macadam *macadam*
tart la torta *torta*
tartar sauce la salsa tartara *salsa tar-tara*
taste[1] vb: **can I taste some?** ne posso assaggiare un po'? *nay pos-so as-sad-jayray un po;* **it tastes of tomatoes** sa di pomodoro *sa dee pomo-doro;* **it tastes good** ha un buon sapore a *oon bwon sa-pohray*
taste[2] n il sapore *sa-pohray*
tax la tassa *tas-sa*
taxi il taxi *taxi*
taxi rank il posteggio dei taxi *postayd-jo day-ee taxi*
tea il tè *te*
teabag la bustina di tè *boo-steena dee te*
teach insegnare *eensayn-yahray*

teacher l'insegnante (m/f) *eensayn-yantay*

team la squadra *skwadra*

teapot la teiera *tay-yera*

tear[1] n (rip) lo strappo *strap-po*; (from eye) la lacrima *la-kreema*

tear[2] vb strappare *strap-pahray*

teaspoon il cucchiaino *kook-ya-eeno*

teat la tettarella *tayt-tarel-la*

technical tecnico *tek-neeko*

teddy (bear) l'orsacchiotto *orsak-yot-to*

teenager l'adolescente (m/f) *ado-lay-shentay*

teeshirt la maglietta *mal-yayt-ta*

teeth i denti *dentee*

telegram il telegramma *taylay-gram-ma*

telephone il telefono *tayle-fono*

telephone box la cabina telefonica *ka-beena taylay-fo-neeka*

telephone call la telefonata *taylay-fo-nahta*

telephone directory l'elenco telefonico *ay-lenko taylay-fo-neeko*

television: on television alla televisione *al-la taylay-veez-yohnay*; **television set** il televisore *taylay-vee-zohray*

telex il telex *telex*

tell dire *deeray*; **I'll tell him** glielo dirò *lee-aylo deero*; **can you tell me the time?** mi può dire l'ora? *mee pwo deeray lohra*

temperature la temperatura *taympay-ra-toora*; **to have a temperature** avere la febbre *a-vayray la feb-bray*

temporary temporaneo *taympo-rahnay-o*

ten dieci *dee-echee*

tender (sore) sensibile *saynsee-beelay*; (meat) tenero *te-nayro*

tennis il tennis *ten-nees*

tennis ball la palla da tennis *pal-la da ten-nees*

tennis court il campo da tennis *kampo da ten-nees*

tennis racket la racchetta da tennis *rak-kayt-ta da ten-nees*

tent la tenda *tenda*

tenth decimo *det-cheemo*

tent peg il picchetto *peekayt-to*

tent pole il palo *pahlo*

terminus (for buses) il capolinea *kapo-leenay-a*; (station) la stazione di testa *stats-yohnay dee testa*

terrace la terrazza *tayr-rats-sa*

terrible terribile *tayr-ree-beelay*

terylene il terital *te-reetal*

textbook il libro di testo *leebro dee testo*

than: more than ten più di dieci *pee-oo dee dee-echee*; **better than this** meglio di questo *mel-yo dee kwaysto*

thank you grazie *grats-yay*; **thank you very much** tante grazie *tantay grats-yay*

that quel, quella *kwayl, kwayl-la*; **that door** quella porta *kwayl-la porta*; **I know that ... so che ...**

so kay; **that one** quello là *kwayl-lo la*

thaw: it's thawing sta sgelando *sta zjay-lando*

the il, (plural) i *eel, ee;* la, (plural) le *la, lay;* **the boy** il ragazzo *eel ragats-so;* **the boys** i ragazzi *ee ragats-see;* **the women** le donne *lay don-nay;* **the orange** l'arancia *laran-cha*

theatre il teatro *tay-atro*

their il loro *eel lohro;* **their shoes** le loro scarpe *lay lohro skarpay*

theirs il loro *eel lohro;* **this table is theirs** questa tavola è la loro *kwaysta tah-vola e la lohro*

them li, le, *lee, lay;* **I see them** li vedo *lee vaydo;* **I wrote them a postcard** ho scritto loro una cartolina *o skreet-to lohro oona karto-leena;* **without them** senza di loro *sentsa dee lohro*

then: then I ate poi ho mangiato *po-ee o man-jahto;* **they will be away then** a quell'epoca saranno via *a kwayl-le-poka sarah-no vee-a*

there li *lee;* **there is/there are** c'è/ci sono *che/chee sohno*

therefore quindi *kweendee*

thermometer il termometro *tayrmo-maytro*

these questi, queste *kwaystee, kwaystay*

they loro *lohro;* **they aren't here** non ci sono *nohn chee sohno*

thick spesso *spays-so*

thief il ladro *lahdro*

thigh la coscia *kosha*

thin magro *magro*

thing la cosa *kosa;* **can I leave my things here?** posso lasciare qui la mia roba? *pos-so la-shahray kwee la mee-a roba*

think pensare *payn-sahray*

third[1] n il terzo *tayrtso*

third[2] adj terzo *tayrtso*

thirsty: I'm thirsty ho sete *o saytay*

thirteen tredici *tray-deechee*

thirty trenta *traynta*

this questo, questa *kwaysto, kwaysta;* **this one** questo qui *kwaysto kwee*

thistle il cardo *kardo*

those quelli, quelle *kwayl-lee, kwayl-lay;* **those men** quegli uomini *kwayl-lyee uo-meenee*

thousand mille *meel-lay*

thread il filo *feelo*

three tre *tray*

thriller il thriller *thriller*

throat la gola *gohla*

throat lozenges le pastiglie per la gola *pasteel-yay payr la gohla*

throttle la leva del gas *leva dayl gas*

through attraverso *at-tra-vayrso*

throw lanciare *lan-chahray*

thumb il pollice *pol-leechay*

thunder il tuono *twono*

thunderstorm il temporale *taympo-rahlay*

Thursday giovedì (m) *jovay-dee*

thyme il timo *teemo*

Tiber il Tevere *tay-vayray*

ticket il biglietto *beel-yayt-to*
ticket collector il controllore *kontro-lohray*
ticket office la biglietteria *beel-yayt-tayree-a*
tide la marea *maray-a*
tidy ordinato *ordee-nahto*
tie[1] n la cravatta *kravat-ta*
tie[2] vb legare *lay-gahray*
tight stretto *strayt-to*
tights i collant *kol-lant*
till[1] n la cassa *kas-sa*
till[2] prep fino a *feeno a;* **till tomorrow** a domani *a do-mahnee;* **till they come** finché arrivano *feenkay ar-ree-vano*
time il tempo *tempo;* **what time is it?** che ore sono? *kay ohray sohno;* **this time** questa volta *kwaysta volta*
timetable board il tabellone degli orari *tabayl-lohnay dayl-lyee o-rahree*
tin la scatola *skah-tola*
tinfoil la carta stagnola *karta stan-yola*
tin-opener l'apriscatole (m) *apree-skah-tolay*
tinted sfumato *sfoo-mahto*
tip (to waiter etc) la mancia *mancha*
tipped con filtro *kohn feeltro*
tired stanco *stanko*
tissue paper la carta velina *karta vay-leena*
tissues i fazzoletti di carta *fats-so-layt-tee dee karta*
T-junction l'incrocio (m) a T

een-crocho a tee
to a *ah;* **to London** a Londra *a lohndra;* **to Spain** in Spagna *een span-ya;* **I want to go** voglio andare *vol-yo an-dahray*
toast il pane tostato *pahnay to-stahto*
toaster il tostapane *tosta-pahnay*
tobacco il tabacco *tabak-ko*
tobacconist il tabaccaio *tabak-ka-yo*
toboggan lo slittino *zleet-teeno*
today oggi *od-jee*
toe il dito del piede *deeto dayl pee-eday*
together insieme *een-see-emay*
toilet la toilette *twalet;* **where are the toilets?** dov'è la toilette? *dohve la twalet*
toilet paper la carta igienica *karta eeje-neeka*
toilet water l'acqua (f) di colonia *akwa dee kolon-ya*
toll il pedaggio *paydad-jo*
tomato il pomodoro *pomo-doro*
tomato juice il succo di pomodoro *sook-ko dee pomo-doro*
tomb la tomba *tomba*
tomorrow domani *do-mahnee;* **tomorrow morning** domani mattina *do-mahnee mat-teena*
ton la tonnellata *ton-nayl-lahta*
tongue la lingua *leengwa*
tonic water l'acqua (f) tonica *akwa to-neeka*
tonight stasera *sta-sayra*
tonsillitis la tonsillite *tonseel-*

leetay

too (*also*) anche *ankay*; **it's too big** è troppo grande *e trop-po granday*

tool l'attrezzo (*m*) *at-trayts-so*

tooth il dente *dentay*

toothache: I have toothache ho mal di denti *o mal dee dentee*

toothbrush lo spazzolino da denti *spats-solee-no da dentee*

toothpaste il dentifricio *dayntee-freecho*

top[1] *adj*: **the top floor** l'ultimo piano *lool-teemo pee-ahno*

top[2] *n* la cima *cheema*; (*of bottle*) il tappo *tap-po*; **on top of ...** sopra ... *sohpra ...*

torch la pila *peela*

torn strappato *strap-pahto*

total il totale *to-tahlay*

touch toccare *tok-kahray*

tough (*meat*) duro *dooro*

tour il giro *jeero*

tourism il turismo *too-reezmo*

tourist il turista *too-reesta*

tourist office l'ufficio informazioni turistiche *oof-feecho eenfor-mats-yohnee tooree-steekay*

tourist ticket il biglietto turistico *beel-yayt-to tooree-steeko*

tow rimorchiare *reemork-yahray*

towel l'asciugamano (*m*) *ashoo-ga-mahno*

tower la torre *tor-ray*

town la città *cheet-ta*

town centre il centro *chentro*

town plan la pianta della città *pee-anta dayl-la cheet-ta*

tow rope il cavo da rimorchio *kahvo da reemork-yo*

toy il giocattolo *jokat-tolo*

track il sentiero *saynt-yero*

tracksuit la tuta da ginnastica *toota da jeen-nas-teeka*

trade fair la fiera campionaria *fee-era kamp-yohnar-ya*

traditional tradizionale *tradeets-yo-nahlay*

traffic il traffico *traf-feeko*

traffic jam l'ingorgo (*m*) del traffico *een-gorgo dayl traf-feeko*

traffic lights il semaforo *saymah-foro*

traffic offence l'infrazione (*f*) *eenfrats-yohnay*

traffic warden il vigile urbano *vee-jeelay oor-bahno*

trailer il rimorchio *reemork-yo*

train il treno *treno*

tram il tram *tram*

tranquillizer il calmante *kal-mantay*

transfer (*money*) trasferire *trazfay-reeray*

transfer charge call la telefonata a carico del destinatario *taylay-fo-nahta a kah-reeko dayl daystee-natar-yo*

transistor (*radio*) il transistor *tran-seestor*

transit: in transit in transito *een tran-zeeto*

translate tradurre *tradoor-ray*

translation la traduzione

tradoots-yohnay

transparency (*photograph*) la diapositiva *dee-apo-zee-teeva*

transparent trasparente *trasparentay*

travel viaggiare *vee-ad-jahray*

travel agent l'agente (*m*) di viaggio *a-jentay dee vee-ad-jo*

traveller's cheques i travellers *travellers*

tray il vassoio *vas-so-yo*

treat trattare *trat-tahray*; **I want to treat you** offro io *of-fro ee-o*

treatment (*medical*) il trattamento *trat-ta-maynto*

tree l'albero *al-bayro*

trifle la zuppa inglese *dzoop-pa een-glayzay*

trim la spuntata *spoon-tahta*

trip la gita *jeeta*

tripe la trippa *treep-pa*

tripod il treppiede *traypee-e-day*

trouble la difficoltà *deef-fee-kolta*

trousers i pantaloni *panta-lohnee*

trout la trota *trota*

true vero *vayro*; **it's true** è vero *e vayro*

trunk (*luggage*) il baule *ba-oolay*

trunks i calzoncini da bagno *kaltson-cheenee da ban-yo*

try provare *pro-vahray*

try on provare *pro-vahray*

T-shirt la maglietta *mal-yayt-ta*

tube il tubo *toobo*

Tuesday martedì (*m*) *martay-dee*

tulip il tulipano *toolee-pahno*

tuna il tonno *ton-no*

tune la melodia *maylo-dee-a*

tunnel la galleria *gal-lay-ree-a*

turbot il rombo *rombo*

turkey il tacchino *tak-keeno*

turn (*handle, wheel*) girare; **to turn left** girare a sinistra *jee-rahray a see-neestra*

turn off (*light etc*) spegnere *spen-yayray*; (*tap*) chiudere *kee-oo-dayray*

turn on (*light etc*) accendere *at-chen-dayray*; (*tap*) aprire *a-preeray*

turning: which is the turning for . . .? dove bisogna girare per . . .? *dohvay beezohn-ya jee-rahray payr*

turnip la rapa *rahpa*

turquoise turchese *toor-kayzay*

TV lounge la sala TV *sahla teevoo*

tweezers le pinzette *peentsayt-tay*

twelve dodici *doh-deechee*

twenty venti *vayntee*

twice due volte *doo-ay voltay*

twins i gemelli *jaymel-lee*

twin-bedded room la camera con letti gemelli *ka-mayra kohn let-tee jaymel-lee*

twist: to twist one's ankle slogarsi la caviglia *zlo-garsee la kaveel-ya*

two due *doo-ay*

type battere a macchina *bat-tayray a mak-keena*

typewriter la macchina da scrivere *mak-keena da skree-vayray*

typical tipico *tee-peeko*

typist la dattilografa *dat-teelo-grafa*

tyre la gomma *gohm-ma*

tyre pressure la pressione delle gomme *prays-yohnay dayl-lay gohm-may*

U

ugly brutto *broot-to*

ulcer l'ulcera (f) *ool-chayra*

umbrella l'ombrello (m) *ombrel-lo*

uncle lo zio *tsee-o*

uncomfortable scomodo *sko-modo*

unconscious svenuto *zvay-nooto*

under sotto *soht-to*

underclothes la biancheria intima *bee-ankay-ree-a een-teema*

underdone poco cotto *poko kot-to*

underground la metropolitana *maytro-polee-tahna*

underground station: where's the nearest underground station? dov'è la più vicina stazione della metropolitana? *dohve la pee-oo vee-cheena stats-yohnay dayl-la maytro-polee-tahna*

underpass il sottopassaggio *sot-topas-sad-jo*

understand capire *ka-peeray;* **I don't understand** non capisco *nohn ka-peesko*

undone slacciato *slat-chahto*

unemployed disoccupato *deezok-koo-pahto*

unfortunately purtroppo *poortrop-po*

ungrateful ingrato *een-grahto*

uniform l'uniforme (f) *oonee-formay*

United States gli Stati Uniti *stahtee oo-neetee*

university l'università *oonee-vayrsee-ta*

unless se non *say nohn;* **unless they arrive** se non arrivano *say nohn ar-ree-vano*

unlock aprire *a-preeray*

unpack: I have to unpack devo disfare le valigie *dayvo dees-fahray lay va-leejay*

unpleasant sgradevole *zgraday-volay*

unscrew svitare *zvee-tahray*

unusual insolito *eenso-leeto*

up su *soo;* **up the hill** su per la collina *soo payr la kol-leena;* **up the road** su per la strada *soo payr la strahda;* **up there** lassù *las-soo*

upside down alla rovescia *al-la ro-vesha*

upstairs di sopra *dee sohpra*

urgent urgente *oor-jentay*

urine l'orina (f) *o-reena*

us ci *chee;* **can you send us**

the . . .? ci può mandare il . . .?
chee pwo man-dahray eel . . .;
after us dopo di noi *dopo dee
no-ee*
USA USA *oosa*
use[1] *n* l'uso (m) *oozo*
use[2] *vb* usare *oo-zahray*
used: I used to do it lo facevo
loh fa-chayvo; **I'm used to it** ci
sono abituato *chee sohno abee-
too-ahto*
useful utile *oo-teelay*
usual solito *so-leeto*
usually di solito *dee so-leeto*
U-turn l'inversione (f) a U
eenvayr-see-ohnay a oo

V

vacancies (*in hotel*) le stanze
libere *stantsay lee-bayray*
vaccination la vaccinazione *vat-
cheenats-yohnay*
vacuum cleaner l'aspirapolvere
(m) *aspee-rapohl-vayray*
vacuum flask il thermos
tayrmos
vague vago *vahgo*
valid valido *va-leedo*
valley la valle *val-lay*
valuable di valore *dee va-lohray*
valuables i valori *va-lohree*
value[1] *n* il valore *va-lohray*
value[2] *vb* (*financially*) valutare
valoo-tahray
valve la valvola *val-vola*
van il furgone *foor-gohnay*
vanilla la vaniglia *vaneel-ya*

vase il vaso *vahzo*
VAT l'IVA (f) *eeva*
veal il vitello *veetayl-lo*
vegetables le verdure *vayr-
dooray*
vegetarian il vegetariano
vayjay-tar-yahno
vegetarian restaurant il
ristorante vegetariano *reesto-
rantay vayjay-tar-yahno*
vehicle il veicolo *vay-ee-kolo*
veil il velo *vaylo*
vein la vena *vayna*
velvet il velluto *vayl-looto*
vending machine il
distributore automatico *destree-
boo-tohray a-ooto-ma-teeko*
Venice Venezia *vaynayts-ya*
venison la carne di cervo *karnay
dee chayrvo*
ventilator il ventilatore *vayntee-
la-tohray*
vermouth il vermut *vayrmoot*
vertical verticale *vayrtee-kahlay*
very molto *mohlto*
vest la canottiera *kanot-tyera*
vet(erinary surgeon) il
veterinario *vaytay-reenar-yo*
VHF VHF *voo ak-ka ef-fay*
via via *vee-a*
video (*machine*) il video *veeday-
o;* (*film*) la videocassetta *veeday-
okas-sayt-ta*
view la vista *veesta*
villa la villa *veel-la*
village il paese *pa-ayzay*
vinaigrette l'olio e aceto *ol-yo
ay a-chayto*

vinegar l'aceto (m) *a-chayto*

vineyard la vigna *veen-ya*

vintage wine il vino d'annata *veeno dan-nahta*

violin il violino *vee-o-leeno*

virus il virus *veeroos*

visa il visto *veesto*

visit la visita *vee-zeeta*

visitor l'ospite (m) *o-speetay*

vitamin la vitamina *veeta-meena*

V-neck (jumper) il maglione con lo scollo a V *mal-yohnay kohn loh skol-lo a voo*

vodka la vodka *vodka*

voice la voce *vohchay*

voltage il voltaggio *voltad-jo*

vomit vomitare *vomee-tahray*

vote votare *vo-tahray*

W

wade sguazzare *zgwat-tsahray*

wage lo stipendio *steepend-yo*

waist la cintura *cheen-toora*

waistcoat il gilè *jeele*

wait (for) aspettare *aspayt-tahray*; **I'm waiting for a friend** aspetto un amico *aspayt-to oon a-meeko*

waiter il cameriere *kamayr-ye-ray*

waiting room la sala d'aspetto *sahla daspet-to*

waitress la cameriera *kamayr-ye-ra*

wake up svegliarsi *zvayl-yarsee*

Wales il Galles *gal-lays*

walk[1] vb camminare *kam-mee-nahray*

walk[2] n: **to go for a walk** fare una passeggiata *fahray oona pas-sayd-jahta*

walking shoes le scarpe da passeggio *skarpay da pas-sayd-jo*

walking stick il bastone da passeggio *ba-stohnay da pas-sayd-jo*

wall il muro *mooro*

wallet il portafoglio *porta-fol-yo*

walnut la noce *nochay*

want volere *vo-layray*; **I want to see it** lo voglio vedere *loh vol-yo vay-dayray*

war la guerra *gwer-ra*

warm[1] adj caldo *kaldo*; **it's warm today** oggi fa caldo *od-jee fa kaldo*

warm[2] vb scaldare *skal-dahray*

warning triangle il triangolo *tree-angolo*

was: I was ero *ero*; **he was** era *era*

wash lavare *la-vahray*; **to wash oneself** lavarsi *la-varsee*; **to wash one's hands** lavarsi le mani *la-varsee lay mahnee*

washable lavabile *lavah-beelay*

washbasin il lavabo *la-vahbo*

washing (clothes) il bucato *boo-kahto*

washing machine la lavatrice *lava-treechay*

washing powder il detersivo *daytayr-seevo*

washing-up liquid il detersivo

per i piatti *daytayr-****seevo*** *payr ee pee-attee*

washroom il bagno *ban-yo*

wasp la vespa *vespa*

waste sprecare *spray-kahray*

waste bin il bidone della spazzatura *bee-dohnay dayl-la spats-satoo-ra*

waste-paper basket il cestino *chay-****steeno***

watch¹ *n* l'orologio (*m*) *oro-lojo*

watch² *vb* (look at) guardare; **will you watch my case for me?** può tenere d'occhio la mia valigia? *pwo tay-nayray dok-yo la mee-a va-leeja*

watchstrap il cinturino dell'orologio *cheentoo-****reeno*** *dayl-loro-****lod****-jo*

water l'acqua (*f*) *akwa*

watercress il crescione *kray-shohnay*

waterfall la cascata *kas-kahta*

water heater lo scaldabagno *skalda-****ban****-yo*

watermelon l'anguria (*f*) *angoo-reea*

waterproof impermeabile *eempayr-may-ah-beelay*

water skiing lo sci acquatico *shee akwa-teeko*

watertight stagno *stan-yo*

wave (on sea) l'onda *onda*

wax¹ *n* la cera *chayra*

wax² *vb* dare la cera a *dahray la chayra a*

way (manner) il modo *modo*; (route) la strada *strahda*; **this**

way di qua *dee kwa*; **which is the way to ...?** può indicarmi la strada per ...? *pwo eendee-****karmee*** *la strahda payr*

we noi *no-ee*

weak (person) debole *day-bolay*; (coffee) leggero *led-jero*

wear portare *por-tahray*

weather il tempo *tempo*

wedding il matrimonio *matree-mon-yo*

Wednesday mercoledì (*m*) *mayrko-ladee*

week la settimana *sayt-tee-mahna*; **this week** questa settimana *kwaysta sayt-tee-mahna*; **next week** la settimana prossima *la sayt-tee-mahna pros-seema*

weekday il giorno feriale *jorno fayr-yahlay*

weekend il week-end *weekend*

weekly rate la tariffa settimanale *tareef-fa sayt-teema-nahlay*

weigh pesare *pay-sahray*

weight il peso *payso*

welcome¹ *adj* benvenuto *baynvay-nooto*

welcome² *vb* ricevere *reechay-vayray*

well bene *benay*; **he's not well** non sta bene *nohn sta benay*; **well done!** bravo! *brahvo*; **well done** (steak) ben cotto *ben kot-to*

wellington (boot) lo stivale di gomma *stee-****vahlay*** *dee gohm-ma*

Welsh gallese *gal-layzay*

went: I went last year ci sono andato l'anno scorso *chee sohno an-dahto l'an-no skorso*

were: you were lei era *le-ee era*; (to friend) tu eri *too eree*

west ovest *ovest*

western occidentale *ot-cheedayn-tahlay*

wet bagnato *ban-yahto*

wetsuit la muta *moota*

what che *kay*; **what is it?** cos'è? *koze*; **this is what I did** ecco ciò che ho fatto *ek-ko cho kay o faht-to*

wheat il grano *grahno*

wheel la ruota *rwota*

wheel brace la chiave a tubo *kee-ahvay a toobo*

wheelchair la sedia a rotelle *sed-ya a rotel-lay*

whelk il buccino *boot-cheeno*

when quando *kwando*

where dove *dovay*

which: which is it? qual'è *kwahle*; **the book which you bought** il libro che hai comprato *eel leebro kay ha-ee kom-prahto*

while: can you do it while I wait? può farlo mentre aspetto? *pwo farloh mayntray aspayt-to*; **in a while** fra poco *fra poko*

whipped montato *mon-tahto*

whisky il whisky *whisky*

whisper bisbigliare *beezbeel-yahray*

whistle fischiare *feesk-yahray*

white bianco *bee-anko*

white coffee il caffelatte *kaf-faylaht-tay*

Whitsun la Pentecoste *payntay-kostay*

who: who is it? chi è? *kee e*; **the boy who came** il ragazzo che è venuto *eel ragats-so kay e vay-nooto*

whole tutto *toot-to*

wholemeal integrale *eentay-grahlay*; **wholemeal bread** il pane integrale *pahnay eentay-grahlay*

wholesale price il prezzo all'ingrosso *prets-so al-leengros-so*

whooping cough la pertosse *payrtos-say*

whose: whose is it? di chi è? *dee kee e*; **the girl whose passport was lost** la ragazza il cui passaporto si era perduto *la ragats-sa eel koo-ee pas-sa-porto see era payr-dooto*

why perché *payrkay*

wide largo *largo*

widow la vedova *vay-dova*

widower il vedovo *vay-dovo*

width la larghezza *largayts-sa*

wife la moglie *mol-yay*

wild (animal) selvatico *saylva-teeko*

will: I'll be back soon torno fra poco *torno fra poko*; **she will go** andrà *andra*

win vincere *veen-chayray*

wind il vento *vento*

windmill il mulino a vento *moo-*

leeno a vento

window la finestra *fee-nestra;* (shop) la vetrina *vay-treena*

window seat (train) il posto vicino al finestrino *pohsto veecheeno al feenay-streeno*

windscreen il parabrezza *parabraydz-za*

windscreen washers il lavacristallo *lahva-kree-stal-lo*

windscreen wiper il tergicristallo *tayrjee-kree-stal-lo*

windy ventoso *vayn-tohzo;* **it's windy** c'è vento *che vento*

wine il vino *veeno*

wine list la lista dei vini *leesta dayee veenee*

wine waiter il sommelier *sommel-yay*

wing l'ala (f) *ahla;* (of car) la fiancata *fee-an-kahta*

wink strizzare l'occhio *streetssahray lok-yo*

winner il vincitore *veencheetohray*

winter l'inverno *een-vayrno*

winter sports gli sport invernali *sport eenvayr-nahlee*

wipe pulire *poo-leeray;* (dishes) asciugare *ashoo-gahray*

wire (electrical) il filo *feelo*

wish volere *vo-layray;* **to wish to do** voler fare *volayr fahray*

with con *kohn*

without senza *sentsa*

witness il/la testimone *testeemonay*

woman la donna *don-na*

wonder: I wonder if . . . mi chiedo se . . . *mee kee-edo say . . .*

wonderful meraviglioso *mayraveel-yohzo*

wood (material) il legno *layn-yo;* (forest) il bosco *bosko*

wool la lana *lana*

woollen di lana *dee lahna*

word la parola *pa-rola*

work (person) lavorare *lavorahray;* (machine, car) funzionare *foontsyo-nahray*

world il mondo *mondo*

worried preoccupato *pray-okkoo-pahto*

worse peggio *ped-jo*

worst il/la peggiore *payd-johray*

worth: it's worth £100 vale cento sterline *vahlay chento stayr-leenay;* **10,000 liras' worth** 10,000 lire *dee-e-chee-meela leeray*

would: I would like vorrei *vorre-ee*

wrap (up) incartare *eenkartahray*

wrapping paper la carta da pacchi *karta da pak-kee*

wreck il naufragio *na-oo-frajo*

wrench (tool) la chiave *keeahvay*

wrist il polso *pohlso*

write scrivere *skree-vayray*

writer lo scrittore *skreet-tohray*

writing paper la carta da lettera *karta da let-tayra*

wrong sbagliato *sbal-yahto;*

sorry, wrong number scusi, ho
sbagliato numero *skoozee o
zbal-yahto noo-mayro*

X

X-ray il raggio X *rad-jo eeks*

Y

yacht lo yacht *yacht*
yawn sbadigliare *zbadeel-yahray*
year l'anno *an-no;* **this year**
quest'anno *kwaystan-no;* **next
year** l'anno prossimo *lan-no
pros-seemo*
yeast il lievito *lee-e-veeto*
yellow giallo *jal-lo*
yes sì *see;* **yes please** sì, grazie
see gratsyay
yesterday ieri *yeree*
yet: they haven't cleaned my
room yet non hanno ancora
pulito la camera *nohn an-no an-
kohra poo-leeto la ka-mayra;* **is it
ready yet?** è già pronto? *e ja
prohnto*

yoga lo yoga *yoga*
yoghurt lo yogurt *yogurt*
you lei *le-ee;* *(with friends)* tu
too; *(plural)* voi *vo-ee;* **I'll see
you tomorrow** la/ti vedrò
domani *la/tee vaydro do-
mahnee;* **for you** per lei/te *payr
le-ee/tay*
young giovane *joh-vanay*
your il suo *eel soo-o;* *(to friend)*
il tuo *eel too-o;* **your house** la
tua casa *la too-a kasa*
yours il suo *eel soo-o;* *(to friend)*
il tuo *eel too-o;* **is this yours?** è
questa il suo? *e kwaysto eel
soo-o*
youth la gioventù *jovayn-too*
youth hostel l'ostello *(m)* della
gioventù *ostel-lo dayl-la jovayn-
too*

Z

zero lo zero *dzero*
zip la cerniera *chayrn-ye-ra*
zoo lo zoo *dzo-oh*